Social Work in the American Tradition

Field · Body of Knowledge · Process

Method · and · Point of View

SOCIAL
WORK

IN THE AMERICAN TRADITION

NATHAN EDWARD COHEN

Dean of the School of Applied Social Sciences
Western Reserve University

HOLT, RINEHART AND WINSTON

NEW YORK—CHICAGO—SAN FRANCISCO
TORONTO—LONDON

To my wife Sylvia, and to David, Ned, and Sue,
without whose patience and understanding
this book would not have been possible.

Preface

ONE OF the best examples of the increasing importance of the helping professions over the past fifty years is the phenomenal growth of social work. Two world wars and a major depression forced social work to hasten its pace before it was fully prepared to walk, and to articulate concepts before it was ready to talk. There has not been sufficient time and leisure to evaluate the direction it has been taking. There is always the danger, in this type of growth, of becoming so involved in the job to be done that earlier purposes and goals fade into the background. In the words of William James:

Most human institutions, by the purely technical and professional manner in which they come to be administered, end by becoming obstacles to the very purpose which their founders had in view. Notoriously the great reforms in many at least of the professions and institutions have been first advocated, or at least have been greatly aided, by laymen rather than by the official keepers of the seal. And there is reason arising from the very nature of a professional and technical institution why it should easily get out of touch with human life. For the scientific and the technical is necessarily the objective, the impersonal, the intellectual, as distinguished from the subjective, the personal, the individual, the emotional. It gives us . . . the world of description, not the world of appreciation.

Social work is so intimately related to human life that it cannot afford such a development. In looking at itself, social work must evaluate not only its present but also its heritage

vii

from the past and its aspirations for the future. This, essentially, is the purpose of *Social Work in the American Tradition*. The book views the field as a whole and examines the many streams that have flowed into it. I have tried to point up the ways in which various threads have been woven into the fabric known today as social work.

One owes much to many in an undertaking of this kind. All of my colleagues at the New York School of Social Work, Columbia University, have at one time or another contributed to the book either through the written word or the informal discussion. I have also received stimulation and guidance from many colleagues in various parts of the country through the numerous sessions at conferences and the meetings of professional associations. I thank them all for their valuable help, and absolve them of any responsibility for those sections of the book where my biases may still be evident. Students, through their critical discussions in class and their written material, forced me constantly to reexamine my formulations. My colleagues Alfred J. Kahn, Muriel Pumphrey, and Margaret Otto contributed to the development of the Selective Bibliography. Margaret Otto and her library staff performed a yeoman task in checking footnotes and references. My secretary, Margaret Acorn, did much to make the production aspects of the work easier. I owe special thanks to my wife and colleague, without whose sympathetic understanding and constant encouragement this book could not have been written. She also read the entire manuscript and made many helpful editorial and content suggestions.

I am indebted to Doubleday and Company, Columbia University Press, and the National Association of Social Workers for permission to use sections of former articles which had appeared in their publications.

N. E. C.

Contents

Social Work in the American Tradition

1

HUMANITARIANISM IN SEARCH OF A METHOD

HUMANITARIANISM may be defined as devotion to the welfare of all human beings. One of its chief characteristics is sympathy for the underdog or the unfortunate. Burgess ranks humanitarianism with individualism and democracy as dominant articles of faith of the American people and describes its basis as follows:

> Its motivation should not be too closely inquired into. It may arise from altruistic sentiments. It may be the outcome of imagining one's self in the place of an unfortunate. It may result from a guilty conscience as penance for personal sins or public wrongs. It may be the expression of a wish to shine before the public as a philanthropist. Or it may be a combination of these and other motives.[1] *

Out of this humanitarian faith the programs of social reform and social welfare have emerged on the American scene. Historically speaking, social work might be viewed as humanitarianism in search of a method. A common impulse to do for others has always been present in the American scene even with its highly diversified ethnic, cultural, economic, and social structure. The method of meeting this concern, however, has varied among humanitarians and with the prevailing philosophy of the times.

To understand why there have been differences as to method, one must view humanitarianism in relation to the other two dominant articles of faith, individualism and de-

* Superscript numbers refer to footnotes, to be found at the back of the book.

3

mocracy, as at times it may be in direct conflict with them. The English colonists who came to settle the country had not been citizens of a democratic homeland. They did bring with them, however, the rebellious spirit of the underdog. It was in rebellion against control and the authority of those who placed little value on the dignity and worth of the individual that the colonists hammered out a system of democratic procedures. There have been various interpretations of the influences that molded the American ideals and the American character. Myrdal, in his projection of the American Creed, describes it as a humanistic liberalism developing out of the epoch of Enlightenment with its emphasis on the "emancipation of human nature"; Christianity, particularly as it took the form in the colonies of various lower-class Protestant sects and split off from the Anglican Church; and English law with its concept of a government "of laws and not of men." [2] The democratic procedures that emerged were consent of the governed, majority rule, and freedom of assembly, speech, and religion. Underlying these procedures was a social philosophy that stressed social equality and equality of opportunity. Government was not to be an end in itself, and in order to insure opposition to authority in all areas including government, there was constant emphasis on the appeal to a higher law. In tune with the spirit prevalent in the founding of the nation, revolt against injustice was the citizen's sacred right and duty. The individual was the fountainhead and was to be protected against the intrusions of government. The most desirable form of government was the least amount of government.

What had emerged was an ideology that placed priority upon the individual and his rights while underplaying concern for society. Born out of a fear of government, it minimized the role of government as a positive force in the service of society. Furthermore, this ideology emphasized procedure and attitudes rather than specific institutions. It was a philosophy that reflected the needs of a relatively simple agricultural society rather than the demands of rapid growth and change which took place.[3] Yet not long after the founding of the nation the political, economic, family, educational, and religious organizations, instituted for meeting the functional needs of the society, were already undergoing change. As the population grew and became more diversified, and as the economy began to feel the impact of industrialization, the question arose of how narrowly or how broadly the democratic attitude and procedures were to apply. Were they to be limited to the political institution or were they to pervade the whole of American life, including the economic and the social institutions? Furthermore, as the society became more complicated and groups with specialized functions began to multiply, the concept of freedom as personal autonomy began to be challenged. Greater heterogeneity demanded increasing interdependence.

Humanitarianism had to find its way from this back‐ ground. The simplest theory was that the society as conceived was perfect and provided the necessary opportunities for all who would seek them. Opportunity and success were there for the asking. Any able-bodied individual who failed to achieve success needed punishment and moral preachments. Reform of the individual was the order of the day. As the problems became more intensive and more extensive, the humanitarians sought, with deep sincerity, better methods of organizing charity and better ways of helping the individual to change his way of life. This group was inclined to accept a simple, highly individualistic morality with little reference to environmental causes or to social responsibility.

Some humanitarians, however, were beginning to relate the problems of the underdog to the democratic article of faith. They felt that the prevailing methods for dealing with deprivation were inconsistent with the ideology that "all men are created equal and from that equal creation they derive rights inherent and inalienable, among which are the preservation of life, liberty, and the pursuit of happiness." As the nation began to experience a series of recessions and depressions, creating great human suffering, they felt that charity was not enough. One had to look for the conditions that were creating the problem and avoid confusing symptom with cause. Under such circumstances they were reluctant to place the blame for failure and dependency on the individual alone. Their democratic interest suggested a course of action, and they turned their attention to reforming the environment through political and legislative means. This point of view was expressed in the following letter by a social worker who had labored diligently in the vineyard of individual reform:

I think there is far more important work to be done for working people. Five hundred thousand wage earners in this city, 200,000 of them women, and 75,000 of those working under dreadful conditions or for starvation wages. That is more vital than the 25,000 dependents. . . . If the working people had all they ought to have, we should not have the paupers and the criminals. It is better to save them before they go under than to spend your life fishing them out when they're half drowned and taking care of them afterwards.[4]

The resort to political and legislative action meant facing up to the fact that government would have to play a more positive role in the service of society. The needs of people in a rapidly growing industrial society could no longer be met through private philanthropy alone. There were problems of a social, health, and economic nature which were beyond the ability of the individual, the family, and the private agency to handle, problems that required the collective action of the political community. A changing role for government was to be created step by step. By the early part of the nineteenth century local community government was taking on responsibilities for health and welfare. Toward the middle of the century state action and cooperation merged. Not until the twentieth century, however, did the federal government assume a major role. President Roosevelt, in an address to Congress, summed up the change that had taken place, as follows:

Security was attained in the earlier days through the interdependence of members of families upon each other and of the families within a small community upon each other. The complexities of great communities and of organized industry make less real these simple means of security. Therefore, we are compelled to employ the active interest of the nation as a whole through government in order to encourage a greater security for each individual who composes it.[5]

The changing pattern of meeting health and welfare needs created conflict in humanitarian ranks. Those who still viewed individualism as sacrosanct found difficulty in helping to build up the role of government. For them government participation in welfare meant a challenge to individul freedom and the introduction of external restraints. They could not agree that freedom is related to the social structure and conditioned by the group membership of the individual. Their view of individualism was such that they rejected the concept that security was basic to freedom and that needs met as a right, rather than as charity, constituted a form of freedom. Only in periods of extreme suffering, therefore, did they give way, and then often with the rationalization that the measures were temporary. It was difficult to accept the fact that these measures were an integral part of a society which was changing, rapidly expanding, and becoming increasingly interdependent.

Both types of humanitarianism were to make their contribution to the rapidly enlarging field of social work. The experience in dealing intimately with the individual and his family was to provide important knowledge for the methodology of the caseworker. The approach of the friendly visitor, fortified at a later date with a more scientific knowledge from psychiatry and the social sciences, and with a democratic approach based on the American ideals, was to become the core of the social work method. The experience of tackling mass problems through social legislation and political action was to provide a way for obtaining the necessary resources through which people could meet their basic health and welfare needs. Furthermore, these two approaches were to feed each other. Knowledge obtained through working with the individual and his family could provide an informed basis for legislative and political action. The emphasis on the importance of the environmental pressures in turn forced those working with the individual to take these into account in their diagnosis of problems and in their proposed remedies. As legislative and political action made better provisions for meeting economic needs, the social worker was freed for dealing with the individual in areas other than economic dependency.

The changes in the material conditions of the nation had brought problems not only of economic dependency but also of human relations and adjustment. Those institutions such as the family, education, and religion, which are part of the non-material culture and have the important functions of child care, socialization, education, and the interpretation of the value system, were caught up in the rapid material changes. The cultural lag between the material institutions and the non-material ones was creating myriad problems in the adjustment and development of the individual. One needs only to pick up a newspaper today to discover the growing concern which such social problems as delinquency, crime, narcotics, alcoholism, broken homes, and mental illness. With the emergence of these problems social work expanded its concern. New services dealing with the group life of children and youth were introduced. Services which dealt formerly with economic dependency were retooled to provide help with problems of adjustment and development. The concept that man does not live by bread alone was highlighted and the psychological dimension took on significance.

Social work today has found a methodology and a two-pronged approach growing out of the two types of humanitarian influence. The two-pronged approach includes concern, on the one hand, for the adjustment and development of the individual toward more satisfying human relations and, on the other, for improving the social institutions within which the individual functions. It seeks through its work with individuals, groups, and the community to help people find within themselves the resources for solving both the problems that affect them alone and those that affect people in general. Thus it is concerned not only with the individual and the social institutions within which he functions but also with the relationship between these two factors. Better family life, improved schools, better housing, more understanding courts, more protected economic conditions, better relations between the various racial and religious groups, and more adequate medical care will all help the individual in his adjustment and development. On the other hand, the achievement of these desirable conditions depends on the use the individual can make of existing institutions and the resources he can mobilize both personally and in cooperation with other people. In a sense, as Gordon Hamilton points out, this is one of the distinguishing features of social work:

Probably all professions would stake out an interest in these same objectives, (economic well-being, or a health-and-decency standard of living, and satisfying social relations), but there is little doubt that social work occupies a peculiarly inclusive position in regard to both. For the social worker the problems involved in economic well-being and social behavior are usually interwoven. It is this essentially dualistic relationship which consistently has shaped social work and gives it its distinguishable if not yet wholly distinctive pattern.[6]

These two are but two sides of the same coin. Both have their roots and expression in the "ideal" values that motivate and guide the democratic way of life. These "ideal" or "ultimate" values of fraternity, equality, liberty, and dignity of the individual are the ever-present guides to the attainable and immediate goals of an adequate economic and health and decency standard of living and satisfying social relations. Integral to these objectives, however, is the method through which we arrive at them. An approach which seems to accomplish the goal but which, in the process, destroys the very values from which it stems is a false accomplishment. On the other hand, without the security of an adequate standard of living, our "ideal" values can be reduced to hollow and empty slogans. For social work, therefore, both objectives must be pursued together through methods that reflect the "ideal" values from which they arise and grow.

There are three primary methods for which social workers are trained to achieve these objectives, namely, casework, group work, and community organization. Basic to all three methods is the understanding and use of relationship. In casework there is a one-to-one relationship between the worker and the client. The worker, however, sees the client not as an isolated individual but as a member of the various groups of which he is a part, especially the family. In group work the pattern of relationship is less intense but more varied, for besides the relationship of the worker to the group and the individuals who compose it, there are the relationships of the individuals to each other, and the relation of each individual to the group as a whole. In community organization the pattern is even more varied, for the worker deals primarily with representatives of the different agencies and groups of the community. Of significance besides his relationship to these representatives as individuals and as members of a group of representatives is the relationship of each individual to the group he represents and the relationship that exists between these groups. Common to all three approaches are the dual objectives described above, but with varying emphases on one or the other. In casework the adjustment of the individual in relation to his immediate social environment is explicit, and always implicit is a concern for those environmental stresses that affect people in general. In social group work the focus on the individual may be less explicit than in casework, but preparation of the individual for dealing with the environment in general, that is, training for citizenship in a democracy, becomes more explicit. In community organization the focus on social goals which benefit people in general is explicit, but always implicit is the meaning of these goals for the individual and the realization that change will come about only through the awareness of the individual and the groups through which he functions.

Also common to all three approaches is a basic set of principles which grow out of our "ideal" values. Lindeman[7] refers to them as rules of conduct which constitute the democratic disciplines. One of these principles is to encourage self-direction and self-determination. The individual, group, or the community must be helped to help himself or itself, with the professional worker playing an indirect or enabling role rather than a manipulative one. As stated by Lindeman, "it implies that good human experience cannot emanate from a relationship in which one person commands and the other obeys, from situations in which one person or one group chooses the ends and thereupon uses others as the means. And it implies further that end-gaining individuals, persons who concentrate upon goals, are likely to become careless respecting their means." [8]

A second principle recognizes the importance of beginning at the level where the individual, group, or community stands and proceeding at a pace that is meaningful to him or it. The perfectionist, busy selling the solution of problems to others, Lindeman points out, cannot enter into the give and take of the democratic process and become "an insulating and separating agent" in good human relations. In the words of John Dewey, "Not perfection as a final goal, but the ever enduring process of perfecting, maturing, refining, is the true aim in living." [9]

A third principle is to deal with the total individual. The professional worker must focus not merely on the immediate problem as seen by the individual, group, or community, but on its relation to the total situation. What may at first seem to be the problem may after examination of all the facts turn out to be merely a symptom.

A fourth principle is to understand and take into account the fact of difference in individuals, groups, or communities. Diversity is an essential part of the democratic process; democracy recognizes that richness and progress ensue from a process which permits individuals to express themselves, rather than forcing them to submerge their differences to a uniformity characteristic of totalitarian movements. Unity out of diversity, rather than unity out of uniformity, would be the true expression of the democratic ideals.[10]

A fifth principle is to recognize that the welfare of any individual, group, or community is inextricably interwoven with the welfare of the whole. All individuals, groups, or communities, therefore, must be concerned with the development of material, human, and social resources to meet all the needs of all the people rather than the vested interest of any individual, any particular group or community.

The three methods of social work, then, share the same general objectives and principles, and give the same central importance to relationships. Because of the different patterns of relationship with which they deal, however, and the varying emphasis on one or the other of the dual objectives, the techniques and skills of the three methods differ. The following are generally accepted definitions and descriptions of each method.

The social caseworker deals with people who are experiencing some breakdown in their capacity to cope unaided with their own affairs. This breakdown may be due primarily to external forces beyond the control of the individual or it may be partially, largely or entirely due to factors within the individual; that is, he may himself create his social dilemma. In either instance the caseworker deals with people who are in trouble and who, regardless of the source of difficulty, are prone to have disturbed feelings about it. . . . The caseworker gives services which meet practical reality needs and takes action which modifies environmental stress and makes available opportunities in areas of deprivation and frustration. These very services, when oriented to feelings and to ways of responding, may ease anxieties, relieve discouragement, give new confidence and enable the individual to manage his own affairs more competently.[11]

The group worker enables various types of groups to function in such a way that both group interaction and program activities contribute to the growth of the individual and the achievement of socially desirable goals. The objectives of the group worker include provision for personal growth, according to individual capacity and need, the adjustment of the individual to other persons, to groups and to society and the motivation of the individual toward the improvement of society; the recognition by the individual of his own rights, limitations and abilities as well as his acceptance of the rights, abilities and differences of others. Through his participation the group worker aims to effect the group process so that decisions come about as a result of knowledge and a sharing and integration of ideas, experiences and knowledge rather than as a result of domination from within or without the group. Through experience he aims to produce these relations with other groups and the wider community which contribute to responsible citizenship, mutual understanding between cultural, religious, economic or social groupings in the community and a participation in the constant improvement of our society toward democratic goals. The guiding purposes behind such leadership rest upon the common assumptions of a democratic society; namely, the opportunity for each individual to fulfill his capacities in freedom, to respect and appreciate others and to assume his social responsibility in maintaining and constantly improving our democratic society.[12]

Community organization for social welfare has been defined as the process of bringing about and maintaining a progressively more effective adjustment between social welfare resources and social welfare needs within a geographic area or functional field. Its goals are consistent with all social work goals in that its primary focus is upon needs of people and provision of means of meeting these needs in a manner consistent with the precepts of democratic living. . . . Its processes involve a) gaining facts about human needs; b) analyzing resources (services) available to meet needs; c) synthesis, correlation and testing of facts; d) relating facts about needs to facts about available services; e) bringing into participation in all phases of the process those individuals and representatives of groups concerned; f) fostering interaction of attitudes and representative viewpoints with the objective of reaching agreement through mutual understanding; g) stimulating citizen interest in social problems and creating motivation for action through participation and education; h) determining priorities; i) developing and improving standards of service; j) identifying gaps or duplications in services; k) adjusting or eliminating existing services or developing new services to meet needs; l) enhancing community understanding through education; and m) mobilizing support—moral and financial.[13]

Social work has not always operated, and does not now always operate, within the values and goals described above, any more than the nation as a whole has ever been able to approximate them. These are our ideal values, or as Lindeman described them, our "directional finders."[14] At times in our history they have stood out clearly as guides to a mature democracy for all people. At other times, however, the "directional finders" have been dim, and we have wandered into a hostile world of war, poverty, unemployment, ill health, racial and religious prejudice, and crime. At times social work has made a courageous and sustained effort to help remove the darkness which from time to time tends to overcast our guiding ideals. At other times the darkness has been so pervasive that it has had a greater effect on social work than social work has had on it.

Social workers, furthermore, like any other group in a democratic society, have not been unanimous in their views or interpretations. Even today there are some who see social work primarily as a network of services to supplement the family, the school, the church, the courts, and the medical institutions. Another group sees it as a unique process for helping the individual, the group, and the community to find within themselves the resources for solving their problems. Still another group regards social work primarily in terms of social policy, with the emphasis less on the individual and more on improving the institutions within which the individual functions. For example, this school of thought would focus attention on unemployment as the problem rather than on the unemployed. The various views of the social workers reflect the different economic, political, social, and scientific philosophies of the day.

To emphasize one view over the others, to seek an all-or-none approach, is to ignore reality. The three approaches merely reflect different emphasis on the "why," the "what," and the "how" of social work. All three are essential, and to abstract one to the exclusion of the others tends to over-simplify complex problems. Most of our problems have more than one cause and demand an integrated multiple approach to their solution. The key problem in social work today is not to place one view against the other but rather to integrate them within a total and meaningful approach that can contribute to the larger aims of democracy.

An integration of objectives, principles, services, and method requires an understanding of the dynamics of social work as a whole. This understanding cannot be attained merely through a description or interpretation of the present pattern of social work. We need more information concerning how we arrived where we are and what our aspirations and potentials are for the future. It is the purpose of this book to contribute to such an approach through an historical analysis of social work's progressive or regressive adjustment to change; its readiness to modify its approach as new circumstances arose, new ideas evolved, and new techniques developed; and an interpretation of the meaning of these events for the present and for future trends.

The analysis will deal with the following periods of American history in terms of two sets of related factors, the "internal" and the "external": from the colonial period to the Civil War; 1860 to 1900; 1900 to 1930; The Great Depression; World War II; World War II to the present. "Internal factors" refers to what was happening within social work as a field, a body of knowledge, a method and a process, and a point of view. "External factors" refers to the social, economic, political, and scientific climate of the period. In brief, it is assumed that social work must be viewed in the perspective of the past, present, and future, and that historical development represents a cause-and-effect relationship rather than a conglomeration of disjointed and fragmentary episodes. Our purpose is to help create an attitude that views the various aspects of social work as parts of a related whole and understands their relationship. Only with this approach can social work make its vital contribution to the nation's efforts—as it grows, develops, and changes —to fulfill its democratic aims and the individual aspirations of its people.

2

DEFEND MAN'S NATURAL RIGHTS

Punish Him for His Weaknesses

(Colonial Period to 1860)

SOCIAL WORK in its present-day form seems to have no roots in social work as practiced prior to 1860. Yet it was during this period that stretched from colonization to the Civil War that the philosophy, values, and mores of American life were being forged, happenings which were to play a large role in the development of social work. Concern for such concepts as individualism, democracy, and humanitarianism was becoming deeply imbedded in the mores of the nation, and the resultant attitudes toward the needs, rights, and responsibilities of the individual and of government have affected the course and direction of social welfare programs, both private and public, to this day. For our purposes the period can be subdivided into three stages: Colonial, 1620-1776; Revolutionary and postwar, 1776-1790; and the rise of national democracy and the beginnings of the Industrial Revolution, 1790-1860.

The population grew from approximately a quarter of a million in 1776 to 2,781,000 in 1780. The earliest settlers were primarily English, with about 70,000 arriving by 1640. Included in this group were a small number of people of property, a larger number seeking religious freedom, and the largest number victims of the economic distress in England.

Many [says Soule] . . . were economic victims of the transformation of the English countryside resulting from the enclosure of land for raising sheep to supply the highly profitable woolen industry. The resulting dispossession of tenants and small farmers filled English towns with "paupers" and "vagabonds." They became a bur-

19

den on the taxpayers and were feared as unruly or criminal characters, though the only crime of most of them was inability to find employment. Some were induced to come to America by shipmasters or labor agents, some were shipped abroad by government authorities.[1]

Crises in other European countries were responsible for additional immigration. The European Wars beginning in 1689, the depression in Northern Ireland, persecution of Protestants in France and Jews in Spain brought immigrants with common cause but with differences in language and religious emphasis. The introduction of the Negro slave from the West Indies began in Virginia in 1619. Between this time and 1700 approximately a quarter of a million slaves were brought into the colonies. Settlement of the white immigrant during this period was primarily along the eastern seaboard. Communication between settlements was by water, and livelihood was through agriculture, shipping, and trading.

The early settlements must be viewed in the context of the changes taking place in the countries of origin of the settlers. Feudal Europe under the domination of the church was a static and repressive society intolerant of any political, economic, social, or scientific change. The economic base of the society was ownership of land. A coalition between the landed aristocracy and the church which also had large land holdings kept the society under rigid controls. By the fifteenth century with the rise of liberalism in Western Europe reaction against the feudal society set in. The reaction represented a coalition of interests, and involved scholars, scientists, a new middle class of merchants, traders, and bankers, religious leaders, and the rulers of newly emerging self-sufficient national states. They all had in common a desire and need to free themselves from the prevailing stranglehold of absolutism, privilege, and rigid class structure. The doctrine of individualism, emphasizing a minimum of interference in all aspects of life, became the dominant keynote of this heterogeneous group. In these early stages, before the full impact of industrialization and urbanization, it was possible for liberalism to include under its banner the economic as well as the political individualist.

Many of the settlers in America were the protagonists of the struggle for liberalism in Western Europe. Special mention should be made of the English settlers in this connection, especially the New England colonizers, since they were to have a marked effect on the mores of the nation. They were in the main Puritans, a religion with a strong individualistic emphasis, who were having difficulty with the State Church of England. Many of them came because they were seeking a setting more conducive to their way of life. "New England differed from the other English colonies in that it was founded largely for the purpose of trying an experiment in Christian living." . . . Many say that the motives were economic . . . this may be so but "the dynamic force in settling New England was English Puritanism desiring to realize itself." [2]

In early New England the ministry provided leadership not only in religious but also in community and government affairs. The first settlers were deeply religious and adhered strictly to the Puritan pattern of the authoritative paternalism of God over man, of pastor over flock, of parent over child, and of conscience over instinctive drive. The Puritans' abiding faith in a paternalistic God who was concerned with every aspect of their way of life—political, economic, and social as well as religious —and in corresponding pragmatic rules of behavior provided both a motivation and a code of living to a people facing the herculean task of settling a wilderness and establishing a new social and economic order. Each member of the colony had to do his share if failure for all was to be avoided. There was little time for play and much need for serious and hard work. A strong moral code limiting man's relation with man was essential in this experiment of cooperative living under conditions that tried men's souls. The Puritan emphasis on the inherent value of work, on the sinfulness of pleasure, and on a moral code centered around the commandments six through ten, met a real need.

In the first century of settlement Puritanism took on an almost fanatical intensity. By the eighteenth century, however, with greater economic security and a more orderly society, a reaction against the extreme theological views began to set in. French rationalism, with its emphasis on the goodness and the potentialities of man and the determination of man's success through his own efforts, became more appealing and more congenial to the new conditions. Puritanism as a way of life, however, had left a marked effect on the character of the nation. The Puritans "developed around the core of 'the New England conscience' a character, which, with all its ugly excrescences, was to form an invaluable strain in the nation of the future." [3] The individualistic tradition with its emphasis on industrious application, thrift, and shrewdness, and its disdain for poverty and failure as sin and moral weakness became deeply imbedded in the attitudinal fabric of the nation. These were self-made men who could best glorify their newly found status by looking down upon economic failures. Success in material things was the road to status and power. Everyone could reach the top if he worked hard, were thrifty, and shrewd. Failure was the fault of the individual, not the society.

To understand the handling of welfare during the colonial period it is necessary to understand its stage of development in England, the ruling power. Poor-law experimentation in England correlated with years of economic distress. The attitude at first was punitive. In 1349, following the ravages of the Black Death, the Statute of Laborers was introduced. This statute was an attempt to fix the wages of labor and to compel all laborers to work. The punishment for "vagabonding" was severe. By 1536 the government began to play a more positive role. A law was passed by Parliament to regulate the collection of alms and to have them dispensed by local authorities. The channel for collection was the church at its weekly Sunday service. In 1572 an act was passed which created the office of the overseer of the poor. Expenditures of tax funds levied upon local communities were to be directed by these civil officers. By the end of the sixteenth century there was sufficient experience and need to

warrant codifying the successful municipal practices. The Elizabethan Poor Law of 1601, which was to remain the basis of
handling relief for the next 233 years, spelled out the existing
practices in a more logical system of poor relief. The law
established three categories of relief: the able-bodied poor; the
unemployable; and dependent children. Almshouses were utilized for the unemployable, and apprenticeship for dependent
children. Two other measures introduced between the passage
of the Elizabethan Poor Law and the next period of major
revision in 1834 were the Settlement Act in 1662 and the Workhouse Test in 1697. The Settlement Act was an attempt to
relieve the parishes of responsibility to new residents and to
prevent movement of the indigent group from parish to parish
in search of relief. The Workhouse Test was a means of forcing
the unemployed to work for their relief. The parishes had
joined together to establish workhouses to lodge the poor and
to provide jobs. The poor were farmed out to neighboring employers at a salary that represented the difference between the
minimum needs supplied by the parish and the prevailing wage.
Farming out was abolished by Parliament in 1782, because it
encouraged exploitation by employers.

The system of poor relief in Colonial America reflected the
Elizabethan Poor Laws. The town, the smallest unit of government, like the parish was responsible for its inhabitants. Up
to about 1700, when almshouses began to appear, cases were
handled individually, usually through discussion at the town
meeting. When the number of cases increased with the influx
of indentured immigrants and children left destitute from war
and disease, the English pattern of overseers of the poor was
introduced. The primary motive of the town was to protect
itself against the poor and destitute. The major responsibility
of the overseer, therefore, was to see to it that the town was not
victimized by the poor. Legal settlement was strictly adhered
to. In towns not large enough to run an almshouse it was not
uncommon to auction the poor to neighboring farmers or to
send them to privately run almshouses. Children received the
greatest consideration, and were the first group to be given

special attention by friends, families, and religious orders. Thus a private home for mothers and children was established in 1729 in New Orleans by the Ursuline Sisters for those left homeless by Indian Massacres. Furthermore, the early settlers regarded the family unit as basic, and felt that every child and youth should be part of a family. Thus indenture became the common practice with children. A similar practice was used in the case of youth who were unruly or unmanageable but who were not criminals.

Another interesting development during this Colonial period was the broadening of the base of responsibility from the town to the province in Massachusetts for a special category of poor. Kelso[4] points out that when refugees from King Philip's War in 1675 sought safety in Boston, their numbers were so great that a special grant had to be obtained out of the province treasury. By 1701 there was provision for reimbursement to the town for relief in all cases of unsettled dependent persons ill with dangerous, infectious, or contagious diseases. By 1720 town records identify a well-defined class of dependents known as the Province Poor. In a sense this represents the first inroad on the concept that the local unit of government could handle total responsibility for poor relief. It took a major crisis to create the change. Once the crisis was over the attempt was made to return to the original pattern, but each crisis leaves a residue which prevents complete return, and this was no exception.

1776-1790

The American Revolution was not an isolated incident but rather part of the contemporary ferment in the hearts of men throughout the civilized world. English seventeenth-century liberalism as represented by Locke and French eighteenth-century humanism and equalitarianism as represented by Rousseau had a deep effect on American political philosophy. Locke's philosophy was an integral part of the thinking of one of America's foremost political philosophers, Thomas Jefferson. This influence is marked in the similarity of the conceptions of Locke about the relations of man to government and the preamble of the Declaration of Independence written by Jefferson. The influence of both the English and French schools bore upon political and civil rights. America, having experienced the tyranny of British rule, was fearful of government. On the other hand, there was great faith in the ability and potentialities of the individual if given an opportunity to develop. This faith was not theoretical but based on the pioneer experiences when settlers had to fend for themselves, to be independent, and to provide their own services. It was a period when the concept of self-help was strong and when individuals had to do for themselves many things now regarded as the normal role of government.

In the America of 1800 [says Commager], men were for the most part, able to take care of themselves. The country was surpassingly rich, and the land was to be had almost for the taking. There was little poverty and no unemployment. The new nation was wonderfully fortunate. There was no standing army to support, no established church to maintain, no idle aristocracy to subsidize. There was little for government to do, and much that men individually and collectively could do for themselves, especially men as virtuous and enlightened as the American of that generation appeared to be.[5]

The focus of the newly evolving political philosophy, therefore, was on guaranteeing and defending the "natural rights" of citizens against the arbitrariness of fellow-man and nature rather than on assigning the state a positive role in meeting the welfare of the individual. The state was to be an organ of defense and order, and it was to protect the freedoms and rights of the individual, so essential to his ability to develop his potentialities. It was in this connection that Jefferson favored public education, for it aided in developing the type of individual essential in a democracy. In its extreme, the highly individualistic view was best expressed by Adam Smith who advised

that man should be left alone, "free to pursue his own interest
his own way . . . as long as he does not violate the laws of
justice." [6]

Dominant American traits were being forged in an agricultural economy, in a land sparsely inhabited and with abundant
resources yet to be tapped. Because the American pioneer had
to begin from scratch, and because of the milieu in which he
found himself, the theories of Locke and Rousseau found a
different emphasis than in populated England and France. The
equal creation of men and their rights to life, liberty, and the
pursuit of happiness were dominant themes. It was liberty, however, that received the greatest emphasis in America. This fitted
into the growing individualistic tradition more readily than the
concern for equality, for the latter involved a more positive role
of government in furthering the welfare of the people. The
individual was not only supreme but had to be of a special
kind. The hard-working, practical man, whose philosophy was
that "every man cannot only look after himself, but is part of
a world in which the capacity to advance is universal," was the
American prototype. This view had a marked effect on the
attitude toward those who needed help. The full impact can
be seen as one views the later development of the psychological
approach in American social work, as described, for example,
by Dr. Davis:

Individualism is tacitly assumed in three ways: 1) The person is
held responsible for his own destiny. In case of neurosis his will is
the object of treatment. In short, he is the entrepreneur. 2) Individual happiness is the ultimate good. Mental health is interpreted
as the satisfaction of individual needs. 3) Human behavior is assumed to be understandable in terms of individuals abstracted from
their society. Needs, desires, and mental processes are frequently
discussed as if inherent in the organism.[7]

It was too early in American life to foresee that the role
of government as protector of life, liberty, and property would
become more complex as society became more complicated. Increased population, the closing of frontiers, industrialization
and urbanization, new inventions, discovery of new resources,

international relations, and so forth, were to bring new types of problems that fell within the definition of common danger and common welfare.

1790 - 1860

The period of 1790 to 1860 saw the theoretical concepts of a democratic government spelled out in practice. From the beginning the question of the role of the national government was a controversial issue. Federalists under the leadership of Hamilton favored a strong central government with vigorous powers to enforce its new responsibilities in the areas of defense, finance, trade, and production. The anti-Federalists under the leadership of Jefferson, "spokesman for the more democratic forces, who feared a strong central government, especially one allied with bankers and manufacturers, favored strong state governments." [8] The constitution finally ratified by the states represented a compromise between these two forces. Events, however, helped determine the direction of the controversy, for problems of foreign relations and internal management necessitated the development of the thirteen states into a union that could function as one nation. The appointment of John Marshall as Chief Justice of the Supreme Court prior to the loss of the election by the Federalist to the Jeffersonian Party in 1800 helped this trend. "In decision after decision he upheld federal power and helped to cement the union. Jefferson himself as President acted as the leader of a nation rather than as chairman of a group of sovereign states." [9] One of Marshall's famous opinions on the issue of national supremacy was that of *Cohens v. Virginia,* 1821:

But a constitution is framed for ages to come and is designed to approach immortality as nearly as human institutions can approach it. Its course cannot always be tranquil. It is exposed to storms and tempests, and its framers must be unwise statesmen indeed if they have not provided for it, so far as its nature will permit, with the means of self-preservation from the perils it may be destined to encounter. No government ought to be so defective in its organization as not to contain within itself the means of securing the execution of its own laws against other dangers than those which occur every day. . . .

"That the United States form, for many and for the most important purposes, a single nation, has not yet been denied. In war we are one people. In making peace we are one people. In all commercial regulations we are one and the same people. In many other respects the American people are one, and the Government which is alone capable of controlling and managing their interests in all these respects is the government of the Union. It is their government, and in that character they have no other. America has chosen to be, in many respects, and to many purposes, a nation; and for all these purposes her government is complete; to all these objects it is competent. The people have declared that in the exercise of all powers given for these objects, it is supreme. It can then, in effecting these objects, legitimately control all individuals or governments within the American territory. The constitution and laws of a State, so far as they are repugnant to the Constitution and laws of the United States, are absolutely void. These States are constituent parts of the United States. They are members of one great empire—for some purposes sovereign, for some purposes subordinate.[10]

The controversy over the role of the federal government was not to be solved once and for all. It remains one of the fundamental questions in the American political system. It is not a question of all or nothing but rather of how much. With the growth of groups with well-defined economic interests, such as the farmers, the workers, the white-collar workers, and the industrialists, there is bound to be a constant struggle to utilize the power of government in the interests of one group or another. In fact, success in elections has always depended on a coalition of some of these groups whose interest merge at a given time behind one party or the other. Jefferson's party was not so much against a central government with power to discharge its responsibilities as it was against a government serving the interests of the bankers and the industrialists rather than the people.

During this early period of the United States, beginning

with the election of Jefferson in 1800, the rights of the common man in the new political democracy were in the ascendancy. Andrew Jackson's election in 1828 was a further victory. A product of the lower classes and a champion of their cause, much of the support for his election came from the city worker and the small farmer. Under his administration, which emphasized faith in the ability of the common man to manage his own affairs, many democratic practices were introduced in all levels of government. These included breakdown of exclusive right of property-owners to vote and hold office; increase in the number of elected as against appointed officers; shortening of the periods of holding office; introduction of the nominating convention; and the establishment of the role of the President as the servant of the people.[11]

The further democratization of government coincided with the period of parliamentary reform in England. The first parliamentary reform bill, which became law in 1832, broke the hold of the aristocracy. Although it certainly did not give the English workingman his share in the political life of the nation, it led the way to a broadening of the suffrage. In both England and the United States the reform of electoral and governmental procedures provided a climate for other types of reforms.

In England the impact of the Industrial Revolution was felt at an earlier period than in America. The depression of 1815-1820 was the worst the nation had experienced. The impoverishment of the working people challenged the accuracy of Adam Smith's philosophy of laissez-faire. John Stuart Mill criticized Smith's theory for placing its emphasis on the increase in the material wealth possessed by the nation and proposed the more equitable distribution of the wealth as the fundamental aim. During this period Jeremy Bentham was redefining the goal of government. He saw utility—defined as "the greatest happiness of the greatest number"—as the chief purpose of government, to be accomplished by legislation.

The climate in England was conducive to the legislative expression of humanitarian reform. Thus the regulation of child labor, agitation for which had started in England in 1796, became law in 1833. Two other major developments during this period were the Act to Abolish Slavery and reform of the Poor Laws, the latter being the first major change in the code of practice for dealing with the poor since the Elizabethan Act of 1601.

Paralleling this period of social reform in England under the Whigs (1830-1846) was the Jacksonian era in the United States (1829-1841). It was during this period that humanitarian movements were initiated to correct the social evils resulting from Industrial Revolution. Prominent among the crusades of this era were those that fought for women's rights, public education, the abolition of slavery, greater religious toleration, better treatment of the insane and other unfortunates, and prohibition.

The nation was also growing physically and economically during this period. The population in 1780 was 2,781,000. By 1860 it had grown to 31,443,321. The increase was due to both immigration and a high birth rate. Between 1820 and 1860 more than 4 million immigrants came from more than twenty different countries. Most of them came from England, Ireland, Germany, and Scandinavia. Ireland was experiencing a serious potato famine in the late 1840's and the unsuccessful revolt in Germany in 1848 brought many political refugees. The English blended with the general population. The Irish settled en masse in the large cities, the Scandinavians in compact and isolated frontier communities, and the Germans made an attempt at collective colonization. The birth rate contributed more to the population than did immigration. Thus between 1820 and 1830, where records are available for birth rates, immigration, and population change, we find that in a population growth of 3,300,000 there were only 138,500 immigrants. The size of households during this period was the highest in the nation's history. The average number of persons per household in 1790 was 5.7 as compared with 3.6 today. Internal migration was also heavy. As reported by Soule:

Movement of persons from one part of the nation to another has usually been more marked than migration into the nation from abroad. As the frontier moved westward, settlers of new agricultural regions were predominantly recruited from native populations not far to the east of them. Major exceptions to these generalizations occurred during the gold rush to California after 1848, or settlement in North Central states west of the Mississippi River by immigrants of Scandinavian origin.[12]

The country began to shift from the agricultural dream envisioned by Jefferson to the industrial nation foreseen by Hamilton. Although the Industrial Revolution did not reach its full rate of growth till 1860, its beginnings were being felt in the first half of the nineteenth century. The growth of urban communities began in 1820. By 1860 New York had a population of over a million. Industry demanded new sources of labor, since in a nation where land was still plentiful and agriculture still dominant, the men did not flock into industry. Labor had to be secured, therefore, from among women, children, and immigrants. The social and political problems arising from a changing economy and large-scale immigration in a young country were numerous.

The family as a social institution felt the impact of the changing times. It was beginning to shift from a producer to a consumer group, and this brought movement out of the home. Women began to give up their traditional role and sought work in the community.

Up to that time the traditional occupations of women who attempted to be wholly or partially self-supporting were domestic service, teaching and sewing. The invention of the sewing machine in 1846 began to change all that. No longer could the paternal or fraternal homestead absorb productively the labors of an indefinite number of "females." Not only had most of the processes connected with the making of clothing—spinning, weaving, dyeing, dressmaking, and tailoring—become factory work through the introduction of machinery, but many of the tasks connected with day-to-day living, such as laundry work and some forms of cooking, were also becoming factory processes. Historically these were woman's tasks, and quite naturally she followed them to the factory, the bakery and the laundry.[13]

Youth also was on the move, especially from the rural areas to the cities. It was a strange and difficult experience for many of these young people. The hazards involved in living away from family guidance were numerous.

The changing times also witnessed a shift from a theologically centered approach in religion to one that reflected the economic and sociological changes that were taking place in the nation. Protestantism did not regard good deeds as a prerequisite to salvation. Faith was the important consideration. Man's motivation and obligation for good deeds were related to his originally being saved by Christ and his acceptance of Christ. This Protestant philosophy influenced the approach to charity. The state rather than the church was encouraged to take responsibility for the poor and their problems. With the growing materialism religion also became pragmatic and turned to "good works" as well as to prayer. "Work, money, God: a new religion took hold of the American Union, to rule a hundred years or more." [14] Reform of the society as well as the individual became part of the growing effort to stem the effects of materialism. "Reform the prisons, the insane asylums. Give rights to women. Abolish debtor prisons—drunkenness—pauperism. Be merciful to the deaf and dumb, teach the blind to live." [15] This was America's moral conscience responding to the destruction of human life being wrought by the economic cyclone.

The emerging industrialization brought growing dependence on wages for the basic necessities of food, clothing, and shelter. The fate of the individual was thus more hazardous during periods of economic difficulty. Between 1800 and 1860 there were five depressions, those of 1837 and 1857 being of major proportions. As the Beards said, "Such crises had often occurred in the past but as long as the overwhelming majority of the people tilled the soil for a livelihood depressions did not create destitution for the masses." [16]

The change in the economic pattern of the nation resulted in a more sharply defined class structure, with industrialists and bankers at one end of the scale and workers at the other. Between 1800 and 1860 the groundwork was being laid for the trade union movement. First came the local crafts unions followed by the coordination of a number of local unions into a city trades union (New York, 1833). By 1836 steps were taken to federate single crafts unions nationally. This was followed by the formation of many unions into a national federation.

The impending economic upheaval also brought new tensions. A struggle for power in government arose between the newly emerging industrialists and bankers, and the common man as depicted in the Jeffersonian philosophy. Jackson's election in 1828 was regarded as a victory for the common man. There was also growing tension between the different sections of the country with their varied economic interests. The demands of industry for more workers brought increased immigration. The new immigrants were of a different religious background than their predecessors, and tensions appeared among religious groups, and anti-alien movements arose. America was feeling its growing pains. The theoretical formulations of the Revolutionary period were being put to a test by the rapid changes in the economic, political, and social life of the country. Certain dominant traits, however, had emerged. As pointed out in Chapter 1, they could best be categorized as individualism, democracy, and humanitarianism.

During this early period of the nation's history social problems were comparatively minor and temporary and could be handled by the people without resorting to the aid of the federal government. Furthermore, when economic problems reached an acute or depression stage, the open frontiers always provided a safety valve. Give the individual the necessary liberties to be on his own and to fend for himself, and if he were not lazy or morally weak he would find the necessary opportunities to succeed.

There were three important developments in social welfare during this period. The first, as we have seen, was the gradual recognition of the special needs of people with particular handicaps. America with its philosophy of individualism still could not accept economic dependence for the able-bodied in other than moral terms, but it could, in the case of the widow, the child, the blind, the deaf, and the mentally deficient, argue in rationalization that these problems were the results of acts of God and not necessarily of moral weakness. In other words, these people did not destroy the basic philosophy that the reason for failure resided in the individual and not in the society. Special institutions, both public and private, were developed for children, for the handicapped, and for the mentally ill. Child labor legislation was the first type of labor legislation enacted in the nation. Connecticut led the attack in 1813 with a law requiring millowners to have children in their factories taught the three R's. Massachusetts improved upon this in 1836 with a law requiring that children under fifteen working in factories attend school for three months a year. In 1842 both states adopted a law which established ten hours a day as the maximum work day for children under twelve. In 1848 Pennsylvania established the first law setting a minimum age. Children under twelve were prohibited from working in textile plants.

The State of Massachusetts also took leadership in regarding the insane as a special group of dependents. The initial motive was again the protection of society. Thus, the Massachusetts legislature in 1797 passed a bill holding that "when it appears that a person is 'lunatic and so furiously mad as to render it dangerous to the peace and safety of the good people, for such lunatic persons to go at large' he may be committed to the house of correction." [17] The "less furious" were sent to the almshouses, mixed in with the paupers, the children, and the criminals. Care of the insane in Massachusetts was still regarded as part of pauper relief until 1835, when the state assumed financial responsibility for all insane who were without settlement eligibility in the newly established state lunatic asylums.

A second important development was the assumption of greater responsibility by the states when local units could not provide adequate care for these specialized groups. "Among pioneering efforts in the several fields were the first juvenile reformatory opened in New York in 1825, the first school for the deaf opened in Connecticut in 1817, and the first school for the blind established in Boston in 1830. Similar facilities soon followed in a number of states." [18] These state institutions soon gave rise to the need for state boards of charity, the forerunners of the present state departments of welfare. The administrators of the state institutions and the members of the state boards were also to play a large role in the creation of the National Conference of Charities and Corrections in 1873.

One person who contributed greatly during this period to the recognition of the needs of people with handicaps was Dorothea Lynde Dix. Miss Dix "popularized institutional treatment for mental diseases and aroused a social conscience; and through her personal activities 32 hospitals were established in America and several in Europe as well." [19] One of her special contributions was her success in getting the states to take responsibility for the care of the mentally ill. As Dr. Felix points out, "the mentally ill were the first victims of chronic disease whose care was recognized to be a public responsibility." [20]

Miss Dix went beyond the level of state, to that of federal, responsibility when in 1855 she drafted the Act of Congress that begins: "The title of the institution shall be the Government Hospital [presently St. Elizabeths] for the Insane and its objects shall be the most humane care and enlightened curative treatment of the Insane of the Army and Navy of the United States and the District of Columbia." [21] The federal government was prepared to help the men in the armed services; it had not, however, reached the point of accepting responsibility in social welfare. In 1854 Miss Dix had presented

to Congress a moving appeal for federal aid in the form of millions of acres of land to be given to the states for the benefit of the insane. A bill to this effect was passed by Congress and vetoed by President Pierce. In his veto message, the President maintained that the welfare clause (Section 8) in the Constitution did not give the Congress the power to provide for the indigent insane outside of the limits of the District of Columbia, nor for any indigent persons.

He argued that if the Congress had power to make provisions for indigent insane outside of the District, it had the same power to provide for the indigent who are not insane; and thus to transfer to the Federal Government the charge of all the poor in all the States.[22]

President Pierce in his veto had articulated the then prevalent philosophy of the role of the federal government in meeting social welfare needs. It was to be more than three quarters of a century before this view would be changed legislatively.

A third important development was the emergence of the private agency, which was to play a major role in the development of social work as it is known today. The social problems growing out of increased immigration, industrialization, and urbanization awakened the humanitarian interest of many citizens. One of many organizations was the New York Association for Improving the Conditions of the Poor, founded by Robert Hartley and associates in 1843. This organization merged with the Charity Organization Society of New York to form the Community Service Society, the largest private family agency in the United States. The Children's Aid Society of New York, the first child placing agency separate from an institutional program was established in 1853. Around 1850 several maternity homes for unmarried mothers were established by the various religious groups. The motivation for these programs was highly moralistic, with a desire to reform the fallen and to protect society from the ever-increasing indigent group. The reformers themselves showed a strange mixture of contempt, fear, and sympathy for these people. The accelerating movement of unattached youth into the cities also met with response from the community. A concern for the morals and the continued identification of these youth with the traditional religious approach gave rise to the YMCA movement.[23] The early YMCA's were organized under the influence of the Protestant concern for evangelization.

The private agency, which was to attain a role of leadership in social welfare in the coming years, was not only established and sponsored by lay people but was also manned by them. The paid worker had not yet arrived on the scene. This was the period of the "Lady Bountiful" stereotype. It was the "morally and socially" superior who attempted to help the less fortunate and the "fallen." It was the period of the missionary utilizing charity not as an end in itself, but as a means of proselytizing the "victim" into their particular creed.

Summary

External Factors

In its first eighty years as an independent nation the United States experienced a population increase of 29 million through immigration and a high birth rate. The pattern of nationality, religious, and racial differences with the numerous problems of intergroup relations that we face today was being established. The sectarian pattern of private social services was also in the making.

Jefferson's dream of a democratic society within an agricultural setting was fading into the background with industrialization and urbanization. Basic views toward individualism, democracy, and humanitarianism, however, had become deeply imbedded in the attitudinal fabric of the nation. They centered around a political democracy with little sensitivity to its interrelations with economic and social democracy.

The change in the economic institution brought changes in such other institutions as government, the family, religion, and education. The family was changing from a producer to a consumer group. Its normal economic, educational, religious, and police functions were being taken over by other institutions. The change in institutional structure brought many social problems, one of which was poverty within a pattern that was entirely new to the nation.

America began with a belief that "the less government we have, the better." It was soon evident, however, that even within a narrow interpretation of government as a policing organ, it would have to enter the domain of regulation if the emerging economic groupings were to enjoy the rights of "life, liberty, and the pursuit of happiness," and if the nation was to function as one rather than as thirteen sovereign states.

A class structure based on economics became more explicit. At one end of the scale were the manufacturers and the industrial bankers—the capitalists—and at the other end the workers. In between were the farmers and the growing number of professional and white-collar workers. The conflict between capital and labor was evident in the emergence of the trade union movement.

The social sciences were still in their infancy. Sociology was social ethics, and psychology was wandering between the shadows of philosophy and physiology.

Internal Factors

If we regard a field of work as composed of the organizations whose major activity is such work, then we can talk of a field of "social services" during this period. It was not an organized or professionally self-conscious field, but there were both public and private agencies serving the needs of people in difficulty. The private agencies were manned by volunteers, but in the public settings there were paid staff. The agencies dealt primarily with problems of economic dependency, but even within this broader category there began to emerge special categories and corresponding special institutions for the insane, orphans, and handicapped children—the blind, the deaf, and the feeble-minded.

There was no organized body of knowledge in the strict sense of the term. Experience was being accumulated, however, on such matters as legal settlement; centralization versus decentralization of charity administered by the states and the local governmental unit; dealing with the special categories of problems in separate settings; administrative and policy issues in the running of institutions; and, institutional versus foster-home placement of children.

There was no scientifically defined method of dealing with people in trouble during this period. The method, which can best be described as punitive and moralistic, grew out of the prevailing philosophy about economic dependency. The fault lay in the moral weakness of the individual and not in the evils of society; the exceptions were those unfortunates who were handicapped through an "act of God," but here again society was not considered at fault. The approach was to protect society against the insane and the feeble-minded by placing them in institutions. Orphans were to be helped sufficiently to prevent their becoming members of the dependent class, but not so agreeably that they would find pleasure in getting something for nothing. In the case of the morally weak, the approach was to try to restore them to grace through moral preachment and punitive measures. Religion at that time was deemed the best source of information for dealing with the morally weak.

If "social work" during this period is to be thought of in terms of social services for the economically dependent, then the point of view of social work has been described above. If, however, one thinks in broader terms of social welfare or social policy then one must include the gains made by the common man during this era in matters of self-government, education, and democratic ideals. Without these gains later changes in attitudes concerning the needs and rights of the economically dependent would not have been possible. Toward the latter part of the period, for example, we find evidence of the reformer merging his humanitarian and democratic conceptions by turning to legislation as a way of improving the conditions of child labor.

3

EXPANDING

INDUSTRIALISM

The Human Side

(1860-1900)

THE HEART OF America began to function at full strength during the Revolution and during the forging of the democratic ideals into the Constitution with the accompanying Bill of Rights. The body for which this heart had to perform was small. As pointed out in the preceding chapter, however, the body grew rapidly. By the time of its first major internal crisis, the Civil War, "the country at large seemed in the grip of feverish excitement; it was like a body that had grown too fast for its heart." Furthermore, it was not merely growing too fast; but perhaps even more important, it was developing unevenly and suffering the breakdown of the mechanisms essential for co-ordinating the parts. The strong feeling of solidarity during the struggle for independence had given way to a view of the nation as made up of discreet sections rather than interdependent units affected by common political, economic, and social forces. There was little recognition that the more complex and interdependent a society became the more organized it must be in order to meet its needs, if by "organized" we mean a recognition by all groups of the relation between their welfare and the welfare of the nation as a whole.

Between 1780 and 1860 the population increased from 2,781,000 to 31,443,321. The increase was running well over 30 percent per decade. Up to 1820 approximately 20 percent of the total population was Negro. With the increase in the white population through immigration and a high birth rate, however, and with the halting of importation of slaves, the percentage of Negroes in the population began to drop off in 1820. An important population factor was the uneven growth in the North and the South. "During the first three or four decades in the history of the Nation, the populations of the north and the south were approximately equal in size and rate of growth, but because of its rapid industrialization the population of the north soon outstripped that of the south. By 1870 the population of the north was double that of the south." [1]

The physical size of the country had also grown by leaps and bounds. During the administration of James K. Polk, 1845-1849, the nation experienced the largest geographical expansion since the administration of Jefferson. Texas had been annexed just before Polk was inaugurated. As a result of the war with Mexico all territories west to the Pacific were also added. By agreement with England the Canadian boundary was established at the Forty-ninth Parallel. The addition of new territory brought conflict as to how it was to fit into the established pattern of the Mason and Dixon Line and the Ohio River as the recognized boundaries between free and slave states. A series of compromises followed, each accompanied by serious controversy, since each not only overturned the original formula but also destroyed the previous compromise. The new territories compounded the problem, which was not solved; the day of judgment was merely postponed.

The economic growth of the country, too, was both gigantic and uneven. The North was a region of industrial and mercantile progress. Well-defined groups such as manufacturers, workers, farmers, merchants, and fishermen emerged, each group with its own specific interests and problems. Because of the industrial development of the North slavery was not found profitable and died out. In the South, on the other hand, there were few industries or large urban areas. It was still a section primarily of farmers. For a brief time in the "Old South" slavery showed signs of dying out, but the invention of the cotton gin by Eli Whitney in 1793 and the opening of the Southwest and Far South brought an abrupt change. After 1800 cotton began to dominate the agricultural economy of the

South. Furthermore, improvements in soil care revivified the plantations of the "Old South."

New inventions brought rapid economic changes, which were almost compulsive in nature. During the administration of Jackson, for example, the invention of the steam locomotive, the steel ploughboard, the sewing machine, and the reaper gave rise to wildcat schemes and speculation. Westward expansion, proceeding at a dizzy pace, was upsetting the economy in other parts of the nation. Paper money and an unsound banking system added to the chaotic conditions. Each new development sharpened the vested interests of the various sections of the country. Free soil and westward expansion exacted their price from the industrial East's labor supply. High tariffs protected the interests of the North at the expense of the South and the newly developing West. The economic system was expanding but not without pain. The five depressions between 1800 and 1860 were symptomatic.

During this period when there was need for a strengthened central government and a reinterpretation of the rules of the game, the basic question of the relation between the states and the nation was being sharply debated. Was the nation merely an organization of states with its power granted and limited by state legislatures, or was it a creation of the people and serving as their agent? Were the states sovereign in their power to the extent of being able to nullify an act of the central government or secede from the Union if they so desired? Could the federal government as an agent of the people protect their rights if these rights were invaded by the states? With the proposals of nullification and secession not yet fully resolved, the important question of the nature and extent of federal authority in economic, political, and social affairs could not be tackled. The South in essence was challenging the existence and power of the federal government as a "political community or corporate unit." Jefferson Davis in his history of the rise and fall of the Confederate government stated "that the term 'people,' in the preamble to the Constitution and in the tenth amendment, is used distributively; that the only 'people of the United States' known to the Constitution are the people of each State in the Union; that no such political community or corporate unit as one people of the United States then existed, has ever been organized, or yet exists; that no political action by the people of the United States in the aggregate has ever taken place, or ever can take place, under the Constitution." The election of Lincoln in 1860 defied this principle, for although only a moderate on the issue of slavery, Lincoln was outspoken in his belief in the Union and federal power.

There have been various interpretations of the cause of the Civil War. They range all the way from the economic to the theoretic in concern for the Union and to the humanitarian. All elements were no doubt involved. For a nation founded in idealism and dedicated to the proposition that "all men are created equal," slavery represented too obvious a contradiction. Within such a nation it could not be condoned, and had to be eradicated. Although a bloody war of four years duration was to be fought to change the policy legally, America was again to discover that the mere enactment of a law does not change the minds and hearts of men. The struggle to give equal rights for the Negro had not ended; in fact it had just begun.

The four years of Civil War ended an era in American life. The Thirteenth Amendment abolished slavery, and the Fifteenth Amendment gave to all citizens the right to vote regardless of race or color. The war also settled once and for all the "question of the right of a State to secede. It brought in its train a constitutional revolution—a transfer of authority from State to Federal Government. This constitutional revolution was at once dramatized and accelerated by the Fourteenth Amendment, the first section of which reversed the traditional relationship of citizen to his government by throwing the protection of the Federal Government around rights that might be invaded by States." [2] This constitutional revolution was important not only in setting forth the rights of the Negro but also was in serving as the basis for broadening the government's interpretation of its responsibility to the welfare of the people in the twentieth century.

The program of political reconstruction following the Civil War represented the first attempt by the Federal government to deal with problems usually regarded as the prerogative of the States. The constitutionality of many of the measures undertaken during this era were constantly under question. One of the fundamental issues was whether reconstruction was within the authority of the President or the Congress. President Lincoln in drawing up his plan for reconstruction had proceeded on the premise that the Southern states had never seceded and that the rebellion against the Federal government could be attributed to individual Southerners. Within this interpretation the problems of reconstruction would fall within the jurisdiction of the executive since the President had the constitutional power to pardon acts against the government. After the death of President Lincoln, however, the plan never had a chance to be fully tested. Congress, under the leadership of such radical Republicans as Thaddeus Stevens and Charles Sumner, attacked the program as too lenient.

The reconstruction governments formed in the South were in the hands of Northern politicians who went South after the Civil War, Southern whites who supported the radical Republicans, and Negroes. The Negroes were inexperienced in the affairs of government and leaned heavily on the leadership of the whites. The record of the reconstruction governments was not a proud one. They found themselves involved in graft, corruption, heavy taxation and wild spending. It must be borne in mind, however, that graft and corruption were rampant throughout the nation during this period. The administration in Washington under President Grant (1869-1877) was having its own difficulties with graft and corruption. In New York State, Boss Tweed was in power.

There were many positives in the reconstruction program which tend to be overlooked. New liberal constitutions were established which emphasized civil liberties, universal male suffrage, and greater democracy in local government. Many important public works projects such as roads, bridges, and government buildings were started. Compulsory free public education was introduced in the South. Although the impact on the South was negative in many respects, the reconstruction program represented the first major effort on the part of government to protect the rights and to raise the standards for a deprived segment of citizens. It represented the beginning of the important idea that government could and should use its power on a large scale for the public weal. Even with its failures, therefore, the program of reconstruction made a basic contribution to the changing role of government.

With the war out of the way, the United States was again free to pursue its interrupted interest in the development of its huge resources and its industrial potential. For the South the era of the large plantation was at an end, and the era of the small farm and industrialization at its beginning. In the period 1865 to 1900 America was to become the leading manufacturing nation in the world. New inventions increased its productive equipment. The output from agriculture, industry, and mining expanded at a phenomenal rate. It was a period dominated by economic interests, which pervaded the total fabric of the nation, its social as well as its political life.

The population increased from 31,443,321 in 1860 to 75,-994,575 in 1900. A combination of high birth rate, declining mortality, and immigration accounted for the rapid increase. Immigration continued at a rate of approximately 2.5 million for each decade from 1850 to 1880. Between 1880 and 1890 immigration reached a new high of 5.25 million. Up to 1865 the immigrants were primarily from Great Britain, Germany, and the Scandinavian countries. After 1865 they came primarily from Poland, Russia, Austria, Hungary, Turkey, Italy, and the Balkans. The bulk of the immigrants in the period 1880 to 1900 were from Eastern Europe, and the largest number were Jews who were the victims of widespread pogroms in Czarist Russia. In 1820 there were only 6000 Jews in the United States, but by 1920 the number had risen to 4 million.

These later immigrants came to a highly urbanized America with over 50 percent of the population residing in the cities. They also came at a time when the supply of free land was drying up. In the census of 1890 the government stated officially that the frontiers were closed. Thus the prediction of Jefferson that the millions of square miles would suffice for a thousand years had been wrong by 900 years. Many of this group could not understand English and settled in the large cities on the Eastern Seaboard at or near the port of entry.

During this period of swift economic development the country's attention turned more to its physical than to its human resources. Between 1865 and 1879 the government sent teams of experts into all sections to make a survey of its natural resources such as agricultural land, coal, oil, iron, and forests. In 1870 with the introduction of the Bessemer process for making steel a great change was brought into the lives of the people. Steel production rose from 380,000 tons in 1875 to over 10 million tons in 1900. By 1900 the country was covered with a network of railroads. Communication was further expanded with the introduction of the telephone in 1876. The gasoline engine was developed toward the end of the nineteenth century. Rapid economic expansion created a need for capital, and in the second half of the nineteenth century the pattern of partnerships gave way to the modern form of group ownership, namely, corporations with their large number of stockholders. In the beginning of the 1800's industry was in the hands of thousands of small businessmen. With the rise of the corporations with their dependence on vast capital, the large industrialists and the corresponding huge banking houses came to control the economy of the nation.

The philosophy of big business was that of laissez-faire. It was rugged individualism rearing its head in the most extreme form with Social Darwinism thrown in as a scientific rationalization. Darwin had published his famous study in 1859; the English sociologist Herbert Spencer had developed Darwin's concept of the survival of the fittest into a social philosophy. His chief exponent in this country was William Graham Sumner, an economist at Yale. For Sumner, competition was a law of nature which should not be tampered with, and the determination of the conquest of nature was entirely in the hands of the individual.

Nature is entirely neutral; she submits to him who most energetically and resolutely assails her. She grants her rewards to the fittest, therefore, without regard to consideration of any kind. If, then, there be liberty, men get from her just in proportion to their works, and their having and enjoying are just in proportion to their being and their doing. Such is the system of nature. If we do not like it, and if we try to amend it, there is only one way in which we can do it. We can take from the better and give to the worse. We can deflect the penalties of those who have done ill and throw them on those who have done better. We can take the rewards from those who have done better and give them to those who have done worse. We shall thus lessen the inequalities. We shall favor the survival of the unfittest, and we shall accomplish this by destroying liberty. Let it be understood that we cannot go outside of this alternative: liberty, inequality, survival of the fittest; not-liberty, equality, survival of the unfittest.[3]

It was difficult for the followers of the laissez-faire philosophy to recognize that one man's liberty was often at the expense of another, and that people were not competing on equal terms. "In America as everywhere else—and sometimes, perhaps, on the average, a little more ruthlessly—liberty often provided an opportunity for the stronger to rob the weaker." [4]

America had come of age industrially but not socially. It was still applying the "moral code of an individualistic, agrarian society to the practices of a corporate and industrial society." It was encouraging millions of immigrants to come to the "promised land," but free land was no longer available. In place of the self-sustaining farm home was the factory with its long hours of work and its insecure jobs. Good living conditions in the city were difficult to find within the income of the worker, and slums with their myriad social problems became the environment into which the immigrant brought his family. Because of the problems of adjustment and the need for security in a strange land the immigrants tended to segregate themselves in language and racial groups. They came seeking a new life, but found a nation so absorbed in making money that it had no time to consider them as people. They were invited to jump into the fast-flowing economic stream without concern for their ability to swim. Human life was expendable in this economic war. America, on the one hand, wanted them because it needed manpower for its growing industries, but on the other hand, feared them and their foreign ways. Robert M. Hartley, founder of the New York Association for Improving the Conditions of the Poor, reflected the prevailing sentiment of the day in the annual report of the association for 1871. Hartley quoted with approval the following:

"How to deal with our own immigrant ignorance and superstition, our colonized Communism, Fenianism, Ribbonism, Atheism, Romanism, and all the other products of ignorance—the mother of all vices—this is our pressing but persistent and patient problem. . . . We are not free in New York City, because ignorance, fanaticism, brutal ferocity, and animal appetites and lusts, unrestrained by self-knowledge or by mental discipline, are always pursuing the orderly and educated classes like a pack of wolves."

What of government during this period? Was it serving as an agent of the people? Although the Fourteenth Amendment had broadened the government's responsibility for, and authority over, the welfare of the people, Congress and the courts managed to keep the government out of social reform. In fact, corporate business made greater use of the amendment to defend itself from government interference than government did in furthering the rights of the people in their struggle for existence. The government, which was in the hands of the Republicans for the entire period except for the two Democratic administrations under Grover Cleveland, had succumbed to a laissez-faire interpretation of a policing power to make sure that no stop signals interfered with the progress of the rugged individualist. Above all, it was not to interfere with business, including the conditions of work and the relationships with the workers. The economic realm was sacrosanct, forbidden territory for governmental authority. Interestingly enough, businessmen showed no hesitation in asking government to put its resources at their disposal. Thus land and financial grants were made to the railroads to help in their development. The protective tariff, which was a contradiction of the laissez-faire principle of free competitive enterprise, was tightened to protect favored domestic interests. In the last two decades of the century, because of the growing pressure against the centralization of power in industry, the government enacted the Interstate Commerce Act and the Sherman Anti-Trust Act, but government as a positive tool in serving the welfare of the people was still in the future.

In this period of phenomenal industrial growth the American dream had become a nightmare for the common man. America was rapidly becoming a land of the privileged rather than a land of promise. Honest stock-taking would have revealed the following:

The continent had been conquered, but the conquest had been attended by an exploitation of soil and forest and water so ruthless that the natural resources of the nation were nearing exhaustion. The agricultural domain had grown beyond the dreams of even Jefferson, but the farmer was on the verge of peasantry. The Industrial Revolution had made the United States the greatest of manufacturing nations but the process had depressed a large element of society and had been accompanied by monstrous perversions in the employment of women and children and in the treatment of the aged, the incompetent, and the infirm. Unemployment and child labor went hand in hand; machinery was marvelously efficient, but no other industrial nation confessed so many industrial accidents. The nation was fabulously rich but its wealth was gravitating rapidly into the hands of a very small portion of the population, and the power of wealth had already undermined the political integrity of the Republic. In a land of plenty there was never enough food, clothing, and shelter for the underprivileged, and cyclical depressions, apparently unavoidable, plunged millions into actual want. In the great cities the slums grew apace, and from the slums spread corrupting disease, crime and vice. Science told how to control many of the diseases that plagued mankind but poverty interposed between science and health, and tuberculosis, hookworm, malaria, syphilis, and other diseases of poverty and ignorance took an annual toll that ran into millions. The churches taught the Ten

Commandments and philosophers the Golden Rule, but man's inhumanity was still illustrated in the penal code, in prison conditions, the treatment of the aged, the poor, the incapacitated, the defective and the insane, and in the attitude toward the criminal and the prostitute. The white race was sure of its superiority, but it had forgotten that code of chivalry which placed upon the strong responsibility for the weak, and the callous indifference toward the Indian and the exploitation of the Negro was a blot on American civilization. The educational system was an object of pride, but its benefits were unevenly distributed, and the census of 1900 discovered over six million illiterates. Everyone gave lip service to the principles of democracy, but political corruption cankered the body politic from top to bottom. On all sides thoughtful men feared that the nation which Lincoln had called "the last best hope of earth" would prove instead the world's illusion.[5]

The nation was facing an acid test of democracy's faith in the common man to assert his rights and to make intelligent decisions about his welfare and his destiny.

The laissez-faire philosophy carried to this extreme was beginning to affect America's democratic and humanitarian traditions. Toward the close of the nineteenth century reaction set in and the philosophy of Social Darwinism was challenged in the economic, political, and social arenas. People from all walks of life joined the protest. They included teachers, sociologists, economists, clergymen, politicians, authors, journalists, farmers, and workers. The publication of *Progress and Poverty* by Henry George in 1879, *Dynamic Sociology* by Lester Ward in 1883, *Looking Backward* by Edward Bellamy in 1889, were attempts to formulate social solutions for the accumulated social problems, and they emphasized the positive and planning role of government in dealing with these problems. People selected different avenues of attack. Some turned to trade unionism, some to political action and social reform, and some to social services. Although all three movements were concerned with the welfare of people they varied in their approach and emphasis.

With the industrialization of the nation had come the trade unions, but the early history of unionism was a chronicle of failure because the open frontiers provided a safety valve in times of economic distress, and the rapid movement of workers created organizational instability. Furthermore, in the early period of industrialization many of the workers were women and children, who were not unionized. The city-wide organizations of the 1830's had as their aim increasing the living standards of the whole community, and resorted to political action as a means of achieving their goal. Among other issues they championed free public education, abolition of imprisonment for debt, complete separation of church and state, democratization of the tax system, and a shorter work week. These unions, however, were not strong enough to survive the severe depression of 1837.

The next large attempt on the part of labor was the formation of the National Labor Union in 1866. Although it made some effort to build trade union organization, its primary interest was in legislative reform. It too turned to politics to achieve its goals, and in 1872 became the National Labor Reform Party, but political moves did not succeed, and the severe depression in 1873 spelled the end of this effort. Paralleling this abortive attempt to build a strong politically-oriented labor movement was the formation of the Knights of Labor in 1869. It started out as a secret society of individual members and swelled its ranks to a million by 1886. Lack of organization and a sharp difference between top leadership and the rank-and-file members on a strike policy weakened the effectiveness of the union. In its final stages it entered the field of politics and soon lost the support of its membership, who were becoming discouraged by the long uphill battle which legislative reform involved. Nevertheless, it was somewhat effective as a forerunner of subsequent movements.

It was not until 1881, with the organization of the Federation of Organized Trades and Labor Unions under the leadership of Adolph Strasser and Samuel Gompers, that a stable trade union movement was born. In 1886 this group became the present American Federation of Labor. In a sense the success of this venture was attained at the expense of limiting membership to crafts groups, thereby leaving out the large number of unskilled workers, and by limiting the goals to immediate gains, thereby pulling labor out of politics.

In brief, the workers were beginning to assert their rights and to make themselves heard, but they found the political climate oppressive. The government and the courts were far from friendly. The use of state militia to break strikes was a common practice. Two black days in the history of labor in this country were written during this period, the Haymarket Square riot in Chicago in 1886, and the Homestead riot in Pennsylvania in 1892. Both involved the use of police and state militia. In the Haymarket riot seven were killed and the strikers all replaced by strikebreakers. Government was utilizing its "policing" power to help the industrialist but not to help the people in their struggle for existence.

Labor should have found an ally in the expanding social service movement, but social work was still immersed in trying to save and reform the individual. Social services at this time were in the hands of volunteers who came primarily from the upper and middle classes, that is, from the employing groups. These groups supplied both the finances and the manpower for these humanitarian projects. Strikes tended to make explicit the conflict of interests. The following statement from the annual report of the New York Association for Improving the Conditions of the Poor during the economic unrest of the 1870's sets forth the prevailing philosophy:

Looking at strikes from an ethical or moral standpoint, their demoralizing and impoverishing effect cannot be overlooked. This, as it directly concerned the working classes, was one of the worst results of the contest. Much has been spoken and written of what would be the elevating effects on the character and condition of the working-man by giving him four hours a day for self-improvement and the benefit of his family. But, unfortunately for this pleasant theory, when he had twelve hours at his command instead of four, as during the recent strikes, the advantages of leisure were not verified by the results. It was found here as elsewhere, that idleness and profligacy too often go hand in hand together. Lounging about street-corners, gossiping and drinking at liquor shops, neither tends to his own elevation nor to the happiness of his household but rather to thriftless, dissipated habits and domestic wretchedness. . . .

The objects of this Association incline it to sympathize with Labor, but not against Capital as such, which is essential to the being and well being of organized communities. It is a truism to say that this Charity is an outgrowth of Capital, and could not exist without it, or that the numerous benevolent institutions in this city and the world, with the gratuitous expenditures of untold millions for the help of the destitute and perishing have a like origin.[6]

Charity organization, however, like trade unions was moving along. The day-to-day contact with the sufferings of millions shifted its attention from the moral inadequacy of the individual to the moral inadequacy of society. By the turn of the century under the leadership of people like Jane Addams, the social services joined the swelling democratic revolt against the concentrated power of "big business," and helped to write the social reform record of the early part of the twentieth century.

The reaction against the crushing power of big business came not only from the workers of the highly industrialized East but also from the farmers of the West and the South. The Populist movement, under the leadership of agrarian reformers like Tom Watson and Jerry Simpson, fought for government aid for the farmers. All of the forces began to coalesce, and in 1896 under the banner of William Jennings Bryan, who had espoused the cause of the people and won the leadership of the Democratic Party, they made their first organized stand. They were defeated in the elections of 1896 and 1900, but they showed enough strength to lay the groundwork for new social attitudes in the next decade. The full meaning of the experience of this era to American life is summed up beautifully by James Truslow Adams:

After we had attained independence as a nation, our national elections had registered what I have called the "heart-beats" of the democratic movement, about once each generation. There was the "Jeffersonian Revolution" in 1800; the Jacksonian in 1828; the election of Lincoln in 1860. In each case the common people, the ordinary Americans, placed their candidate in the White House. In another generation, in the Bryan campaign of 1896, they failed

. . . For the fourth time the ordinary American had made a fight, whether with the right ideas or not, for what he thought was his share of the good life, of opportunity, of the American Dream, and he had been licked. . . . Both sides had been frightened, and disgusted. Even so staunch a party man as Theodore Roosevelt wrote to a still stauncher and more hard boiled one, the late Senator Lodge, that the stench of corruption that had been necessary to win the election sickened him.[7]

Within the economic, social, and political climate of this period the sciences were developing. The climate gives to social work its philosophy and motivation, the sciences are responsible for its methodology. In general, the social sciences were still in an undifferentiated stage during the greater part of the nineteenth century. Toward the end of the century the over-all American Social Science Association began to give way to specialized groupings interested primarily in theory and research. For example, the American Psychological Association was formed in 1892 under the leadership of G. Stanley Hall. The National Conference of Charities and Corrections, organized in 1874, was at first part of the American Social Science Association, but became an independent body in 1879. As the social sciences became more differentiated and more interested in pure science, the "social work" group found the setting of the American Social Science Association less congenial to its interest in broad social welfare problems and to the goal of improving social living.

There are several important landmarks in the development of the social sciences during this period. Beginning in 1800 medicine had started its rapid progress toward modern concepts. The work of Joseph Lister in antisepsis, Crawford Long and William Morton in anaesthesia, Louis Pasteur and Robert Koch in the germ theory of disease, and Paul Ehrlich in chemotherapy were all basic to modern medicine. In the same way the work of Auguste Comte, Charles Darwin, Francis Galton, Frederic Le Play, and Wilhelm Wundt were basic to the developments of our modern concepts of sociology and psychology.

Auguste Comte, a French mathematician and philosopher,

is regarded as the father of sociology and the first to use the term. Comte founded the philosophy of positivism, which differentiates scientific or positive knowledge from theological and metaphysical knowledge. For Comte the only real knowledge was factual reality, or knowledge of things having objective existence. He saw sociology as an over-all science, as the tool of integrating the results of the various social sciences. Comte's new approach encouraged the study of society.

In the middle 1800's men like Frederic Le Play, who introduced the case method in the study of social problems, began to apply mathematical formulations to their work. They were trying to make of sociology an exact science rather than an over-all philosophy. Le Play, a metallurgist by training, was deeply interested in people.

This deep interest in the people who earned their living and lived out their lives in and around a particular place of occupation led Le Play to bring the methods of natural science to the observation of social facts and their inductive analysis. He took the family for the elementary social unit and used the family budget as the quantitative expression of family life and the basis for quantitative analysis of social facts. . . . Social scientists have used this case study method for social investigation and for social description. Social workers have applied it to the analysis and treatment of individual problems and needs.[8]

The efforts of social reformers to improve the living conditions of the masses by studying and exposing the conditions of various social institutions contributed to developments in sociology. John Howard, concerned with the inhumane treatment of prisoners, made a study of English prison life in 1777. More than a century later, Charles Booth made a similar study of slum conditions in London. In the United States, Jacob Riis, Jane Addams and others found the survey type of study useful in exposing various social problems. These studies helped to establish a definite pattern for dealing with community problems which has become the interest of both sociologists and social workers. The community survey as a formalized tool in social work was given prominence in the Pittsburgh Survey in 1907-1908 and has been widely used ever since.

Before 1850 there was practically no scientific attempt to interpret and explain the behavior of people. The first psychological laboratory was established by Wilhelm Wundt in Leipzig in 1878. Wundt is best known for his psychology of elements and his development of the experimental approach. Many Americans went to Germany to study with Wundt. Through them and the Anglo-American E. B. Titchener and the German Hugo Münsterberg, both disciples of Wundt who were brought to America in 1892, the Wundtian approach to psychology soon influenced American thought. American psychology was to have another channel of influence, however, through the work of Charles Darwin and Francis Galton. As E. G. Boring notes, American psychology "inherited its physical body from German experimentalism, but got its mind from Darwin" [9]

Charles Darwin published his *Origin of Species* in 1859, and *The Descent of Man*—the application of his theory of evolution to the human race—in 1871. Reference has already been made to the application of his theory to society by Herbert Spencer in England and William Graham Sumner in this country. Darwin's theory was important to all studies of human data, biological and social, in that it established the thesis of "the unit of living matter" and examined the causal relations of change. Changes in the individual and in society could be studied and the causes for change analyzed. To some social scientists such as Lester Ward, it meant reinforcement for the view that there was a two-way process between man and his environment, and that man could change environment just as environment could change man.

Darwin's views had a pronounced effect on American psychology. They stimulated an interest in problems of animal psychology and of mental inheritance. Francis Galton, a cousin of Darwin, developed at this time his thesis on the inheritance of intelligence. Aside from his studies on heredity, one of Galton's major contributions was the application of the statistical method to this study of human data. It remained for William James, the pioneer American psychologist, with his background in physiology and philosophy, to lay the groundwork for an integration of German experimentalism with the Darwinian emphasis on mind in the process of adaptation and survival into the theoretical formulation of American functional psychology. James reacted against the Wundtian conception of elements. For him mind was a process with a definite use which could be observed. Consciousness had evolved with a specific function as a steering apparatus for the complicated nervous system. American functional psychology, later given its structure and philosophical formulation of pragmatic instrumentalism by John Dewey, with its emphasis on "mind in use," paved the way for the growing interest at the turn of the century in psychopathology, educational psychology, mental testing, and applied psychology.

Pragmatism, sometimes referred to as an indigenous American philosophy, represented a reaction against the prevailing idealism. The basis of interest in pragmatism was the impact of the emerging scientific method. It represented an approach closely related to the method of science. The pragmatist did not believe that anything was "self-evident." All ideas had to be judged by how they worked rather than how they looked or sounded. For the pragmatist the life experience was the laboratory for testing hypotheses about man and his environment. Thought was not an esoteric process to be studied in a vacuum but rather a tool in adjustment to the life situation. Thought, furthermore, was to be viewed, not as an isolated individual process but as a social process as well. Pragmatism with its emphasis on integrating theory and practice, thought and deed, brought philosophy out of the ivory tower, out of highly theoretical speculations on the ultimate nature of reality, and into the arena of everyday problems. For example, truth and good were not to be dealt with abstractly, but in terms of their meaning in life situations.

Another development during this period which bore upon both the social sciences and the economic, political, and social events of the day was the work of Karl Marx (1818-1883). Marx was both a theorist and an active participant in the political struggles of the period. He was the founder of the modern theories of socialism, as well as the organizer of the International Workingmen's Association in 1864. Marx devoted his later years to the completion of his world-shaking treatise, *Das Kapital*. It was his thesis that economic factors were the determinants of all history, and that the building of a better society necessitated ownership and control of all the tools of production by the state rather than by individuals. Marx's theory was directly opposed to the philosophy of laissez-faire and rugged individualism. Many of the social reformers in the United States in this period took their stand somewhere between these two extremes. They were less interested in changing the basic structure of American society than they were in reforming its methods of operation. Although they did not advocate government ownership of the tools of production, many of their objectives for social change were similar to those expressed by Marx and Engels in the *Communist Manifesto* of 1848, and, therefore, they were frequently accused of being Communists.

The social sciences were on their way but had not yet reached a point of being able to provide a methodology for dealing with problems of the individual and of society. The economic, political, and social climate was trending rapidly in the direction of "Social Darwinism" with its emphasis on laissez-faire and "rugged individualism." It was not a climate conducive to furthering human welfare through the democratic channels of government. Humanitarianism, however, continued to prick man's conscience in a period troubled by social problems and social corruption. The natural step, therefore, was, if possible, to satisfy that conscience without upsetting the basic philosophy of the day. The answer was an expansion of private charity. Aid was still a privilege and not a right, and the more fortunate could bestow this privilege on the less fortunate, without betraying their belief that social problems were not the fault of the society, but merely evidence of the moral weakness of some individuals. If there were an increasing number of underprivileged, the answer was to be found not in looking for causal factors in the society, but in applying better business methods of coordination and efficiency. Professor Francis Wayland of Yale University "warned in 1877 that receiving public assistance would come to be looked upon as a right, and that the recipient would come to believe that he was living by 'decent means.' " [10] Wayland, however, did not regard assistance by private agencies, individuals, and religious bodies in the same light as public assistance. It was his opinion that the former's more accurate and continuing knowledge of the applicant made their approach more efficient. Furthermore, assistance from private sources would not build up among recipients the attitude that aid was theirs as a right.

In the area of public welfare the earlier principles still held sway. These included: local autonomy; strict enforcement of the settlement law; the liability of relatives; the principle of less eligibility; and, keeping government services at a minimum. Following the earlier expansion of services for children, the handicapped, the deaf, the blind, and the ill, the period 1870 to 1900 saw significant changes in the attitude toward the delinquent. Reform rather than punishment became the new emphasis. In Massachusetts, for example, beginning in 1869 an agent of the State Board of Charities was present at the hearings of all juvenile cases. The function of the agent was to give advice to the judge or to have the child assigned to him. Around this new approach there developed an active group of women volunteers to help with investigations, the supervising of probationers, and the keeping of case records. The first juvenile court was not established until 1899 in Chicago. In 1876, however, the first reformatory was established in Elmira, New York, with an emphasis on rehabilitation rather than punishment.

After the Civil War, jails, which were always badly run, became even worse because the appointment of prison officials was purely political. Under their management the jails became a source for graft; the officials leased convicts for labor and also pocketed funds. Sanitary conditions were deplorable; children, women, and men were housed in the same prison, and little distinction was made between the indigent poor and the hardened criminal. Under the leadership of people like Enoch C. Wines and Zebulon R. Brockway, reforms were initiated. The National Prison Association was begun in 1870 with Wines playing a major role in its organization. The association became interested in the problems of children in prisons, because they felt that prisons had become a breeding ground for crime. They also were concerned with the role of state boards in correcting the deplorable standards in penal institutions.

The reformatory at Elmira was erected in 1876. Through the efforts of the National Prison Association, Brockway, who had developed a new approach in Detroit, was invited to become the warden. Brockway advocated reform rather than punishment, and utilized as his method both the emotional appeal and a program of educating the whole man. Under his leadership Elmira became an experimental center in penology.

With the expansion of the numerous public institutions for these special problems there was need for a more coordinated approach. Institutions had become political footballs. They competed with each other for state appropriations. The state boards of charities were established to deal with this problem. The first state board was organized in Massachusetts in 1863. New York created its Board of State Commissioners of Public Charities in 1867. The boards in the beginning had an advisory rather than a supervisory or administrative function. "While the Board had no power to act directly in correcting abuses in welfare institutions, the publicity given to its exposures frequently resulted in remedial action by the localities." [11]

The pattern of state boards varied, and in the early years of the National Conference of Charities and Corrections there was constant debate as to the merits of the various patterns. The debate centered primarily upon the question of the advisory versus the administrative type of state board. It was the opinion of some that the board which had administrative power and control tended to be most efficient and economical. Others felt, however, that this type of structure thwarted the imaginative and destroyed the creative approach to be seen in an advisory relationship.

The importance of the creation of state boards to the furthering of human welfare is pointed up sharply in the following evaluation of the experience in Massachusetts:

The establishment of this board (State Board of Charities) was an epoch making step in Massachusetts charities; for upon its erection the State's policy in poor relief became a fact. That which before had been chaos and strife, born of local jealousy, became first a groping and then a steady progress toward a social programme looking to the welfare of the community in the large. Warfare was immediately waged upon the absurd practise of herding dependent children with hardened criminals. First, children were to be housed in buildings apart; then they were to be placed in institutions entirely separated from adults; finally, they were to be taken from the institutions altogether and given foster family care wherever there was not discovered such abnormality as to call for special treatment and custody. The insane were to be separated from inmates of normal mind, and the furiously mad were to be given asylum by themselves. Finally, the State was to care for the insane as a special problem of the central government. And it was not enough to relieve the towns of their unsolved problems; a proper staff system called for oversight of the local administration of outdoor and indoor relief. The State, in a series of wise statutes, took supervision of the town almshouses, eliminating the children who could be cared for elsewhere, requiring isolation of consumptives and syphilitics, and inspecting the plan and all its facilities in minute detail. In like manner the State assumed authority to visit all adults placed out by the overseers.[12]

The state boards varied not only in the extent of control or power but also in the types of institutions included. At first the tendency was to cover health institutions as well as those dealing with the dependent, the handicapped, the insane, and the legal offenders. In some states health institutions, and in others penal institutions, were placed under separate jurisdictions. In Massachusetts, for example, the legislature passed an act in 1878:

. . . which abolished the State Board of Health, the Board of State Charities, and the nine several boards in charge of the State institutions and established a State Board of Health, Lunacy and Charity; to consist of nine members; to be unpaid; and to have all the powers and duties of the agencies which it replaced. Oversight of institutions for the instruction of the deaf, dumb, and blind had, meantime, in 1875, been transferred to the State Board of Education, while in the same readjustment of 1879 the supervision of the correctional institutions went to a Board of Commissioners of Prisons.[13]

This pattern continued for seven years. In 1886 with the rapid development of its public health program, Massachusetts established a separate Board of Health.

Massachusetts had established the first Board of Health in the nation in 1869. The study and report of Leonard Shattuck presaged a new era in the field of sanitation. The report recommended not only local and state departments of health but also a sanitary police force and a program of public education to help combat and prevent the spread of disease. By 1880 the example set by Massachusetts was followed by sixteen states. The American Public Health Association was organized in 1872. One of the important aspects of Shattuck's report was that it established a pattern for combining regulation and education in dealing with social problems.

The superintendents of the public institutions and the members of the state boards of charities provided the early leadership in the formation of the National Conference of Charities and Corrections in 1873. As might be expected, the programs in the early years of the conference were focused on problems of public services. Under discussion were such questions as: (1) the merits of the administrative type of state board as compared with the advisory; (2) institutional care of children versus foster care; (3) subsidies by states to private agencies caring for children; (4) administrative and personnel problems of institutions.

The more extensive developments during this period came in the private or voluntary field. Even during the colonial period social service programs under the auspices of religious and civic groups had begun to emerge to supplement the local programs of public financial assistance. With the rapid progress of the Industrial Revolution immediately after the Civil War, the local public-assistance program proved increasingly inadequate and supplementation by private effort became greater and greater. As the number of privately sponsored programs increased, especially in the urban areas, there was great variation in standards and frequent overlap and duplication of efforts. As Watson points out, the need for some rules of the game, for some coordination of services, was recognized as early as 1850.[14] Competition between agencies drove the poverty stricken to become consumers of many similar services at the same time.

Although the need for coordination was apparent by 1850, it took a major crisis—as is often the case—to bring the concept into operational fruition. The severe depression in 1873 created a national problem of unemployment. It pointed up the inadequacy of the existing programs of assistance and catapulted agencies with meager resources into attempts to bring order out of chaos. Kellog asserts that it was the 1873 depression that afforded "the starting point for the examination and reformation of the prevailing methods of charity." [15] Various attempts at better coordination of relief programs were undertaken. The most successful was that introduced by the Reverend S. H. Gurteen in Buffalo in 1877. The Reverend Mr. Gurteen, who had been connected with the London Charity Organization Society—established April 22, 1869, as the London Society for Organizing Charitable Relief and Repressing Mendicancy—helped to develop a similar program. The Charity Organization Society, which was to be the forerunner of both the council of social agencies and the family agency operated on the following four general principles:

(1) Detailed investigation of the applicant;
(2) A central system of registration to avoid duplication;
(3) Cooperation between the various relief agencies;
(4) Extensive use of the volunteer friendly visitor.

The main functions of the charity organization societies were threefold: "First and basic, the rehabilitation of families which for any reason fail to be self-sufficient; second, the education of the community in correct principles of relief; and third, aid in the elimination of the causes of poverty." [16]

Although the emphasis in the beginning was on the first and second functions, the orderly way of doing things led not only to a better understanding of individual and family needs but also to a growing interest in community conditions.

Earlier European attempts to organize the system of charities had affected the development in England. One such effort, which had an influence on the reform of the poor laws in England in 1834 and the formation there of the charity organization society movement in 1869, was the plan developed in Hamburg. The plan called for the following steps:

(1) To create a central bureau to supervise all work done for the poor, and to bring all charitable agencies under one management, in order to prevent "overlapping," and also to put a stop to indiscriminate almsgiving.

(2) To sub-divide the city into small districts, in each of which a competent citizen should personally investigate the condition of all paupers and semi-paupers, that the exact needs of all might be known, that the deserving might be discovered and the undeserving rebuked, and that no more relief should be given than was absolutely necessary.

(3) To remove the causes of distress and pauperism by compelling the able-bodied to work, by making the homes of the poor more healthy, by providing work for the unemployed and by giving the children of the destitute an industrial training that they might grow up self-dependent citizens.[17]

In the early efforts of the charity organization societies one sees the roots of many present-day programs and practices. Among these are the social service exchange, the case conference, social action, and planning. The first Social Service Exchange, which represented a way of coordinating the efforts of the variety of agencies, was organized by the Associated Charities of Boston in 1879. Each agency furnished the exchange with a full history of the families with which they were dealing. The fuller records were later replaced with a card index system containing the necessary identifying information. The purpose of the exchange was to serve as a clearing house in order to prevent duplication of services and to spare the clients from unnecessary investigation.

The case conference method, in its beginnings, brought representatives of various agencies together to share their information about a particular family and to discuss a possible plan of action. These conferences not only served the purpose of better planning but also proved to be a source of education for those who participated.

The publication of directories of charities was seen not only as an important tool for locating services but also as a way of determining gaps in the services available.

Zilpha D. Smith, in giving the first report of the National Conference of Charities and Corrections "Committee on the Organization of Charity," noted in 1888 that four societies had published directories of charities in book form. She said also that charity organization society offices were a bureau of information about all the charities of a city. By gathering the necessary information the charity organization societies would discover unknown societies and reveal gaps in services. According to Miss Smith, part of the work of organized charity was to see that gaps were filled by individual benevolence, by legislation, by extension of old organizations or by the establishment of new ones.[18]

Reflecting the contemporary emphasis on social reform, prevention came into major focus in the charity organizations toward the end of the century. Watson, commenting on the period 1896-1904, pointed out that the outstanding characteristic was the emphasis placed by charity organization societies upon the prevention of poverty, as reflected in the various movements to change social conditions. In the report of the Committee on Organization of Charity in 1893 the chairman presented an impressive list of charity organization endeavors in the area of social action,[19] including among others housing, health, child labor, and sanitation.

By the end of the century the charity organization societies began to employ paid workers, to engage in social reform, and to recognize the need for trained staff. Many of these societies established training courses for their workers. The New York

Charity Organization Society expanded its in-service training program into a more organized effort and established the first school for training social workers in the country in 1898. It was called the New York School of Philanthropy, and is now known as the New York School of Social Work, Columbia University.

Paralleling this development of relief work was the settlement house movement. Again the pattern was set in England in 1884 with the founding of Toynbee Hall in London under the leadership of Samuel Barnett, the Vicar of St. Jude's Parish.

[Vicar Barnett] used the word "settlement" to describe a group of people living in a neighborhood and identifying themselves with its life as a means of understanding and improving conditions. He was seeking a way to bring people together to enable them to learn from each other and through shared experiences to build a richer life for themselves and for the nation as a whole.[20]

In essence, it was the use of the friendly visitor on a more sustained basis by having him live in the settlement house and become better acquainted and more identified with the problems of the neighborhood through this intensive face-to-face experience. The first settlement in the United States was established on the Lower East Side of New York under the leadership of Stanton Coit, under the name of the Neighborhood Guild (now the University Settlement). The settlement movement caught on rapidly and by the turn of the century under the leadership of people like Jane Addams, the head of Hull House in Chicago, played an important role in the crusade for social reform.

The friendly visitor, who came primarily from the middle class, was provided with an opportunity to view at first hand the social breakdown and social injustices growing out of rapid industrialization and urbanization. Settlement houses were organized in many of the large urban communities. The staff was frequently made up of women who found the challenge of the program a natural channel for expressing their own struggle for emancipation. They were, in a sense, a minority group taking on the battle of other minority groups within the principle that the solution of any minority problem is with the community rather than through it. This legion of courageous and dedicated women was to write history in the fight against social injustice.

Many remained within the settlement house movement, but others, stimulated by their experience in the local community, were to move on to national social action projects such as the National Consumers League, the Women's Trade Union League, and the Association for Labor Legislation. A name that stands out in the history of social reform is that of Florence Kelley, who came originally from Hull House. She found in the National Consumers League, organized in 1899, an even more effective vehicle for her deep interest in fighting social injustices. Under her leadership the league made many important contributions in the legislative field. Blessed with a good head as well as a warm heart, Florence Kelley helped to create one of the basic approaches in social action. It involved gathering the facts, making them known to the public, preparing legislation to remedy the situation, and utilizing public pressure to have it enacted.

The settlement house and the charity organization society movements had much in common but they differed in one major respect, namely the degree of emphasis on self-help. As pointed out by Steiner, "The social settlements never accepted the traditional idea that leadership was a divine right of the upper classes. At a time when such an idea was widely prevalent, the social settlements set themselves firmly against attitudes of condescension in their relations with the poor and sought to break down the undemocratic cleavage between social classes." [21] As charity began to undergo a change in its approach, the two groups drew closer together. Thus Mary McDowell reported in a paper at the National Conference in 1896, charity was undergoing a change at the hands of science . . . "the settlement could not cooperate with charity if it were nothing more than a relief society, but could cooperate with it if charity offered a friendship that could change life. The settlement could not stand still and ignore the physical needs of its neighbors. The problem of both the settlement and organized charity, she believed, was how to meet these needs in a way that would leave the neighbor on a higher spiritual plane. The settlement, she said, worked from within while the charity organization society, with its voluntary friendly visitors and its paid agents, was the force coming from the outside into the neighborhood. They differed in method and approach, yet complemented each other. Together they did what neither could completely do alone.[22]

During this period the YMCA movement continued to expand, and was joined in a similar effort for women by the YWCA movement, the first local YWCA being established in Boston in 1866. The stated purpose of the organization was to promote "the temporal, moral and religious welfare of young women who are dependent on their own exertions for support." [23] Membership was open to any Christian woman who was a member in regular standing of an evangelical church. By 1875 there were twenty-eight YWCA's in the United States. In 1873 the movement found its way onto the college campus. The student movement grew quickly, and participated in the formation of the World's Young Women's Christian Association in 1894 and the World's Student Christian Federation in 1895. By the end of the century the YWCA program had expanded to include work with young girls, rural work, work with minority groups, and work with special economic groups.

The YMCA had made some strides prior to the Civil War. At first it appeared that the war would destroy this young and hardly formulated movement. The program for assisting the fighting men, which emerged during the war, however, tended to stimulate and influence the underlying motivation of the movement. By 1869 the fourfold program of serving the social, spiritual, intellectual, and physical needs of young men was enunciated. Reflecting the changing complexion of the nation, the YMCA program expanded as follows:

(1) The Railroad Y.M.C.A. Unit was introduced in 1872, and by 1900 there were 160 such units.

(2) Work with Negroes was introduced in 1872, and by 1900 there were 23 Negro associations.

(3) Work with the Indians was initiated in 1897, and by 1900 there were 44 Indian Associations.

(4) In 1877 the Intercollegiate Student Movement was organized.

(5) In 1890 special training schools were introduced at Springfield, Massachusetts, and Chicago, Illinois.

(6) Work with young boys was introduced in 1869, and by 1900 there were 401 associations providing special programs for boys.

In the middle of the century under the leadership of Charles Loring Brace the movement for child placement in homes, as opposed to institutional care, was initiated. Brace's plan was to send the destitute and homeless children from the streets of New York to homes in western states. By 1875 some 35,000 children had been sent out of the city. Brace's objectives reflected the attitude of the time.

My great object in the present work, is to prove to society . . . that the cheapest and most efficacious way of dealing with the "Dangerous Classes" of large cities is not to punish them but to prevent their growth; to so throw the influences of education and discipline and religion about the abandoned and destitute youth of our large towns; to so change their material circumstances, and draw them under the influence of the moral and fortunate classes, that they shall grow up as useful producers and members of society, able and inclined to aid it in its progress. . . . In the view of this book, the class of a large city most dangerous to its property, its morals, and its political life are the ignorant, destitute, untrained, and abandoned youth; the outcast street-children grown up to be voters, to be the implements of demagogues, the "feeders" of the criminals, and the sources of the domestic outbreaks and violations of the law.[24]

Opposition to Brace's approach came not so much to challenge his political philosophy as to halt his method of placement and indiscriminate selection of children without regard to religious faith. A study made by Hastings Hart of the results of placements made by the Children's Aid Society found that "58% had turned out badly, could not be found, or there was no report available."

The whole problem of child welfare was complicated by the sectarian question: ". . . the development of Protestant and nonsectarian agencies, which for the most part represented a philosophy not in accord with the Catholic philosophy of life, was a challenge to Catholic groups, who felt impelled to set up an organization which would more nearly express the Christian concept of justice and charity." [25] In 1863 the New York Catholic Protectory was established and grew rapidly. The Society of St. Vincent de Paul discussed the problem at their third General Assembly in 1876. Through their efforts the Catholic Home Bureau of New York was established in 1898. Mr. Mulry, one of the leaders in the movement, wrote:

Experience has shown us that in the City of New York alone hundreds of children of Catholic parentage are every year placed in non-Catholic institutions, or families where their faith must almost inevitably be lost.

We realize too that our Catholic institutions are in danger of becoming over-crowded, and their highest usefulness in a measure at least impaired by the necessity of retaining and properly caring for children long after the age when they might safely be placed in private families.[26]

The development of the private agencies was rapid. Its leadership began to dominate the social work scene toward the end of the century and continued this role up to the depression of the 1930's. The private agency moved ahead in a period of mass immigration that brought to this country large numbers of people with varied nationality and religious backgrounds. The early efforts of providing services for the unfortunate were predominantly Protestant in sponsorship. Although the sponsors looked upon their endeavors as nonsectarian, the immigrant saw them as religious in motivation.

The immigrant entered into a civilization essentially Protestant. . . . Before the Civil War the immigrant who needed assistance had to look to Protestant sources. In fact, the public institutions were just as Protestant in character as those operated by the individual denominations. Their agents were often ministers or ex-ministers, or women who were aggressively evangelistic.[27]

The immigrant accepted the economic help offered but resisted the attempt to impose new cultural norms. There arose, therefore, a pattern of sectarian and nationality sponsored services.

The early Jewish settlers had developed their social services around the synagogue. The Jewish community was affected by the factors at work in the general community. "In the latter part of the century a trend toward secularization set in. In the late 1870's, under the impetus of the charity organization society movement, congregational ladies' aid societies began to merge into United Hebrew Charities." [28] The Jewish group had learned through years of persecution and ghetto living the concept of interdependence and the need for an organized community machinery. The idea for federated financing evolved in the Jewish community. In 1896 eight Jewish agencies in Cincinnati formed a successful federation.

In the child care field Jewish activity was early; a Jewish children's home was in existence in Charleston, South Carolina, in 1807. The expansion of children's homes followed the increase in Jewish population through immigration. By the turn of the century there were sufficient facilities in Jewish children's homes to accommodate approximately 4,000 children. Homes for the aged were also established as a religious responsibility. In the field of health two Jewish hospitals were already in existence by 1855. Between 1860 and 1900 many more were established in the large urban communities.

One of the major developments during this period was the emergence of the Young Men's Hebrew Association, increasingly known today as the Jewish Community Center. Whereas the early YMCA's had a strong religious basis, the motivation for the YMHA's was more secular. Their purpose was to provide educational, cultural, and recreational activities. The first YMHA was organized in Baltimore about 1855. By 1875 there were 20 more in existence, and by 1890 approximately 125. The Jewish community also developed settlement houses and educational alliances to aid the immigrants in their Americanization.

The large number of immigrants with varied religious and

nationality backgrounds necessitated an extensive program of Americanization. Various theories of ethnic adjustment began to emerge. At first it was the opinion of some that America could best be looked at as a "melting pot" into which people of varying backgrounds were placed to emerge as typical Americans. Many soon realized, however, that although assimilation to new work habits was easily attained, cultural and ethnic patterns were not readily discarded. Some educational leaders believed that the answer lay in assimilation to the dominant culture. E. P. Cubberly, in his book *Changing Conceptions of Education,* wrote: "Our task is to break up these groups or settlements, to assimilate and amalgamate these people as a part of our American race, and to implant in their children, so far as can be done, the Anglo-Saxon conception of righteousness, law and order, and popular government." [29] There later began to emerge a concept of America as a multi-group society with each group contributing to the whole and being affected by it.

Summary

External Factors

Between 1860 and 1900 the population of the country had increased by 44,551,254, an increase of 141 per cent. One of the chief sources of increase was immigration. The immigrants who came during this period were primarily from Eastern Europe, Italy, and the Balkans. They came with a markedly different culture pattern and added substantially to the Catholic and Jewish populations of the country. They came at a time when the frontiers were closing, and they tended to settle in the urban communities, thus adding to the rapidly growing slums. They were in the main unskilled workers entering the industrial arena with language and cultural handicaps.

America was feeling the full impact of the Industrial Revolution. By the end of the century it had attained the status of the leading industrial nation of the world. The pattern of small businesses owned by thousands of individuals and companies gave way to the all-powerful giant corporations and banking firms. The lines between big business and labor became sharply defined, with labor making numerous attempts to organize in defense of its rights. It was an uneven battle, however, for the industrialists were not only hostile but able to align government on their side.

The rapid technological change was not accompanied by a necessary corresponding change in social institutions and ideologies. The philosophy and attitudes born of a pioneer and rural period were not adequate to meet the problems of a rapidly expanding industrial and urban society. Emphasis was not on utilizing the emerging technology for the furthering of common human needs, but rather on utilizing people to further the technology. The democratic philosophy of Jefferson had broken down and had given way to crass materialism with property rights placed above human rights. A new philosophy, a sort of bastardized interpretation of Jeffersonian individualism with an underpinning of Social Darwinism, reigned supreme.

The decline of the institutional functions of the family evident in the previous period moved rapidly under the impact of the Industrial Revolution. The family was no longer the center of the nation's system of production, having become a consumer rather than a producer group. The teaching, religious, and protective functions had also moved out of the home. These changes in function also brought changes in the social conditions of the family which had been inherent in its structure as a producer group. The changing roles of wife and children as part of an economic institution brought a corresponding change in attitude toward marital age, size of family, and divorce. The supreme authority of the father in matters of conduct lessened. The role of the home as a center for recreational activities and vocational training now had to be artificially maintained, since it was no longer an inherent part of an economically producer-centered group. As the family became weaker in terms of its kinship structure and status it began to provide less protection to its members in need of aid. Increasingly the members had to turn to the community for assistance.

The development and expansion of social agencies during this period represented an attempt to take up the slack and fill the ever-widening gap created by the uneven pace of technological development and by the change in social institutions and ideologies. There was little recognition or understanding at first, however, of the causes of the numerous social problems, and the individual was asked to bear the total blame. The emphasis, for example, was on the elimination of pauperism, not poverty. Economic failure was the result of individual weakness or unfitness. "Broader social causes—such as mass unemployment, substandard wages, bad housing—were largely overlooked."

Government, whose leadership was essential in dealing with the interests and welfare of the nation as a whole during this period of cataclysmic change, tended to identify itself with only the technological change, leaving people to struggle for themselves. The earlier philosophy of a minimal government prevailed. Furthermore, the nature and extent of the authority of the federal government in economic, political, and social affairs was still a moot question. Although the Fourteenth Amendment represented a reversal in the interpretation of the traditional relation of the citizens to his government, it was almost as if a reaction set in after this step had been taken. Government went back to a narrow interpretation of its policing function and accepted little responsibility for regulation let alone seeing itself as a positive tool in furthering human welfare. It saw its duty as that of keeping the competitive process open; the fact that conditions had changed and that midgets with bows and arrows were being asked to compete against giants with guns was forgotten. There was growing resentment toward this interpretation of government, and by the end of the century the people rallied to bring about reform.

The social sciences were still in a highly undifferentiated stage in the middle of the 1800's. By the end of the century the movement toward differentiation was well on its way. With it came a growing emphasis on theory and research, and a tendency to withdraw from dealing with the life situation. It was still too early for the social sciences to provide in any organized form the necessary underpinnings for the applied social fields. The beginnings were there, however, and with them the dangers of too early and too general an application of untested theories and hypotheses.

Internal Factors

The number and types of social service agencies increased during this period. With the increase came a better defined sectarian pattern of services in the private field. With the organization and development of the National Conference of Charities and Corrections great self-consciousness came to the field. There was as yet, however, no common methodology to bind workers together. The agencies had a social purpose in common, in that their programs were operated "not for personal profit by private practitioners, but under the auspices of local and state governmental and/or non-governmental organizations established for the benefit of the community." They also had in common the fact that they were dealing with individuals and families in need of assistance with economic problems. The introduction of the paid worker was just beginning, and it was too early for any attempt to see social work in terms of what the worker does and how he does it.

The body of knowledge of social work was expanding rapidly through experience. It dealt more, however, with the problems of administration and policy than with those of program. Toward the end of the century recognition of the need for some form of training began to emerge. With the introduction of a more formalized training program at the turn of the century came the challenge to go beyond the level of mere exchange of experience. There was need for crystallizing the various experiences if they were to be transmitted through education. The period of conceptualization, however, was still around the corner in the early decades of the twentieth century.

Social work was only beginning to grope its way into a clearly defined and orderly methodology. Terms like investigation, interview, records, cases, individualization, separation into special groups, research, and so forth, began to appear in the literature. Social work, however, could not move toward a scientific approach at a pace more rapid than the speed the social sciences showed in providing the necessary theory and research data on social behavior. There was still little available information on the dynamics of learning and behavior itself. The one area in which a more orderly procedure was developed through the efforts of the charity organization societies was in investigating the needs of the client. The focus, however, was on the commodity given as service rather than on the individual. It was basically an authoritative top-downward approach of telling the client what to do, rather than involving the client in the formulation of the plan. It was doing things for him, rather than with him.

The point of view in social work reflected generally that of the society as a whole. The sponsors and volunteer workers of the social agencies came from the upper classes, and in general they accepted the prevailing laissez-faire philosophy. Their motivation arose from humanitarian aims, more than from any concern for furthering the democratic philosophy on which the nation was founded. As summarized by Watson, "The point of view—the philosophy of the pioneers in both England and America, steeped as it was in the Manchester School of Economics, was philanthropic individualism. The stress was on personal influence, neighborly intercourse with the poor." [30]

Toward the end of the century with the introduction of the paid worker and the growing interest of various groups in the nation in creating a better society, the agencies began to turn their attention to social reform. They began to look beyond the individual to the conditions under which he lived.

4

EXPANSION, WAR,
AND AFTERMATH
(1900-1930)

AMERICA ENTERED the twentieth century as the greatest industrial power of the world. It was struggling internally, however, for its democratic faith, for its continued existence as a nation "of the people, by the people, and for the people." The problem was further complicated by its acquisition through the war with Spain of a colonial empire. Puerto Rico, Hawaii, the Philippines, and, economically, Cuba were now under the American tent. Again America faced a contradiction in its fundamental conceptions of the rights and equalities of people. In the prevailing social climate of the period the Supreme Court supplied an interpretation of the problem which heightened the contradiction and gave the United States a colonial policy of absolute authority over the dependencies. The Supreme Court held that "Fundamental rights belonged to those under the sovereignty of the United States, but civil rights need not be applied to those in unincorporated territories unless Congress so desired." [1] Military and economic expediency was to dictate the policy toward these colonial possessions for years to come. To set the house right was not an easy task, for the nation was still growing rapidly and accumulating additional problems.

Between 1900 and 1930 the population increased from 76,-000,000 to 123,000,000, a gain of approximately 47 million. Immigration continued to represent a substantial source of the increase. "The number of immigrants . . . reached an all-time peak of almost 8.8 million from 1900 to 1910 . . . total immigration remained at fairly high levels through 1930, constituting 5.7 million between 1910 and 1920 and 4.1 million between 1920 and 1930." [2]

The Immigration Act of 1924, which established a quota system, brought a sharp drop in the stream of immigration after 1924. During this period the chief sources of immigrants were Italy, Russia, and Austria-Hungary. "Italian stock increased from 727,844 in 1900 to 3,336,941 in 1920, and stocks of Russian and Austro-Hungarian origin from 2,069,865 to 8,408,088 with foreign born predominating." [3] The Italians came primarily from the agricultural regions of Southern Italy at a time when Italy was in the throes of political, economic, and social unification. Max Ascoli has said that they became Americans before they became Italians. With little agricultural opportunity available to them they settled in the large urban areas and worked as manual laborers. They were ill-prepared for the complexities of city life in a rapidly moving industrial economy.

Age distribution of the population continued to show an increase in the older groups with the median age rising to 26.4 in 1930, as compared with 16.7 in 1820, and a decrease in the age group under five. The percentage distribution of the total population by age for the period 1900 to 1930 is shown in the accompanying table.

Year	Under 5	5–19	20–44	45–64	65 and over
1900	12.1	32.3	37.8	13.7	4.1
1910	11.6	30.4	39.1	14.6	4.3
1920	11.0	29.8	38.4	16.1	4.7
1930	9.3	29.5	38.3	17.5	5.4

The aging of the population can be attributed to the declining birth rate and the increase in the span of life with the advances in medicine. The change in the role of the family in an industrial society brought with it a change in attitude toward family size. Large families were no longer an economic asset as they were in an agrarian society. The conflict over birth control reached a crescendo during this period. The change in the composition of the population introduced new economic and social problems.

Another significant demographic factor during this period was the mobility of the population. The trend from the rural areas to the cities and the nonfarm rural towns continued. By 1920 over 50 per cent of the population lived in the 2722 urban places in the United States. The trek from the metropolitan areas to the neighboring suburbs also began. The greatest internal shift in population distribution during this period occurred among Negroes. Economic and social conditions in the South and the demand for cheap labor in the North resulted in a huge outmigration from the rural South to the large cities in the North. All of these shifts brought problems of adjustment to the complexities of city life. This was especially true in the case of the Negroes, who had the additional problem of prejudice to contend with. The only places available to them were the old and dilapidated tenements of the worst sections of the slums.

America continued to move ahead industrially and to increase its productive capacity. By 1930 the machine as the main source of energy had practically replaced human and animal power, machines providing 84 per cent of the total energy, animals 12 per cent, and men 4 per cent. The composition of the labor force changed markedly with a sharp decrease in the number engaged in farming and a more than doubling of those engaged in nonagricultural pursuits such as mining, manufacturing, trade, transportation, and clerical services. The mass production method first introduced in the automobile industry set new horizons for the productive capacity of the nation. But although man could now produce more in a shorter period, he did not yet have the benefits of the shorter working day or a guarantee of his share of the increased productivity. If anything, the increased productivity without a plan for its just consumption made his economic position more hazardous. He was not to receive his share of the potential good life for all without a step-by-step struggle.

The trend toward huge holding corporations begun in the

last decade of the nineteenth century continued. Between 1898 and 1903 a total of 236 new corporations was added to the 82 already in existence. These corporations controlled natural resources, transportation, and finance and had a total capitalization of $7 billion. With their interlocking directorates they were gaining a stranglehold on the competitive economy. Their power was such that government and the courts gave a broad interpretation to the Sherman Anti-Trust Act, rendering it practically useless in dealing with the problem. Money was being made, but its distribution was uneven. The largest number of people received a disproportionately low percentage of it, and were in an unfavorable position to withstand the ups and downs of an economy that had little planning. Furthermore, the power of the small group running the corporations was increasing to the point where government by the people was being challenged.

The Spirit of Reform

The struggle of the common man for reform, which took shape in the 1890's, gained momentum during the first two decades of the twentieth century. The assassination of President McKinley brought to leadership Theodore Roosevelt, whose heart belonged to the reform movement. Although he could not shake off his identification with the Republican party of his day, neither could he accept their negative attitude toward social reform. In a sense, he aided and abetted the cause of the reformers by providing an important voice through which they could be heard, even if his words at times were louder than his deeds. During his administration (1901-1909), which he dubbed the "Square Deal," he nibbled at some of the problems created by the huge corporations, but he never managed to bite into them sufficiently to make an adequate dent.

Progress was further impeded by a conservative court,

which tended to identify itself with the interests of the corporations.

Roosevelt, like the Supreme Court, was not against bigness as such; he made verbal discrimination between "good trusts" and "bad trusts." He did prosecute and win dissolution of the Northern Securities railroad holding company, and began suits against Standard Oil and American Tobacco, which were not decided until after William Howard Taft had succeeded him. But his Antitrust Division in the Department of Justice consisted of less than a dozen lawyers and stenographers, pitted against the concentrated legal talent available to the greatest aggregation of giant corporations the nation had ever known.[4]

Theodore Roosevelt's administration made its greatest contribution in the areas of (1) conservation of natural resources; (2) civil service reform; and (3) strengthening the powers of the Interstate Commerce Commission.

Taft, who succeeded Roosevelt, was heavily identified with the "Old Guard" of the Republican party, and although carried along to some extent by the momentum of the reform movement, he tended to slow its pace. The interests of big business were protected through higher tariffs, even though the party platform promised a lowering of tariffs. The "big stick" policy of Roosevelt in dealing with Latin America and China was supplemented by "Dollar Diplomacy." Two important amendments, one dealing with income tax and the other with the direct election of senators, were adopted during this administration. Other positive developments were the furthering of civil service reform, a continuation of some anti-trust suits, and the creation of the Children's Bureau.

Theodore Roosevelt had shown some understanding of the problems of the Industrial Revolution. He did not, however, follow through on his intellectual grasp of the situation, because he could not free himself sufficiently from the traditional concept of government held by his party. The times called not for slight changes in the usual way of doing things but rather for a major change in the basic philosophy of government. It remained for Woodrow Wilson, the successful standardbearer of the Democratic Party in 1912, to articulate this new conception of government. In his campaign speeches Wilson made it clear that the free-enterprise system was no longer free, with the stranglehold big business had on it, and that laws were necessary to prevent the strong from destroying the weak.

We used to think in the old-fashioned days when life was very simple that all that government had to do was to put on a policeman's uniform, and say, "Now don't anybody hurt anybody else." We used to say that the ideal of government was for every man to be left alone and not interfered with, except when he interfered with somebody else; and that the best government was the government that did as little governing as possible. That was the idea that obtained in Jefferson's time. But we are coming now to realize that life is so complicated that we are not dealing with the old conditions, and that the law has to step in and create new conditions under which we may live, the conditions which will make it tolerable for us to live.[5]

In his first inaugural address Wilson spelled out further the concept of the use of government as a positive tool in furthering the welfare of people.

We have been proud of our industrial achievements, but we have not hitherto stopped thoughtfully enough to count the human cost, the cost of lives snuffed out, of energies overtaxed and broken, the fearful physical and spiritual cost to the men and women and children upon whom the dead weight and burden of it all has fallen pitilessly the years through. . . . Nor have we studied and perfected the means by which government may be put at the service of humanity, in safeguarding the health of the nation, the health of its men and its women and its children, as well as their rights in the struggle for existence. This is no sentimental duty. The firm basis of government is justice, not pity. These are matters of justice. There can be no equality or opportunity, the first essential of justice in the body politic, if men and women and children be not shielded in their lives, their very vitality, from the consequences of great industrial and social processes which they can not alter, control, or singly cope with. Society must see to it that it does not itself crush or weaken or damage its own constituent parts. The first duty of law is to keep sound the society it serves. Sanitary laws, pure food laws, and laws determining conditions of labor which individuals are powerless to determine for themselves are intimate parts of the very business of justice and legal efficiency.[6]

Over forty years had passed since the enactment of the fourteenth Amendment, but its full intent was just being fulfilled. Government was beginning to recognize its responsibility to protect the rights of people, economic as well as political and social.

Wilson was able to make good on many of his promises early in his first administration. The Underwood Tariff Act in 1913, the Federal Reserve Act in the same year, and The Clayton Anti-Trust Act in 1914 brought long-needed reform in tariff, banking, and monopolistic practices. The Clayton Anti-Trust Act also contained within it a provision for exempting labor from anti-trust prosecution. This was an important measure for labor, for the corporations had been successful in utilizing anti-trust legislation as a means of keeping labor unions from growing strong. Although there were loopholes in the act, it represented a starting point in labor's struggle for recognition by the government; it was referred to by Gompers as labor's Magna Charta. Other reforms enacted prior to World War I included better credit facilities and vocational and agricultural education for the farmers; better working conditions for the merchant marine; a workmen's compensation law for federal civil service employees; establishment of the eight-hour day for workers on all interstate railways; a law excluding from interstate commerce the products of child labor; and federal aid to states and local communities for the construction of highways. Wilson's accomplishments might have been even greater had not the war intervened.

It was an impressive record of gains for the common man and was made possible by the previous twenty-five years of struggle for social reform by the trade unions, the "muckrakers," the social workers, and the political actionists. The AFL and the Railroad Brotherhoods were in business to stay by 1900. The rights and place of unions in a democratic society, however, were not recognized by industry, and labor had to fight every inch of the way for its gains. The anthracite coal miners organized in 1902 and staged a walkout. After a bitter struggle and the intervention of President Roosevelt, arbitration was accepted by the employers. It was an important victory for labor and marked the "beginning of a strong union and collective bargaining in hard coal." In 1903 the National Association of Manufacturers, fearful of the growing strength of labor, threw down the gauntlet and entered into a fight to the finish with labor. "The warfare was carried on by publicity, blacklists, 'yellow dog contracts,' employment of detectives, court action." [7] The growth of the AFL was checked until 1910, but in the meantime a new union group arose, the Industrial Workers of the World, committed to militant tactics and to a philosophy of not mere reform but change in the social order. Their program went beyond the AFL's limited interest in wages and resorted to strong political action.

The Industrial Workers of the World, formed in 1905 by a merger of radical unions, set out to mobilize the laborers and others whom the A.F.L. had not organized. It believed in industrial unions, preached "direct action," would not make agreements with employers, and looked forward to a time when there would be "one big union" conducting "one big strike" in which the workers would take over the factories and mills. Its appeal at the beginning was to the migratory agricultural workers, metal miners and lumbermen of the West; later it lead large strikes in industries of the East, especially in textiles.[8]

It was probably the stimulation and competition of the IWW that lead the AFL in 1906 to change its tactics and to enter the political arena on a nonpartisan basis "to support friends and defeat enemies." It was active in the Congressional elections of 1906. With the adoption of its bill of particulars in the Democratic platform, which included among more general progressive measures exemption of the trade unions from antitrust prosecution and the curbing of injunctions, the AFL supported Bryan against Taft. The support of the workers in the North helped to elect a Democratic Congress in 1910, which was to be helpful to the Wilson administration in its effort at reform.

An important aid to massing public opinion behind first Roosevelt and later Wilson came from the literary protest of the muckrakers. In its earlier phase, with the writings of George Bellamy and Thorstein Veblen, this group represented a philosophical and social science approach. It soon became, however, a more specific attack on evils of the day under the pen of good journalists. Among the muckrakers' numerous writings were those by Jacob Riis on the New York slums, by Ray S. Baker on the exploitation of the Negro, by John Spargo on child labor, by George Kibbe Turner on political corruption and white slavery, by Ida Tarbell on the corrupt methods of Standard Oil, by Charles Edward Russell on the beef trusts, by Gustavus Myer on how the great American fortunes were amassed, and by Lincoln Steffens on the political corruption of the large city political machines. The new emerging popular magazines like *McClure's, Everybody's, Cosmopolitan, Collier's,* and the *American Magazine* provided a channel for bringing these writings in serial form to the general public.

Sin and Society, by E. A. Ross, was one of the classics of the day. It dealt with the inadequacy of our system of ethics, woven in the period of a pioneer and highly individualistic agrarian society, but now lagging behind the demands for a new code to meet the problems of a highly industrial society. Ross wrote:

The stealings and slayings that lurk in the complexities of our social relations are not deeds of the dive, the dark alley, the lonely road, and the midnight hour. They require no nocturnal prowling with muffled step and bated breath, no weapon or offer of violence. Unlike the oldtime villain, the latterday malefactor does not wear a slouch hat and a comforter, breathe forth curses and an odor of gin, go about his nefarious work with clenched teeth and an evil scowl. In the supreme moment his lineaments are not distorted with rage, or lust, or malevolence. One misses the dramatic setting, the time-honored insignia of turpitude. Fagin and Bill Sykes and

Simon Legree are vanishing types. Gamester, murderer, body-snatcher, and kidnapper may appeal to a Hogarth, but what challenge finds his pencil in the countenance of the boodler, the savings-bank wrecker, or the ballot-box stuffer? Among our criminals of greed, one begins to meet the "grand style" of the great criminals of ambition, Macbeth or Richard III. The modern high-power dealer of woe wears immaculate linen, carries a silk hat and a lighted cigar, sins with a calm countenance and a serene soul, leagues or months from the evil he causes. Upon this gentlemanly presence the eventual blood and tears do not obtrude themselves.

This is why good, kindly men let the wheels of commerce and of industry redden and redden, rather than pare or lose their dividend. This is why our railroads yearly injure one employee in twenty-six, and we look in vain for that promised "day of the Lord" that "will make a man more precious than fine gold."

Because of the special qualities of the Newer Unrighteousness, because these devastating latter-day wrongs, being comely of look, do not advertise their vileness . . . it is possible for iniquity to flourish greatly, even while men are getting better. Briber and boodler and grafter are often "good men," judged by the old tests, and would have passed for virtuous in the American community of seventy years ago. Among the chiefest sinners are now enrolled men who are pure and kindhearted, loving in their families, faithful to their friends, and generous to the needy. . . .

The conclusion of the whole matter is this:—Our social organization has developed to a stage where the old righteousness is not enough. We need an annual supplement to the Decalogue.[9]

The evils growing out of this social and cultural lag, described so vigorously by Ross, still represent one of the most perplexing and challenging problems of modern society. As man moves on ever more rapidly to technological discoveries, he lacks the accompanying social know-how to utilize progress for the good of society rather than for its destruction.

The groundwork for the success of progressive legislation in the Wilson administration was also being laid by political efforts on state and local levels. Among others Wilson was forging his New Freedom platform as Governor of New Jersey; John Altgeld was writing a progressive record as Governor of Illinois with reform of penal code, prisons, charitable institutions, and city transportation; Robert LaFollette broke the

corrupt machine in Wisconsin and introduced successful legislation for regulating utilities and railroads and reforming taxation; Charles E. Hughes as Governor of New York fought the
utilities; and Hiram Johnson helped destroy the corrupt political machine in California. All of these men were to play an
important role in the conflict on the federal level. Wisconsin
established direct primaries in 1903 and Oregon in 1905.
Woman suffrage was introduced in Wyoming in 1903. By 1912
thirty states had changed their election procedure to direct election of senators, and many of them had introduced the secret
ballot. "In many states, social workers and others obtained the
passage of workmen's compensation laws, child labor laws, laws
limiting hours of work for women. Laws limiting hours for
men and establishing minimum wages were passed as well, but
were either declared unconstitutional by courts or were left in
doubt." [10]

Another political force in the evolving progressive scene
on both the local and national levels was the Socialist Party.
Under the leadership of Eugene Debs, it grew from a membership of 94,768 in 1900 to 901,873 in 1912. In the elections of
1912 and 1916 Debs, as Socialist Presidential candidate, drew
the largest vote the party has ever enjoyed.

Although social workers had been active for some time in
the local communities, their efforts did not reflect a consciousness of their common cause with the other progressive movements until 1910, when Jane Addams became president of the
National Conference of Charities and Corrections. In her
presidential address Miss Addams took social work to task for
its slowness in recognizing the relationship of poverty to modern industrialism, and spelled out "the gradual coming together of charitable groups and Radicals" in their common
concern for better social conditions. "It is as if the Charitable
had been brought," she said, "through the care of the individual, to a contemplation of social causes, and as if the Radical
had been forced to test his social doctrine by a sympathetic observation of actual people.[11]

For her, social work was part of the larger social movement, and to fulfill its aims it had to engage in social action. She urged social workers to step up the study of social conditions, and to use their close contacts with day-to-day problems to supply the necessary substantiating data for social action. Among the issues she outlined for action were: state care for widowed mothers and children; feeding of school children; adequate recreation for adolescents; proper vocational training in schools; a continued fight against tenements; a better system of public relief. It is interesting to note, in view of the strong emphasis on psychiatry in social work today, Miss Addams' reference to possible help from the newly emerging psychiatry. She expressed in her speech "the need to know from psychiatry how far the fear of the future, arising from economic insecurity, has superinduced insanity."

The growing liberal trend in social work became more explicit in the report to the 1912 conference of the Conference Committee of Standards of Living and Labor headed by Owen R. Lovejoy. The report, which represented three years of work by a representative group, recommended the following "platform of social standards":

1. "A living wage for all 'who devote their time and energy to industrial occupations,' which would provide enough to secure education and recreation, care for immature members of the family, maintain the family during periods of sickness, and permit a reasonable saving for old age. The report recommended the establishment of minimum wage commissions to inquire into industrial wages and to determine minimum standards.

2. The establishment of an eight-hour day, six-day week, with special standards of work for women and minors.

3. Federal investigation of all industries with a view to establishing standards of sanitation and safety and a basis for compensation for injury, together with standardized health and safety inspection.

4. "Social welfare demands for every family a safe and sanitary home; healthful surroundings; ample and pure running water inside the house; modern and sanitary toilet conven-

iences for its exclusive use, located inside the building; adequate sunlight and ventilation," and so forth.

5. Prohibition of all wage-earning occupations for children under sixteen; regulation of factory work for women; government review and regulation of "intermittent employment" in industry; and special training programs to rehabilitate the "unemployable."

6. Workmen's compensation for the victims of industrial accidents and diseases, and social insurance to cover old age and unemployment.[12]

The platform presented by this committee was identical in many respects with the economic and labor platform of Theodore Roosevelt's Bull Moose Party in 1912. There is no available record of how this happened, but it is known that many social workers participated actively in the campaign of this third party. Jane Addams, for example, was not only a delegate but one of the seconders of Roosevelt's nomination.

It is interesting to note that the same controversy that existed in labor concerning its role in partisan politics also arose in social work ranks. In a symposium in the *Survey*, Edward T. Devine took the view that social work should proceed carefully on a nonpartisan basis. It was his opinion that if social work was to achieve its goals it was necessary to "maintain such relations with men of social good will in all parties as will insure their cooperation in specific measures for the promotion of the common good." [13] Jane Addams, on the other hand, defended a policy of political action:

Certainly we have all learned that new ideas can never gain wide acceptance unless the persons who hold them confess them openly and give them an honest and effective adherence. When the ideas and measures we have long been advocating become part of a political campaign, which is after all but an intensified method of propaganda, would we not be the victims of a curious self-consciousness if we failed to follow them there? [14]

In a sense the reaction of the public to social work's entrance into the political arena, and the conflict within the field itself, reflected a healthy stage of growth. Social work had at last left behind the era of belief in the moral inadequacy of the individual, and was groping for a new direction in furthering its concern for people.

One of the major contributions of the period between 1900 and World War I was the change in the attitude toward public problems. As Frederick Lewis Allen pointed out, we learned that we could repair and improve the government machinery. We developed a continual, evolutionary, cooperative, experimental change. It was a reform period marked by evolutionary progress rather than major reorganization. Commager also notes that the political leaders of these transition years— Bryan, Roosevelt, LaFollette, Wilson—agreed that centralized economy required an increasingly centralized political control. The old distrust of the state gave way to the realization that only the state was prepared to act in crises of national affairs.

World War I

World War I was upon the nation before the New Freedom program of Wilson was firmly established. Internal reform was forgotten and hostilities between the various groups in the nation were generally postponed in the all-out effort to fight a common enemy. The method essential for organizing the nation into a war machine had little resemblance to the spirit and aims of the New Freedom. The President was given extraordinary powers to mobilize and coordinate physical and human resources. America was introduced to a system of controls and regulations hitherto unknown to its people. It was the nation's first taste of economic planning with the government assuming full authority. The planning was born of necessity, however, and did not represent a new economic philosophy. Rugged individualism was no longer the order of the day, but as later developments showed, it was merely stored away for safe keeping until the emergency was over. As with other crises, however, this one left its residue. The war was a situation where indifference to the interrelations of the various parts of our huge social system could not be afforded or condoned. Even powerful groups could not go their own way alone. For a brief time they had to face the fact that no man liveth unto himself. A high degree of coordination between agriculture, industry, labor, government, education, religion, and science was necessary for the survival of all.

For a brief period, the nation stumbled into the realization that what affected one part of our society also affected the other parts. Increasing interdependence meant a more organized society; and this in turn meant that all institutions had to be concerned with the material, human, and social resources to meet total needs rather than the special needs of any one segment of the population. In this total approach, forged in an emergency climate, through authority rather than education, each group participated and contributed according to its state of readiness and ability, and benefited according to its own needs and power.

Labor found itself in a new position. Prior to the war labor unrest had been great. There were 9927 strikes and lockouts involving 2,531,000 workers between 1913 and 1915. With the advent of war unemployment decreased rapidly and labor shortages emerged. In addition to the increased demand for war goods several other factors were responsible for the shortages, such as the virtual halting of immigration and the entrance of more than four million men into the armed services. Labor's increased bargaining power enabled it to fight against unfair working conditions and the increased cost of living. There were 4,450 work stoppages in 1917, most of them in the segments of heavy industry essential to war production. Here labor had made little progress toward union recognition and feelings between management and labor were far from friendly. The wartime needs of the nation, however, helped to create an informal truce in the campaigns for such pre-war issues as the closed or union shop and equal pay for equal work for women. By April 1918 the government created the National War Labor

Board, consisting of representatives from labor, employers, and the public, to help settle disputes which could not be handled by the usual procedures of collective bargaining. One of labor's major gains during the war was the eight hour day.

Although labor was in a stronger position it could not press its advantages without affecting the primary goal of defeating the country's enemy, and it was weakened by the passage of the Espionage Act in 1917 and of the Sedition Act in 1918. The chief victims of the witchhunt that followed were the Socialists and the leaders of the militant Industrial Workers of the World. Labor, in the main, participated in the war in the spirit of helping "make the world safe for democracy." Its economic gains were less than those of the farmers and big business. Furthermore, it was to discover after the war that industry's concept of democracy did not include increased affection for trade unions. The extent to which planning was regarded only as a necessary evil was borne out by the rapidity with which all controls were abandoned soon after the completion of the war.

Return to "Normalcy"

In the meantime disillusionment and dissatisfaction had set in. Wilson returned from his triumphant tour of Europe with a treaty and plan for a family of nations to a homeland that was hostile and rebellious. Unity prevalent during the war gave way to partisan concerns. Various ethnic groups were indignant over the treatment accorded their countries of origin, and there was a general feeling that America had been tricked and "taken" by the crafty European diplomats. The progressive forces had lost considerable ground and were in no position to wage a fight. The people, tired and disillusioned, turned back to the security of the old, and elected for three successive administrations the Republican standardbearers Harding, Coolidge, and Hoover.

From 1920 to 1930 the nation experienced a serious recession, then a seven-year period of economic expansion, and then the beginning of the severest depression in its history with the stock market panic in the fall of 1929. The nation had dusted off its idol of rugged individualism and returned it to a prominent place in the political house of worship. National administrations friendly to big business were again in power.

In no decade of American history has the regime of "private enterprise" been more enthusiastically celebrated by its adherents. In the latter days of the Coolidge administration, it was said that the nation had entered a "New Era" of perpetual prosperity and expansion; it had discovered the formula for success, and the chief duty was to safeguard that formula against pollution from unorthodox sources either at home or abroad. . . . The economic function of government was conceived to be mainly to clear the track for business and finance, partly by inaction, partly by reducing taxes.[15]

Hoover's campaign slogan was: "A chicken in every pot and two cars in every garage." In his speech of acceptance of the Republican nomination he oozed the same optimism, saying that "we in America today are nearer to the final triumph over poverty than ever before in the history of any land." Unfortunately for the people, the day of "not a pot to cook in" and "no garage to house a car in" was just around the corner.

The breakdown following World War I was more than economic. It was a breakdown of our value system, our social philosophy, and the conception of social policy which had begun to emerge before the war. As Adams commented,[16] the sudden end of the war left us emotionally unsatisfied, whereas it had left Europe emotionally exhausted.

For two years we had been devoting ourselves, with the energy of fever to building up a great fighting machine; the propaganda services had skillfully played on every nerve to concentrate emotion on fighting; and then, just as we were ready to leap in earnest at the enemies' throats, a hand had suddenly pulled us back. Abnormality was bound to ensue from this extraordinary situation in mass psychology. The mob demanded sacrificial victims and found them in all who differed from the conservative and the stereotyped.

There followed a period of disunity in economic, political, social, and religious life. It was a time of reaction, marked by an attempt to divide and destroy the liberal movement. Beginnings in this direction had already been made during the war with the enactment of the espionage and sedition acts. The latter act practically foreclosed any criticism of the administration, and both acts silenced the press and the liberal channels of opinion and created a nationwide spy system, setting neighbor against neighbor. The fears of change were further heightened by the proletarian revolution in Russia in November 1917.

Immediately after the war there began an open season on Communists. Six thousand arrests were made, in many cases without due process of law. Bolshevism became the emotionally charged word with which one could attack and destroy non-Communist projects and activities. All groups involved in democratic education came under attack. The list included, among others, periodicals like the *Nation,* the *New Republic*, the *Freeman,* and the *Survey;* nonpartisan political groups such as the League of Women Voters and the Foreign Policy Association; and religious organizations such as the Federal Council of Churches. Textbooks and teachers were also targets in this period of retrogression.

The fear of alien ideas and change also had its impact on our immigration laws. By 1924 the new quota system went into effect. It not only reduced the total number of openings for immigrants but reduced especially the numbers that could enter the country from eastern and southern Europe. The total quota under the 1924 law, after some modifications, was 164,667, broken down into the following numbers for each national group: Great Britain and Northern Ireland, 65,721; the Irish Free State, 17,853; Germany, 25,957; Italy, 5802; and Russia, 2712. Such leaders in social work as Edith Abbott and Jane Addams spoke out vigorously but in vain against closing the doors to those who wanted to enter and pointed out the social consequences of this type of law.

With the launching of the new Prohibition Law on January 16, 1920, all of America's hidden and repressed moral and legal attitudes were given a channel for expression. In this period of the bootlegger and the speakeasy, murder, corruption, and gangsterism reached a new high. The breakdown of morals and values in all age groups and the accompanying evils that emerged were beyond the imagination of any of the citizens involved in bringing about the Eighteenth Amendment.

The nation's paralysis and bewilderment were written large in the nomination of Warren G. Harding, the apostle of normalcy and serenity. Harding swept the nation by a record vote. As pointed out by the Beards,[17] normalcy meant the repeal of taxes on income and inheritance and excessive profits—higher incomes, subsidies, and bounties for owners of industries and merchant vessels. It meant no government interference with business; no official meddling with mergers, combinations, stock issues; no resort to harsh price-fixing or regulation schemes; less privileges for organized labor, which had acquired some status, an extended membership, and some power in industry and public affairs. Harding summed up his philosophy of life and government in a speech to captains of industry in Boston in May 1920: "America's need is not heroics but healing, not nostrums but normalcy, not revolution but restoration, not surgery but serenity."

Such a philosophy provided what America, fearful of change, wanted to hear. The results were tragic. The Harding Administration was involved in one scandal after another including the famous Teapot Dome Scandal. It was the most flagrantly corrupt administration in American history. Harding, however, was merely a spokesman for a nation that was refusing to face its problems and was clinging to the hope that when the storm passed the house could be repaired and life would go on as usual. It was a concept of normalcy born out of abnormality. America was refusing to show any awareness of its internal problems and, in its search for security, was projecting and seeking escape mechanisms rather than face reality.

Summary

Between 1900 and 1930 the population of the country had increased by approximately 47 millions. Immigration was one of the main sources of increase until the war period. With the Immigration Act of 1924 the nation had shifted its original philosophy of providing a haven for the poor, the wretched, the homeless, and the "masses yearning to breathe free." Other changes also affected the demographic character of the nation. New attitudes towards the size of the family came with its changing role in an expanding industrial society. As a result the birthrate continued to decline. The movement from rural areas to the cities continued ahead and by 1920 over 50 per cent of the population lived in urban centers. The Negro group was an important part of this shift in population.

America's rapid economic expansion was hastened by the demands of war. The expanding industrialization brought with it a shift in the pattern of employment. There was a drop in the size of the labor force in agriculture and a marked increase in non-agricultural pursuits. The trend toward huge holding corporations evident in the previous period continued.

As industry expanded and labor began to grow in organizational strength the struggle between management and labor became acute. Government found that in a period of rapid change it could no longer stand by as a disinterested spectator or as a silent partner of big business. Theodore Roosevelt talked about the role of government in bringing about a greater equality of opportunity. Woodrow Wilson's "New Freedom" was aimed against the growing concentration of economic power in the hands of a small number. It was a period of groping for a new role for government that would accomplish the goals for the common man as expressed by Jefferson.

The war forced these goals and the new attempts to achieve them into the background. The conservative reaction after the war pushed them even further out of the main stream of consideration. The liberal forces which had begun to emerge before the war found no platform around which to rally during the administrations of Calvin Coolidge and Warren Harding.

The breakdown following the war effected more than the economic situation. It was a period of groping and disunity in all aspects of life including the political, social, and religious. Under attack was not only the pattern of social policy which had begun to emerge under Theodore Roosevelt and Woodrow Wilson, but also our value system and our American Tradition. Social work, which through some of its leaders had begun to play an active part in the formulation and implementation of the new social philosophy, found it difficult to keep focused on the goals of a New Era. Dependent on and intimately related to the cultural fabric within which it operates, social work began to move toward a more fragmented approach with greater emphasis on adjusting the individual than on changing the society.

5

SOCIAL WORK

IN SEARCH OF A

METHOD

(1900-1930)

WHILE THE EMPHASIS in social work up to 1900 had been on affecting the "moral" behavior of the individual through personal influence and neighborly intercourse with the poor, by the turn of the century attention began to shift to the conditions under which the individual lived. The term charity began to give way to the concept of philanthropy with its more positive emphases on prevention of social disorder and the promotion of human welfare. Social work swung sharply toward a program of environmental improvement in order to solve the problems of poverty, dependency, and disease. Through education, surveys, and legislation, change was to be brought about in the economic and political scene, change that would alter the conditions under which people lived. The workers sought to establish principles that would affect people in general and thereby lessen the task of having to deal with specific individuals, families, or groups.

It is Deutsch's interpretation that social work's learning "to tie up economic facts with social conditions" paralleled the introduction of paid staff at the end of the nineteenth century.

The introduction of paid social workers and the trend toward professionalization, dating from the last decades of the century, were important factors in breaking down the barriers that had long existed between organized labor and social work. . . . The professional . . . was a worker who actually thought as a worker, and was more likely, although not always, to appreciate the real problems of her clients . . .

It was about this time that social work began to throw off its false emphasis on individual moral inadequacy as the basic factor in most problems of poverty, dependency and disease. People active in the new profession started to reach out into the homes and factories in which their clients lived and worked. They familiarized themselves with such basic economic factors as wages, rents and profits.[1]

1900 to World War I

The Growth of Specialized Agencies

The welfare field was moving from a highly undifferentiated stage toward the establishment of agencies with specific areas of function.

In the early stages great emphasis was placed on the role of health. For example, Homer Folks, one of the pioneer social workers of this period, saw himself as "more a part of Public Health than Social Welfare. Underlying all his work in the Public Health field, was his belief that public ill health was one of the main causes of society's evils—economic and emotional dependency, unemployment, neglected and destitute children, alcoholism, etc."[2] This approach still dealt with symptoms rather than basic economic and political factors, but in its day it represented a step in the direction of prevention, since it involved looking outside the individual as well as within him for the solution of his problems.

With the emphasis on the problems of health as a central factor in society's evils, special programs were shaped on the local and national levels. For example, on the local level the charity organization societies became concerned with overcrowded housing and lack of adequate light and ventilation, and they began to agitate for improved housing conditions. On the national scene numerous campaigns in the area of health resulted in the organization of several national agencies. Thus in 1904 the National Association for the Study and Prevention of Tuberculosis was organized; in 1912 the National Organization for Public Health Nursing; in 1913 the American Cancer Association; and in 1914 the American Social Hygiene Association.

National organizations with legislative functions were also emerging. In 1904 the National Child Labor Committee was organized, and in 1906 the American Association for Labor Legislation. A further indication of the tenor of the times was the first American conference for the prevention of infant mortality in 1909 and the first national conference on social insurance in 1912.

All along the line, the present division of services was emerging: family; child care; health and medical; mental hygiene; courts, probation, and parole; leisure time; civil rights; aid to migrants, transients, and travelers; help for immigrants, aliens, and foreign born; assistance for specific racial groups. Among the new organizations that came into being in the early 1900's (besides the health and medical services already noted) were the following: (1) family services—The Family Service Association of America was organized in 1911; (2) child care services—on recommendation of the Conference on the Care of Dependent Children held at the call of President Theodore Roosevelt in 1909, Congress created the United States Children's Bureau in 1912; (3) mental hygiene —efforts to reform the existing institutions for the insane and treatment of mental disease led to the organization of the National Committee for Mental Hygiene in 1909, with the purpose of preventing mental disease through the promotion of sound mental hygiene;[3] (4) probation and parole—the National Committee on Prisons and Prison Labor was organized in 1909, and the National Prisoners Aid Association in 1910; (5) leisure time—the YWCA formed a national organization in 1906; and the National Federation of Settlements was created in 1911. New programs included the Boy Scouts (1910), the Camp Fire Girls (1910), the Girl Scouts (1912), the Pathfinders of America (1914), the National Jewish Welfare Board (1917); (6) aliens and foreign-born—the Federated Council of Churches of Christ in America was established in 1908, the Hebrew Sheltering and Immigrant Aid Society in 1911, the American Joint Distribution Committee in 1914, the Common Council for American Unity in 1918, and the National Catholic Welfare Conference in 1919; (7) migrants, transients, and travelers' aid—the National Travelers' Aid Society of America was organized in 1917; (8) civil rights—the American Jewish Committee was organized in 1906, and the National Association for the Advancement of Colored People in 1909; (9) services for special racial groups—the National Urban League was organized in 1910.

The Foundation

Another development during this period was a new form of organized philanthropy, the foundation. Between 1900 and 1917 ten of the major foundations were established. Only a small part of their funds was directed toward social welfare activities, but the Russell Sage Foundation, established in 1907, devoted a major part of its efforts to a study of social conditions, the methods of social work, and stimulation of action for social betterment. The establishment of a charity organization department in 1909, and the leadership given to the Pittsburgh Survey in 1907-1908, represented valuable contributions by the Russell Sage Foundation to the future development of social work. The survey set a pattern for applying social research methods to the evaluation of community progress. The charity organization department sponsored annual four-week institutes, beginning in 1910, for workers of charity organization societies throughout the country. These training institutes were under the leadership of Mary Richmond, who was beginning to formulate a conceptual basis for casework methodology.

Sectarian Agencies

The present-day pattern of services sponsored by private sectarian agencies had been clearly defined by 1910. With the establishment of the National Conference of Jewish Charities (1899), the Federal Council of the Churches of Christ in America (1908), and the National Conference of Catholic Charities (1910), each religious group had begun to develop a network of social services such as family and child care, homes for the aged, and hospitals.

The pattern varied with each of the three major religions. In a sense, this diversity revealed the freedom in our nation for each group to organize its cultural life with few restraints. The Protestants, as the majority group, felt less need, perhaps, than the others for their own social work activities as a means of preserving and furthering a way of life. For the most part they operated through the agencies conducted under non-sectarian auspices in the general community. This was in line with their philosophy that social service like education is a community responsibility. Not all the Protestant denominations, however, accepted this philosophy in full. Many of them, in varying degrees, developed church-related social service programs.

The Catholics, in line with their philosophy of a "supernatural motivation" in the care of the needy, saw social work as an integral part of their religious structure. They developed their numerous services as a function of the official church organization. At first these services developed independently with the parish as the unit of operation. They were then brought under the coordination of the diocesan arm of Catholic Charities as the agency of the bishop. Catholics have viewed their social work services as one means of preserving and furthering Catholic ideology. Thus with each new development in social work they sought and emphasized special content and principles based on Catholic theology. In order to further this approach they established their own schools of social work.

By the end of 1930 there were three Catholic schools of social work in operation: The school at Loyola University was established in 1914, the school at Fordham University in 1916, and the school at St. Louis University in 1930.

The Jews, following a philosophy of cultural pluralism, developed a pattern somewhere between the Catholics and the Protestants. Religion, although important, represented only one aspect of Jewish community life. The common thread was historical and cultural: the desire of the Jewish group to live as Jews and to have a communal life and certain institutional forms of their own. The American Jewish community continued during this period to develop a network of social services, but in the main on a secular basis. In many areas Jewish social work was indistinguishable from general social work.

In the Jewish community, however, as in the Protestant, a conflict existed. The question at issue was: How much of social service programs should be a general community responsibility and how much should emphasize Jewish ideology? There was then, as there is now, a difference of opinion as to whether or not there is a special Jewish content in social work, especially in casework. In 1925 The Training School for Jewish Social Work was established. As immigration slowed down in the 1920's, however, and as the Jewish community began to identify more closely with the American culture, the need for a special school dwindled. The school went out of existence in 1940.

Jewish social work, operating as it did primarily on a secular basis, was most receptive to the newly emerging techniques in the field in general. Through the participation of staff members of Jewish agencies in the National Conference of Social Work, the experimental attitude of many of these agencies, and the professional interests of the National Jewish Conference of Social Service, Jewish social work helped further progress in all three fields of casework, group work, and community organization.

Family Welfare

In the first decades of the century social work began to feel the impact of the new science of sociology, with its concern for the family as an institution and its examination of the changes taking place in family function and structure because of the changes in the society in general. The charity organization society movement was shifting from its earlier concentration on individual economic dependency and pauperism to a concern with the total family and its relationships. How to help families stay together and become self-maintaining and responsible units in the community became the chief objective. Social work was moving from a philosophy of individual defect to an emphasis on environmental determinism. And family welfare was becoming the mainstream of social work.

Along with this new focus, social work had begun to develop its method, with investigation as the core. The technique of investigation was not new, but it was being utilized with a new set of objectives and values. The goal was no longer the determination of the worthiness or the unworthiness of the individual, but rather the gathering of information about all facets of the condition of the family in order to help more effectively. With the needs more scientifically determined, it was then possible to bring to bear the necessary resources, including those of other agencies. Thus a pattern of cooperation between agencies around a specific plan was evolved to meet the needs of the client. Relief was becoming not an end in itself but rather a tool in building the responsible and self-maintaining family unit. Within this philosophy, cash relief became important as an occasion for helping the family with budget planning. The study of all factors in the family situation, the determination of the basic problem, and the establishment of a plan to bring the necessary resources to bear laid the groundwork for the modern concept of study, diagnosis, and treatment. Treatment, however, had not yet been formulated in present-day terms, for it still involved a top-down, authoritative approach.

Coordinated Planning

As a result of the growth of specialized agencies and the growing concern with bringing a variety of specialties to bear on a single problem, a new need arose for an organization to coordinate the efforts of the various welfare groups and to set up standards of performance. For the charity organization societies that had set out to do these jobs were now increasingly preoccupied with their own specialty of family service.

Credit for finding a solution should probably be given to Francis H. McLean, associate director of the charity organization department of the Russell Sage Foundation, for his suggestion that the two functions be separated: the charity organization should concentrate on its services to families; and to set standards, there should be a new organization, to be called a "central council of social agencies," composed of representatives of social agencies that wished to unite in a common project of establishing and improving standards, thereby taking the ungracious and impractical responsibility of setting standards away from a single agency, and placing it upon the entire group.[4]

This was an early recognition of the principle that he who operates cannot coordinate. The first council to be organized was in Pittsburgh in 1908, under the name of the Pittsburgh Associated Charities. Councils soon followed in Milwaukee, St. Louis, Cincinnati, Seattle, and Portland, Oregon.

The council idea, as might be expected, made slow headway because of both philosophical and economic difficulties. The council, representing as it does a cooperative process, required recognition of the importance of interdependence. Such a concept had not been accepted as yet by the society in general. It was difficult, therefore, to obtain the necessary financial support for the venture in most communities. Even if the agencies accepted the principle, they were hardly in a budgetary position to support a central planning body. The full development of the council movement was not to come until the heightened interest in federated financing during World War I.

Federated financing was first tried in Denver in 1888. The real beginning in present-day terms, however, was the Cleveland experimental undertaking in 1913. By 1917 a plan of federated financing was in operation in fourteen communities. In that same year Cleveland took the important step of integrating the work of its Welfare Council and Federation of Charities and Philanthropy, thus recognizing the relationship of planning to finance. The reactions were mixed. Some aspects were approved, but it was feared that control of social work would now be shifted to the business community. A committee of the Association for Organizing Charity appointed to study the problem raised the following questions, and recommended a policy of "watchful waiting":

1. The effect of federation on standards of workmanship. Are low standard organizations by the mere fact of membership in a federation given a standing of respectability and a prolonged lease of life?
2. The effect of federation upon new forms of social effort in a community. Does an ultra-conservatism lead the federation to refuse to admit the proposed new organizations?
3. The effect of organized business interests, e. g. Chambers of Commerce, where they name a certain number of the federation directors. Does the business man dictate standards or is he to be educated by the professional worker?
4. The effect on the contributor's interest in and knowledge of the city's social work. Are contributors better informed and more interested in social work through only one gift a year to charitable work? [5]

The step toward the integration of fund-raising with planning served to allay some of these fears on the part of charity organization workers.

Experiments were also being undertaken to build neighborhood and community planning around public institutions. An example was the Rochester demonstration in 1906-1907 of how public schools could be utilized as centers around which the leisure-time activities of the community could be organized.

Another was the establishment of the first municipal board of public welfare in Kansas City, Missouri, in 1910 with "broad powers to devise and execute plans to fulfill the duties of the city toward all the poor, the delinquent, the unemployed, the deserted and unfortunate classes in the community, and to supervise the private agencies which solicited money from the public for these purposes." [6]

Social Work in Host Settings

Ida Cannon reports in her *Social Work in Hospitals* that the use of social workers in hospitals had its roots in the after-care of the insane, the lady almoners in the London hospitals, and the nursing services and field work training of the medical students at Johns Hopkins Medical School and Hospital. In its 1907 report, the Massachusetts General Hospital, where Dr. Cabot had introduced a medical social work program in 1905, proposed that social workers be trained especially for the treatment of psychoneurotics. Medical social work was introduced in the psychopathic wards at Bellevue in 1906, and in the New York State Hospital for Mental Diseases in 1910. A more formalized service was initiated at the Psychopathic Hospital in Boston in 1913, under the leadership of Mary C. Jarrett. Through this program the role of the social worker in a psychiatric setting became clearly defined.

The first program of school social workers was introduced in 1906-1907 in Boston, Hartford, and New York under private agencies. The first public school sponsorship of the program was in Rochester in 1914. "As in the medical and psychiatric fields, the social worker was brought in because of the recognition that the problems of the child stemmed from his living experiences in the home and community. The social worker was the person who could work with both the child and his environment." [7] By 1916 eight states were utilizing a total of forty-one visiting teachers in their program.

The emphasis on understanding the individual and his environment and the causal relationships between childhood personality problems and adult problems made the field of delinquency a natural area for study and research. In fact, up to World War I the major focus of child guidance clinics was work with delinquents. With the establishment of the first Juvenile Court in 1909 in Chicago under Dr. W. Healy, a program of research was instituted which set the pattern for studies of delinquency. *The Individual Delinquent,* published by Healy in 1915, pointed up the importance of early childhood experiences and the impact of environmental forces in shaping the personality of the delinquent.

Public Welfare

Developments in public welfare during this period were not of as great moment as those in the private field. Between 1900 and 1917 the public field consolidated its grounds and was more concerned with problems of personnel, standards, recording, maintenance of buildings, administration, and coordination than with "actual reorganization, legislative and administrative development and technical study of programs and principles." The latter emphasis came after 1917.[8] There were two developments during this period, however, which represented important steps along the road to a new role by government in dealing with problems of social welfare: the program of "mother's aid," now administered as "aid to dependent children," and "workmen's compensation," which introduced the principle of insurance systems as a means of promoting human welfare.

As in previous eras, the first shift in attitude toward aid to the poor came in the case of children and other dependents whose assistance did not represent a denial of the basic philosophy of individualism. Out of the Conference on the Care of Dependent Children in 1909 (the first White House Conference) came a reaffirmation of the importance of home life to the child and the need for strengthening family life. "Home life is the highest and finest product of civilization. It is the great moulding force of mind and character. Children should not be deprived of it except for urgent and compelling reasons." With this principle as a guide, the states responded quickly to the recommendation of the conference and beginning in 1911 enacted legislation providing the administration of "mother's aid" under local auspices.

Another important outcome of the conference was the creation of the Children's Bureau in 1912. As stated in the creating Act of Congress, its purpose was "to investigate and report upon all matters pertaining to the welfare of children and child life among all classes of our people." The establishment of the Children's Bureau could be traced to the articulate and dedicated women of the settlement house movement. They had recognized that the solution to the problems in their local community frequently could be found only on the state and national levels. They had also learned from experience that the answers to these problems were to be found in the political arena as well as in education. The architect of the Children's Bureau was Lillian Wald, headworker at Henry Street Settlement in New York. The first two chiefs of the bureau, Julia Lathrop and Grace Abbott, also came from the settlement house movement: both were from Hull House in Chicago.

The 1909 White House Conference was itself an expression of the growing awareness of the federal government that it had a share of responsibility for the nation's health and welfare. White House Conferences have been held about every ten years since their inception.

Workmen's compensation, the earliest form of social insurance, was first enacted in 1908. "By 1917 this modern legislative remedy had been accepted by a majority of the states, and in that year it was upheld by the Supreme Court of the United States." [9] Workmen's compensation represented another peg in the structure for meeting the economic problems of individuals. With its emphasis on the cooperative responsibility of the employee, the employer, and the government, it pointed the way for later attacks on problems of unemployment, health, and medical care.

Social Work as a Profession

Social workers operating in this variety of host settings found themselves part of a team with some of the older and more developed professions. The association stimulated the interest of the social workers toward professional concerns and also began to provide valuable knowledge and skills for the profession in general. A pattern of specialization in terms of settings, however, was being forged, and social work was soon to find itself in the interesting position of having built up a series of specialties before a generic or common core had been developed.

As new programs were introduced under both private and public auspices, the need for more than enthusiastic and inspirational leadership became apparent. Workers with administrative abilities and training in the methods of social work were needed. The example of the New York Charity Organization Society in sponsoring a six-week summer institute for social workers from all parts of the country was followed by other agencies in Boston, Chicago, Philadelphia, and St. Louis between 1900 and 1915. These experiments with summer institutes resulted in the establishment of full-time schools of social work. By 1919 there were seventeen such schools, and they had organized the American Association of Schools of Social Work. The training program was technical in nature, in that it emphasized the acquisition of techniques without much theoretical background. "As is shown by Dr. Steiner in his monograph, *Education for Social Work,* the first schools for the training of social workers grew out of the needs of philanthropic agencies and have been largely under the guidance and control of those directly engaged in social work. They did not originate with educational authorities who had seen a need and were moved to meet it." [10]

With the increase in the number of paid workers and the introduction of a more formalized plan of training, a greater interest began to emerge in the findings of modern science, accompanied by a growing professional consciousness. Timothy Nicholson in his presidential address before the National Conference of Charities and Corrections predicted that the immediate future was to be the scientific age of our work.[11] Although social work was beginning to show a greater sensitivity to the developing social sciences there was as yet no organized use of this material. For example, how much preparation in the social sciences and which particular ones should be given priority was a moot question. In 1915 Abraham Flexner, who had made a study of medical education in 1910, addressed the National Conference on the question: "Is Social Work a Profession?"[12] He applied the same criteria which he had utilized in his medical study and found that social work in its then stage of development could not qualify as a bona-fide profession. Some of the areas in which it was found lacking were the following:

(1) Basic preparation in the social sciences.

(2) A body of exclusive and distinctive knowledge and a transmissible professional technique.

(3) Definite educational and professional qualifications tested under state supervision.

(4) Professional organizations.

(5) A code of professional practice.

Flexner's evaluation came just a few years before social work moved rapidly toward a professional technique and the creation of professional associations. He placed his greatest emphasis on the lack of a transmissible professional technique.

The effect of Flexner's paper was profound and far reaching. The challenge was accepted at its face value, and has set social workers to defining and perfecting their methods with a singleness of purpose that has all but blinded them to the fact that method is only one test. Philosophy—what it is all about; why it is undertaken; what are its ultimate goals and its relationships to other activities— is as essential to a profession as method. [13]

One would want to add to this statement the fact that the search for a method occurred just at the time that the impact of psychoanalysis was being felt. Did social work in its haste for professional status reach out for a ready-made methodology for treating sick people, thus closing itself off from the influences of developments in the other social sciences?

The Impact of the Social and Medical Sciences

Before examining further the development of social work as a field, as a body of knowledge, and as a method and a process, it will be helpful to take a look at developments in the social and medical sciences. For, as Grace Coyle asserts, social work is always dominated by two factors: the social climate in which it moves and the state of the sciences on which it is dependent. During the first twenty years of the twentieth century scientific patterns were being developed that were to color the whole future of social work.

Pragmatism, the prevailing philosophy of the early twentieth century, gave backing and substance both to scientific and to social thought. With its emphasis on facts and experiences which favored change and flexibility as against fixed principles, it stressed man's ability to remake society and saw empirical science as a vital tool for accomplishing such an objective. Under the influence of pragmatism the social sciences began to turn from a concern with man as an isolated individual, to be studied as an element or a unit in society, to a consideration of the psychological and moral relatedness of all men.

Pragmatism also brought new approaches in the law, in history, and in religion. O. W. Holmes Jr. introduced the concept of continuous change in legal principles through change in interpretation. R. Pound brought a sociological view into jurisprudence, pointing up the importance of economic and psychological factors in interpreting the law. An economic interpretation of history began to emerge, with Beard's *Economic*

Interpretation of the Constitution in 1913 an outstanding example of this trend. Religious thought and activities were also developing along reform lines. The clergy began to use their parishes for social service programs. Walter Rauschenbusch, of the Protestant faith, wrote *Christianity and the Social Order* in 1912. His thesis was that political equality could not be joined with economic inequality. He called for a Christian socialism. Reform Judaism produced Felix Adler, who established the Ethical Culture movement. In the Catholic group, Father Ryan was promoting a program of social reconstruction and in 1906 wrote a book on *A Living Wage*.

Psychology

Like social work itself, the social sciences were moving toward a specialization. Although scientific methodology was still in its infancy, it was developing rapidly by about 1910. Psychology, which was to supplant sociology and anthropology in feeding social work, began to be differentiated into special areas such as educational, experimental, social, and abnormal psychology. The work of the French psychologist Alfred Binet and his collaborator T. Simon on mental tests in the first decade of the twentieth century found warm reception among American psychologists with their focus on "mind in use." Binet's conceptions of the growth of intelligence and mental age were valuable contributions. Work with the armed forces during World War I was to provide an enormous human laboratory for the psychologists interested in testing. Utilizing group techniques they were able to test approximately 2 million men. Valuable information was obtained about both the method of testing and the role of social factors in intelligence. The use of the Intelligence Test found its way quickly into the educational systems and related fields.

At the turn of the century John Dewey was beginning to make his influence felt in American psychological circles with the organization of the functional school of psychology at Chicago. Dewey was deeply interested in the application of psychology to social practice, and in his presidential address before the American Psychological Association in 1900 he presented a plea and outlined a program for educational psychology. He was called to Teachers College, Columbia University, in 1904 and had a marked influence on educational philosophy. At about the same time G. Stanley Hall at Clark University began his work on genetic psychology, that is, human development. Hall was one of the first psychologists on the American scene to become interested in the work of Freud and Jung. "Hall's geneticism brought him to child psychology, to pedagogy, and presently to the special study of adolescence." [14] Hall's interest in children led him to attempt the organization of an institute of child study in 1909, but he was unsuccessful in obtaining the necessary financial backing. The newer psychology brought changes in the conceptions about childhood. The importance of individual differences and the influence of early childhood on later life were articulated. Furthermore the child came to be looked upon "not as a small size adult, but as a growing, developing, ever changing individual, whose treatment must differ not merely in degree but in kind from that received by the adult."

The new psychology, with its reformulation in dynamic terms, began to provide a methodology for studying and dealing with problems of the individual. It found common ground with the new psychiatry, for they both emphasized the whole individual and saw problems of adjustment as the major concern. Psychology moved toward a study of behavior, taking into account both the physiological and psychological factors involved.

Sociology

At the turn of the century sociologists were busying themselves with the problems of human behavior and social causation. E. A. Ross became interested in the "social pressures which operate within society to make the individual conform to the group norm." Charles Horton Cooley "analyzed human nature as the accumulation of habits acquired out of social experience," a view based on Plato's conception of society as a system of human relationships which was devised by man and into which the individual was forced by the process of education. Within this view the behavior of both the individual and society could be modified. There were varying theories of social causation, ranging from the positivism of Comte to the determinism of Spencer.

There was therefore the utmost confusion in regard to the origins of human behavior, until 1908 when William McDougall pointed the way out by a fallacious certainty. Possibly more than any other individual, he was responsible for the revival of the Aristotelian view. His was an instinctivistic interpretation of individual behavior and thus of social causation; it was acclaimed and adopted by a majority of sociologists and not a few psychologists.[15]

For McDougall society and social phenomena were the consequence of the instinctive urges and drives with which all men are born. This point of view, although palatable to the sociologists at that time in their search for a simple solution to a complex problem, was not as acceptable to those who were dissatisfied with their society and were seeking ways to change it.

The heightened interest in environmental factors between 1900 and World War I brought social work close to sociology. As late as 1919 Professor Chapin delivered a paper at the National Conference of Social Work on the "Relations of Sociology and Social Case Work," claiming that there were common goals and common methods, at one point referring to casework as applied sociology. But this interest was giving way gradually to the impact of psychoanalysis on social work theory.

Psychoanalysis

By 1910 the work of Sigmund Freud was being studied by psychologists and sociologists in the United States. Freud, a physician by training, had become interested in problems of neuroses. Up to this time little was known about neurotic symptoms and there was no method of cure. Freud, who had studied the psychic nature of hysteria with Charcot in Paris, and the phenomenon of post-hypnotic suggestion with Bernheim at Nantz, began by applying the method of hypnosis in the treatment of hysteria. This early work was done in collaboration with Breuer, another Viennese doctor. By 1895 Freud had gathered a body of basic observation data which led him to the development of his ultimate method and ideas.

Freud, with his medical background, was strongly influenced by Darwin and sought for psychic factors a unifying principle similar to the systematic arrangement promulgated by Darwin for the biological development of man. From observation he noted that symptoms of hysteria were connected with emotional happenings in the past, that the patients were unaware of the forces that created the problem, that the neurotic symptoms were caused by factors that could be traced, and that in all the cases sexual difficulties were present. He then broadened his study to the sexual life of patients suffering from many different types of neuroses. Freud discovered that his original hypothesis that one could understand neurosis by its objective symptoms did not hold and that observable clinical data could be understood only in terms of their symbolic meaning. He then proceeded to build his theory and refine his method of approach. Freud's interest was primarily in psychopathology, but in the development of his theories it was necessary for him to spell out the role of society in the adjustment of the individual. Freud saw society not as a resultant of common instincts but rather as a repressor of presocial instincts. For Freud, in his earlier period, the sex instinct was the basis of practically all "psychical energy and striving." Interpreted narrowly "the view that society is a direct outcome of man's inherited instincts and the idea that society arises to suppress his presocial instincts imply that society is largely unmodifiable." [16]

The work of Freud opened up new and valuable vistas in understanding and dealing with problems of maladjustment.

Freud projected his concept as a theory of adjustment, however, and not as a social philosophy. For those looking for simple solutions to complex problems it offered a panacea without an awareness of the dangers involved in making it a theory of social causation. This was especially true on the American scene, where the deeply rooted concept of individual moral inadequacy as the basic factor in most problems of poverty, dependency, and disease could easily be supplanted by an overemphasis on personal (psychological) inadequacy without sufficient regard for the social realities which the individual had to face in a highly industrialized and competitive society.

In any given situation there is a mixture of internal and external reality factors. . . . One of the great problems in psychoanalysis, to which some of its practitioners have unfortunately fallen prey, is the failure to realize this constant admixture. They have sought a unitary and exclusive "cause." They have fallen prey to the mechanistic will-o'-the-wisp of simple cause and effect. . . . Such thinking cannot be applied in the psychological and social spheres. It is "pretty" because of its simplicity, but basically fallacious. We must be careful of the "either-or" and look for the "both-and." For practical purposes we must recognize that in some situations the external environmental factors dominate so completely as to minimize the role of internal factors and vice versa. Theoretically, however, neither the one nor the other can be completely excluded.[17]

The Freudian theories were finding their way into American thought through the efforts of people such as A. A. Brill, who translated Freud's work into English, and William White and Smith Ely Jellife, who introduced the Freudian concepts into practice in mental hospitals. By 1911 the New York Psychoanalytic Society was organized. There were two streams of development emerging: on the one hand, the group who were taking over the Freudian approach in its entirety and whose major focus was the medical and clinical aspects; and, on the other, a group who were attempting to integrate the newer psychiatry within the context of the new psychology and the American culture.

Social Psychiatry

Adolph Meyer, who is frequently referred to as the father of American psychiatry, gave leadership to the latter group. "Through Meyer's capacity to see essentials clearly," Barbu points out, "his work took on an aspect of a philosophy of psychiatry. Much of this seems to be quite original and I believe that it will endure. . . . Meyer saw clearly the interrelationship of the psychodynamics of the individual and the pathology of society. Social forces, he asserted, can be detrimental as well as beneficial to the individual." [18] In his approach to emotional disorders as problems of adjustment rather than merely as diseases of the nervous system, Meyer introduced the procedure of taking family and community as well as individual factors into account. Through the "developmental survey" of a case Meyer brought all these aspects into his treatment plan. Thus, educational retraining became part of his approach. He had projected a philosophy of "social psychiatry."

Meyer's approach was at first attractive to social work, for it represented an effort to integrate the two prongs of social work's approach, that is, concern with both the individual and his environment. His point of view was influential in the early development of the child guidance and mental health movements. The emphasis on "social psychiatry," however, was soon to give way to a narrower concentration on the medical and the clinical. The major attempt at integration of individual, social, and cultural factors was not to come for several decades.

Social Psychology

Some writers saw in the developing social psychology the kind of integration of individual, social, and cultural factors essential to social work and were of the opinion that it should be a basic part of the training program of the social worker.

Fay B. Karpf expressed this view in her writings on social psychology.

The whole trend of modern psychological and social thought has been in the direction of a growing recognition of the importance of the social aspects of personality development and conduct. So important has this movement been in modern thought that it has given rise to a new field of scientific investigation which is specifically concerned with this approach. As a result of its efforts a body of literature has been built up which is of the utmost importance for social work and for all the applied social arts. How personality is built up in its social setting; what role culture and social organization play in one's mental development; how one's ideals, standards, morals, and outlook change with the social situation; what the processes and instruments of social control are; what importance the intimate contacts of family and primary group life have; how these vary from the more formal and transitory contacts of larger group life; what happens when one is transplanted from one social milieu to another; what the effects of group suggestion, contagion and inter-stimulation are; what role language plays in mental growth—these are some of the subjects with which social psychology is concerned. That this subject matter has a most intimate bearing on social work seems to be self-evident . . . where if not in the developing field of social psychology, connecting as it does with psychology and biology on the one hand and with sociology and anthropology on the other, is the answer to such questions to be sought? . . . That social psychology is still a very young field and cannot give full-blown answers to most of these questions is merely a challenge for its further development, for if social psychology does not have full-blown answers to these questions, neither has any other field. And meanwhile social psychology has what some other related fields do not—an inspiring and hopeful outlook on the problems of human nature and social life from the standpoint of the possibilities of change and improvement and that is surely indispensable to the social worker as well as to constructive social work.[19]

That social work did not fully follow this lead but identified itself more specifically with psychoanalytic theories may be attributed to various factors. Social psychology, as pointed out by Karpf, was still in the stage of inspiration and hopeful outlook, and could not supply the methodology that social work was anxiously seeking. Psychoanalysis was more than a theoretical concept and was developing specific methods and techniques for dealing with one segment of the social worker's concern, namely, the immediate problems of adjustment of the individual. Second, the social sciences were becoming highly specialized and were giving little thought to an interdisciplinary approach that would integrate the emerging concepts of psychology, biology, sociology, and anthropology. Social work with its emphasis on practice and its limited experience in the social sciences could not be expected to play a role which the social sciences themselves were not in a position to undertake. Third, the impact of World War I and the conservative social climate of the period after it was conducive to a refocusing of attention on the individual and on methods for dealing with his personal problems, and away from the broader societal factors.

The War Period

World War I opened new vistas for social work and forced it into new directions before it had an opportunity to consolidate and integrate the experiences of the previous quarter of a century.

The 1917 meeting of the National Conference of Social Work, which convened in Pittsburgh the day after the initial military registration, was pervaded by the urgency of the war situation, and to quote the words of the president-elect, "no national conference has ever before been so charged with the sense of actuality, so invested with fateful significance, so informed with singleness of purpose, so wrought together with a quickening scheme of thought, of faith, of practise." Nineteen hundred and seventeen was indeed one of the turning points in the Conference. Only the year before it was still called the Conference of Charities and Corrections, and the change in name was, in a sense, prophetic of the enlarged responsibilities and wider horizons which World War I was to bring to social workers; for the growth of the social services in the next twenty-five years was to be far greater than it had been in the previous half-century. Few of the delegates could foresee clearly what these changes would be, and so the discussions embodied some concepts that were already inadequate to the time and some ideas suggestive of the future, while the majority of the papers were concerned with the current problems created by the war.[20]

Out of the experience came a new direction for casework; an expansion of social work services beyond the economic dependent; more rapid movement toward a professional organization; joint financing and planning for social work services; and further expansion of the system of insurance for meeting social welfare needs.

New Directions for Casework

Prior to the war casework's chief stock in trade had still been investigation and relief giving. The need for trained workers had been recognized but the early workers were not much beyond the level of the volunteer with their brief and vocationally focused preparation. The attitude of the worker, like that of the volunteer, was authoritative, with the emphasis on planning for the client rather than with him. There was little understanding of human behavior and its meaning for the problems with which the social worker was concerned. Social work, however, was groping for a fuller understanding of the meaning of the situations and experiences with which it was dealing, an understanding which would relate its methods to the emphasis on values which had emerged from the social reform period. And Freud's work and writings had turned the attention of psychiatrists to the broader concept of emotions in the behavior pattern of the individual. As the psychiatrist began to work with others than the mentally ill some social workers began to see a common element which had special meaning for their work. As Bruno reports:

Very early, both disciplines recognized their common elements. Mary Richmond consulted frequently with Dr. Adolph Meyer, of Johns Hopkins, in the development of her principles of social casework. (It should again be noted that in 1911, the year in which social casework was first mentioned in the program of the Conference, Dr. Meyer read a paper on "Case Work in Social Service and Medical and Social Cooperation in Nervous and Mental Diseases.") In a few favored cities psychiatrists were being consulted by social caseworkers as early as 1915.[21]

The methodology that began to emerge as a result of these developments represented a growing recognition that individuals differed in their types of problems and in the ways in which they handled them, and a new awareness of the importance of having the individual take responsibility in the plan developed to meet the problem. But though the importance of the relationship of the worker to the client was emerging, there was no scientific knowledge of the dynamics of relationships and their meaning to the worker and the client. With the growing information available from psychiatry and psychology, the field was ready for a leader with a conceptual mind to begin to systematize the rapidly expanding body of experience and knowledge. Mary Richmond played this role.

Miss Richmond's *Social Diagnosis* in 1917 marked the development of a body of knowledge and skills which comprised a casework method of helping people. . . . She enlarged the scope of social casework in exchanging the concept of the "poor for that of the client"—who was conceived of as a person whose character, physical condition or circumstances or combination of these have made him incapable of full self-maintenance in his social setting. . . . *Social Diagnosis* was the definition of the social situation and the personality of the client. It was arrived at through a process of collecting and evaluating information and drawing inferences. It was conceived as a common procedure to all casework. In this period the situational aspects of the case were mainly stressed; the history gathering was emphasized with the belief that if we could get enough facts we would know what to do. The diagnosis and planning were still very much in the worker's hands because of her objective view and know-how in dealing with environmental resources. However, the psychological basis is laid down with Miss Richmond's emphasis on the influence of mind upon mind or mental interaction. . . . Miss Richmond gave a conceptual underpinning to social casework as well as a method. The two key concepts in her philosophy are: individual differences and the wider self—that is, man as a product of his social relationships. . . . One might almost summarize Miss Richmond's orientation by her three inscriptions in *Social Diagnosis*—Cooley's need to understand; Putnam's significance of social relations; and Gross' need for training.[22]

Psychiatric Social Work

The war neuroses and the new attitude of the army toward them increased the need for psychiatrically trained social workers to help provide treatment to former servicemen. The work of the new Division of Neuropsychiatry within the army was followed closely by social work and was a subject of great interest at the National Conference of Social Work in 1917 and 1918.

The story of the beginnings of psychiatric social work is colorfully told in the report of the first class of the Smith College School for Social Work given by Esther Cook at the Alumnae Reunion in 1953.[23]

In the spring of 1918, there appeared on the bulletin board of women's colleges and social agencies throughout the United States and Canada, the following simple notice:

"On July 8, 1918, Smith College and the Boston Psychopathic Hospital, under the auspices of the National Committee of Mental Health, will open at Smith College a training school for psychiatric social workers to assist in the rehabilitation of soldiers suffering from shell-shock and other nervous disorders. This had been a dream of Miss Mary Jarrett and Dr. Ernest Southard to establish a professional school which would emphasize the importance of social work in the practice of psychiatry. Shortly after its opening in 1913, the Psychopathic Hospital had taken students from Simmons for field placement and also had its own apprentice course of 8 months for a few students. With the war pressure of soldiers suffering from emotional shock, there was more need than ever for a large number of workers trained to deal with the mentally disturbed."

To this clarion call, came many requests for admission but only 70 were chosen. One of the bases of selection was that they be women as Dr. Southard felt that women passed through more changes of an emotional sort in one year than men do in five, and yet are more rational than men. The women ranged from 20 to 46 years of age. Forty-three were college graduates, four had advanced degrees. The rest had special experiences but only one had been psychoanalyzed. Jarrett expected that they would be sturdy pioneers from which the faculty could expect keenness, eagerness, endurance and adaptability. During the planning of course content there had been much speculation as to whether in the teaching of the fundamental principles of human behavior, both normal and abnormal, social and anti-social, the faculty could lecture on materials not supposed to be talked about in the presence of young girls. They could and did. The class was able to take it all including the blown-up pictures of syphilitic lesions and male anatomy. Although the course was well-balanced with emphasis on casework, sociology and psychology, the main focus was on social psychiatry. The students had ten and a half hours a week of class with two two-hour sessions (clinic) at Northampton State Hospital. . . .

For faculty they had Miss Mary Jarrett, Chief of Social Service of the Boston Psychopathic Hospital, as Director; Professor S. Stuart Chapin of the Smith Faculty was in charge of the sociology courses and Professor David Rogers of the Psychology courses, Miss Betsey Libbey of Philadelphia, Jessie Taft of New York, and Anna King of the Boston Red Cross discussed casework. As for social psychiatry, there were many famous people: Lawson Lowry, young and handsome, Dr. Cheney, Dr. Kirby of Wards Island, New York, Abraham Myerson of the "nervous housewife" fame, Dr. William Healy of the Judge Baker Guidance Center, Dr. Adolf Meyer of Phipps, Dr. Frink, an analyst, Dr. A. A. Brill, translator of Freud, Dr. Walter Fernald with his ten-point scale to determine feeblemindedness, and an occupational therapist.

There was one dissenting note; one group was not sure that we would remain normal after being told about conflicts and sex. This was the faculty at the Mount Holyoke summer school who were preparing leaders to look after the health of women in industry. These students were not permitted to visit Northampton for fear they would become contaminated.

At the National Conference of Social Work in 1919, Mary Jarrett presented a paper on the "Psychiatric Thread Running Through All Social Case Work." Soon casework, which had not yet fully acquired a method and philosophy, was embracing without discrimination the new developments in psychiatry and psychoanalysis. Psychiatric content began to outweigh other subject matter in the curricula of the schools of social work. It was a process of addition and substitution, however, rather than one of integration. Social work was facing the challenge of integrating its immediate past of social reform, whose emphasis was on the socioeconomic, with the newly emerging concepts of medicine and psychiatry, which concentrated on the emotional and on the individual. The integrated two-pronged approach of the psychological and the socioeconomic within a democratic frame of values, however, was difficult to apply. At best the tendency was to utilize the two approaches as parallel efforts, with greater emphasis on one or the other depending on the existing social, economic, and political climate. Some social workers saw in the methods of psychiatry not only a more meaningful but also a more democratic relationship between worker and client. Furthermore, it was an approach that had use beyond the needs of the economic dependent.

The Red Cross

The work of the Red Cross during the war period helped to further the potential of social work as a service for more than the economic dependent. The Red Cross, with its task of serving as a liaison between the man in the service and his family, developed the Home Service Bureau to carry out the community part of the responsibility. The national office with its workers in all of the military installations and its network of Home Service Bureau programs in more than 3,000 communities provided a fairly complete channel of communication between the men in the armed services and their families.

The Red Cross experience produced, among other benefits, the following positive results for social work: (1) it brought social work services into every corner of the nation, extending them beyond the walls of the large urban areas; (2) it brought these services to all regardless of economic need or background; (3) it brought services that were other than relief giving; (4) it stimulated a program of training for chapter chairmen and their assistants, which was carried on in cooperation with the schools of social work and the social science departments of the universities.

Coordinated Planning

Another important development during the war period was the advance made in coordination and joint financing. The need for better coordination of social services had already been recognized before the war. In the public field state boards of charities were performing the function of organizing and coordinating the public institutions. On the local level in the private field charity organization societies and the settlements were attempting to further better neighborhood and community planning, and beginnings had been made in the creation of councils of social agencies and in federated financing. Progress had also been made toward a better relationship between the public and the private efforts.

It was the experience of World War I, however, that provided the greatest impetus to coordination and federated financing. Just as the general climate favored putting aside difference for the common effort, so too in social work the attitude was one of cooperation. The programs of mobilizing the civilian population for national defense and the efforts of the War Camp Community Service on behalf of the men in the armed forces all met with a positive response. The financial appeals of the national agencies engaged in war and relief services tended at first to create confusion in the local communities. But under the leadership of Newton D. Baker, Secretary of War, who had been mayor of Cleveland at the time of the local experiment in federated financing, steps were taken to bring greater cooperation and planning into the situation.

In 1918, the second year of our participation in the war, Secretary Baker induced seven national agencies to join a United War

Activities Fund, to establish a joint national budget, and to assign local quotas to be raised locally by war chests. Although the period set for raising the money was the week of Thanksgiving, and the Armistice was signed on November 11, the war chests throughout the country were a tremendous success, both in amounts raised and in numbers of contributors. It is supposed that more than three hundred communities organized war chests, in contrast with the less than twenty cities which had adopted federated giving by 1916. Some of the new war chests absorbed the budgets of the peacetime agencies; most of them did not. But the experience of donors in combining all of one individual's contributions in one pledge exerted a powerful influence on the chest movement; and although most of the war chests went out of existence with the end of the war, the development of the chests kept on at an accelerated pace, until at the present the principle of the chest has been more widely adopted than almost any movement in social work.[24]

The American Association for Community Organization, the forerunner of the present Community Chests and Councils of America, Inc., was formed in 1918.

Public Welfare

The war also saw further extension of the philosophy of the workmen's compensation laws. Prior to World War I men in the armed services were rewarded with gratuities or pensions, but there was no organized plan for meeting the economic needs of either the serviceman or his family. Under the chairmanship of Judge Julian W. Mack, president of the National Conference of Charities and Corrections in 1912, the plan for the amended War Risk Insurance Act was drawn up.

Based upon the philosophy of the workmen's compensation laws this measure provided for the various risks or hazards which war entails, including compensation in case of death or disability incurred in line of duty, a voluntary system of insurance, and medical, surgical, and hospital care, and anticipated the later program of vocational rehabilitation of the permanently disabled. In addition, a provision for allotments from the enlisted man's pay and family allowances from the Federal Treasury were important departures from any previous Federal legislation.[25]

Again a crisis situation had thrown the nation into the future and had forced the government on a federal level to assume more than a policing or regulating role in dealing with the welfare of the people.

The Social Work Profession

The number of paid workers in the field had increased considerably with the demands growing out of the war. The special short-term training courses carried on frequently with the cooperation of the schools of social work were exposing larger numbers to some formalized training. Group consciousness was developing. The National Conference served as one vehicle for exchange between paid workers; another was the social worker's clubs in the larger communities, where members could discuss their common problems as individuals rather than as agency representatives.

The increasing opportunities and interest in social work as a field had led the Intercollegiate Bureau of Occupations of New York City to establish a special department for social work. The responsibility for vocational counseling and placement was taken over by the National Social Workers' Exchange in 1917. As the only organization of people engaged in social work with a specific concern for matters of personnel, and with the growing professional consciousness emerging through the training programs and the local social workers' clubs, the exchange found itself under pressure from its membership to take on additional functions pertaining to professional standards. In the meantime social workers in hospital settings, both medical and psychiatric, formed the first professional organization in social work in 1918, the American Association of Hospital Social Workers (later called the American Association of Medical Social Workers and now a section of the National Association of Social Workers). During the war membership in the exchange, which was open to both paid and volunteer workers engaged in social work, increased substantially. By 1921 social workers would be ready to move from this informal structure to a more formal professional organization with specific membership requirements and limited only to paid workers. The National Social Workers' Exchange became the American Association of Social Workers in 1921, and in 1922 the functions of counseling and placement were turned over to a newly created organization, the Joint Vocational Service.

Mixed motives were undoubtedly involved in the striving for professional status in this period. For some it represented social status, for others it represented a way of drawing a line between the volunteer and the paid worker, and for a small group, conscious of the emergence of a unique methodology, it represented the recognition of a "functionally specific technical competence." If one keeps in mind the observations of Flexner in 1915 that social work was not meeting professional criteria, and the fact that the American Association of Hospital Social Workers was organized in 1918, three years before the general professional organization came into being, one cannot help but draw the conclusion that the impact of psychiatry on social work was a strong influence in precipitating it toward professional status.

Post-War to Depression

The disillusionment and dissatisfaction that set in following the war was accompanied on many fronts by conservatism and reaction. Social work, too, reflected the climate of the day. Absorbed, furthermore, in the new-found concepts of psychoanalysis, it shifted its concern from socioeconomic factors to the individual and his adjustment.

Mary Richmond saw the development of personality as the basic aim of social work. Social casework for Miss Richmond consisted "of those processes which develop personality through adjustments consciously effected, individual by individual, between men and their social environment." [26] Social work for Miss Richmond also had other processes for furthering personality adjustment, namely, group work, social reform, and social research. "Group work serves it by dealing with people face to face but no longer one by one; . . . social reform serves it by effecting mass betterment through propaganda and social legislation; . . . and social research serves personality by making original discoveries and re-interpreting known facts for the use of these other forms of social work.[27]

This broad conception of social work in general and of social casework in particular was not acceptable to the field as a whole. Casework tended to take on the coloring of the particular setting in which it was practiced. Definition was more in terms of field than in terms of a generic social casework which could be utilized in a variety of settings. Workers were referred to not as social caseworkers, but as family caseworkers, children's caseworkers, psychiatric social workers, hospital social service workers, and so forth.

Social Casework

The concept of a generic social casework was the major matter of concern at the Milford Conference in 1929. Out of the deliberations of the conference came "the emergence of a strong conviction unanimously held by the members of the Conference that a fundamental conception which had come to be spoken of as 'generic social case work' was much more substantial in content and much more significant in its implications for all forms of social case work than were any of the specific emphasis of the different case work fields." [28]

The definition of social casework agreed upon at the conference, however, was more limited in scope than that projected by Miss Richmond in 1922. It was the opinion of the conference that social casework "deals with the human being whose capacity to organize his own normal social activities may be impaired by one or more deviations from accepted standards of normal social life." [29]

Miss Richmond's objective went beyond changing the behavior of the deviant in conformity with accepted standards of social life. Hers was a more dynamic concept of personality development in general and the "inner" and "outer" factors which affect it. Her approach, therefore, laid stress on the processes involved in personality development, such as:

1. Insight into individuality and personal characteristics.

2. Insight into the resources, dangers, and influences of the social environment.

3. Direct action of mind upon mind.

4. Indirect action through the social environment.

The conference, on the other hand, spelled out its approach in more static terms and listed twenty-five techniques or methods for social casework such as adoption, after-care, diagnosis, evaluation, first interview, institutional care, investigation, re-education, relief allowance, transportation, treatment, use of documents, and so forth. Within Miss Richmond's concept it was possible to integrate the two-pronged approach of the psychological and the socioeconomic. The emphasis in the Milford Conference Report, however, was such that it tended to limit casework to the adjustment of the deviant individual to his environment, without considering how the environment might also be changed to make it more suitable to the fulfillment of human life. A later definition of social casework by Miss Richmond further articulates the integrated approach: "Social case work may be defined as the art of doing different things for and with different people by cooperating with them to achieve at one and the same time their own and society's betterment." [30]

Miss Richmond's attempt to integrate the new psychiatry into the sociological emphasis of the earlier period was not successful. *Social Diagnosis* had formulated the sociological base of social work but, as Virginia Robinson points out, by 1930 we had departed from the social point of view it represented. *Social Diagnosis* was a creative attempt to formulate the logic and science of social diagnosis, and started with the premise of the family group as the unit of study and the unit in which reconstruction must take place. It stressed the importance of relationship but more in terms of being friendly and helpful than in the dynamics of psychoanalytic theory.[31]

Others in the 1920's were involved in the losing effort to remind the field of social work of its heritage in the social sciences. In 1923 Professor Ernest W. Burgess outlined the relationship between social work and sociology. It was his thesis that, although independent in origin, they had a common ground in research. He was of the opinion that the newly emerging research findings in sociology could be adapted for use in social work.

Recent studies in sociology have fashioned tools for the analysis of personality and group behavior not yet fully appreciated by social workers. Outstanding among these concepts are social forces, the human wishes as indices of the normal life, the role of folkways and mores in behavior, human nature as the product of social life, the person as the individual with status, and isolation, mobility and unrest as diagnostic symptoms.[32]

And in 1924 A. Irving Hallowell was asserting the dangers of neglecting the social and cultural approach. In his paper on "Anthropology and the Social Worker's Perspective" he warned:

Most of the literature of the psycho-biological schools which treats the social aspects of personality stresses "instinct" or other innate dynamic factors and neglects or fails to make clear the role played by culture in determining the habits of individuals. Of course the human organism is said to react to its "environment," but this term is not analyzed or clearly defined, so that it is next to impossible to grasp the connection between it and the human beings which in some way or other are supposed to respond to it. Some comprehension of the cultural heritage of a group, particularly a foreign one where the cultural values take on a more objective aspect than our own, enables us to understand what it is to which the individuals of that culture respond.[33]

Similar pleas were being made for including economics, political science, and philosophy in the training program for social workers. But social work had borrowed so heavily from psychiatry that it could not set its own directions. It had adopted, among other ideas, the concept of determinism in psychic life—holding that each psychic event had a history; an emphasis on the need basis of behavior as opposed to the intellectual; and a concentration on the impact of family relationships on individual development.[34] Individual needs and the way they expressed themselves had become the focus of social casework. Knowledge of the family was less for the purpose of dealing with the family as a unit than for understanding the effect of the family constellation on the attitudes, behavior patterns, and personality of the individual. Dr. Salmon had foreseen the new emphasis clearly in 1920 with the observation, "There has been a change of direction in social studies, which after playing upon scenery, and chorus, the audience, and the orchestra finally cause the spotlight to rest upon the individual actor." [35]

Although there were differences in definition and emphasis, social casework expanded rapidly after the war. The mental hygiene movement had shifted from its earlier preoccupation with the care and treatment of the mentally ill in institutions to an interest in prevention. In the 1920's, aided by the financial support of the Commonwealth Fund, it was active in the establishment of child guidance clinics. Psychiatric social workers were part of the clinical team. By 1926 there were enough psychiatric social workers in the hospitals for the mentally ill and in the clinics to warrant the creation of a separate professional organization, the American Association of Psychiatric Social Workers.

The use of caseworkers in other than social work settings continued. The number of hospitals with social service departments increased considerably by 1930, and it is estimated that there were approximately 2000 social workers in hospitals and clinics in the country by 1931. With the financing of demonstration programs of visiting teacher work in some thirty centers throughout the country by the Commonwealth Fund in 1921, the number of visiting teachers grew from 41 in 1916 to 275 in 1931. In 1919 they organized the American Association of Visiting Teachers (now the School Social Workers Section of the

National Association of Social Workers). There was also an increase in the use of caseworkers in religious, court, and industrial settings. By 1930, the first year in which the Bureau of the Census classified social workers as a professional group, a total of 31,241 paid workers was reported. This did not include the 15,020 "keepers of charitable and penal institutions," and the 4270 "public probation and truant officials." [36] It is estimated that over 50 per cent of those classified as social workers were caseworkers.

The experience of social caseworkers in these new settings did more than increase the ranks numerically. It also forced them to think in interdisciplinary terms and to broaden their horizons. Bertha Reynolds is of the opinion that the experience in the child guidance clinics in the 1920's played an important part in the democratization of social casework.

Psychiatric work, like the Red Cross Home Service, brought a new clientele from the child guidance clinics into the field of case work. They were business and professional families who could not get the combined service of four professional people such as made up the clinical team (psychiatrist, psychologist, pediatrician, and psychiatric social worker) in any other way. They were people who were used to paying for professional service, and sometimes did so when the local medical society permitted the clinic to charge a fee. They brought with them a self-respecting, voluntary use of professional help. . . . Secondly, the new clients could not help realizing that people who were referred by social agencies to the same clinics had some of the same problems with their children, and were troubled parents like themselves. The problems dealt with by the clinics could not be assumed to be associated with poverty or mental abnormality, for some of "the best people" had them. Thirdly, the kind of problems encountered demanded an approach on the basis of respect for the dignity and worth of the client. One might give coal and remain at spiritual distance from the recipient, but one could not even learn the story of bewilderment and mental anguish without coming close to the person. Patronage, coercion simply would not do. At the very least, the humility of a scientific spirit was required.[37]

Just as physical health recognized no economic boundaries, so too mental health was not a problem limited to the economic dependent. As social casework moved into settings which went beyond giving relief assistance to the economic dependent, it began to see its potential as a "professional service available to any member of the community in need of help in removing obstacles to productive living." A fuller conception of this potential, however, was not to come until the experience in the depression, when a third of the nation found itself in need of such help.

Group Work

During the 1920's, group work began to take on a formal pattern. Several main channels of influence helped speed its emergence. Industrialization and urbanization threatened the primary group experiences so important in the development of the individual in a democracy. Social agencies like the Young Men's and Young Women's Christian Associations, settlements, centers, the Scouts and the Campfire Girls which offered group experiences, expanded to fill the vacuum. The workers in these leisure time agencies were profoundly affected by the work and philosophy of John Dewey and Mary Follett. Dewey and Follett, fearing that the loss of the intimate, face-to-face relationships represented a danger to preparation for citizenship in a democracy, encouraged the use of the small group for dealing with social problems. Following their lead, adult education circles in the 1920's became interested in the discussion method as a means of furthering the creative and intimate democratic group procedure.

In the meantime, the new concepts of human growth and development and the emphasis on individual and group relations were being dealt with in schools of social work. As the workers in the leisure time agencies turned to the newly developing educational psychology of Dewey and Kilpatrick for guidance, they began to find more common ground with social work. The new progressive education emphasized the value of group education with the focus on the individual and the importance of relationship. These various influences brought workers from education, recreation, and youth-serving agencies together to discuss their common interest in the group approach. By 1933, courses in group work were established at the Y.M.C.A. Schools and at the School of Applied Social Science at Western Reserve University. Informal study groups of workers in these related fields emerged in many communities. By 1936 they became organized on a national scale as the American Association for the Study of Group Work (later called the American Association of Group Workers and now the Group Work Section of the National Association of Social Workers).

Social Work Research

"Social work research" in its present form is of recent vintage. The term "social research" was used originally without any attempt to differentiate between social science research and social work research. Mary Richmond, in her *What Is Social Case Work?* (1922), included social research as one of the methods in social work and defined it as follows: "Social research with its precious freight of original discovery in all fields covered by social work, has also the secondary task of assembling facts in order to re-interpret them for use in social reform in group work and in casework." [38] The first *Social Work Year Book,* which was published in 1929, included an article entitled "Social Research" by Harry L. Lurie.[39] The second volume of the *Year Book,* published in 1933, also contained an article by the same author, but the title was changed to "Research in Social Work." [40] As Hasan notes, "this change of title indicated the growing consciousness in the field that social work research or research in social work was something different from social research." [41] Both terms, however, have continued in use interchangeably until recently.

The main emphasis in research in social work during this period, and through to the 1940's, was in the area of needs and services. The method of tackling such problems was the social survey. The social survey was an integral part of social work's interest in reform.

> The desire to seek facts, regarding the society, its needs and problems, for using them as weapons in the fight for social reform, in the struggle against poverty, suffering and misery, led to the beginning of the survey movement. . . . Social work, which was in its infancy at the turn of the century, and which was anxious to fill the gap of unmet needs, took the social survey to its heart as its main instrument for justifying its own growth and even existence. The facts collected through social surveys would be used both for advocating social reform, as well as for soliciting more funds, for the expansion of social services, charity organization societies, settlement houses and other social agencies, all contributed to the survey movement.[42]

Eaton and Harrison prepared a Bibliography of Social Surveys in which they listed a total of 2775 titles or projects completed up to January 1, 1928. Of these, 154 were general surveys and 2621 were in specialized fields covering 125 special groups in almost all parts of the country.[43] The character of the survey changed during this time. "The first surveys covered a broad range of subjects: they were general studies of entire communities. A tendency set in, however, after a few years, toward employing the survey to appraise some major phase of the community life." [44] As might be expected, these surveys which had varied sponsorship and varied purposes, were not always of a standard which could qualify as research. Some of the surveys were on a high level, but the majority of them "usually contain little of permanent value as research because of haste in preparation, inadequate methods and limited perspectives." [45]

Social Work Education

Expansion of social services and of the number of paid workers was accompanied by an expansion of training programs for social work. Prior to 1915 there had been only five schools of social work. Between 1915 and 1930, because of the growing demands for personnel the number of schools rose to over forty. Twenty-eight of these schools were members of the American Association of Schools of Professional Social Work, and the majority of the schools in the association required a year of graduate professional work. Many of the schools, however, also had a provision for a certificate for those who did not have the necessary undergraduate requirements. Of the other fifteen-odd schools providing training for some aspect of social work, some were within the undergraduate social science departments of universities and several were sponsored by national agencies. The total enrollment of all of these schools was approximately 2000, with only about 10 per cent enrolled as full-time graduate students. If one compares this number with the total of 31,241 paid workers in the 1930 census, it is obvious that the schools were not even providing for the normal turnover due to marriage, death, and retirement, let alone for the growing demand for additional workers. Part of the difficulty which continues to this day to plague social work is that the salaries for beginning workers did not warrant the financial investment in graduate training. Another factor in the period under discussion is that a large part of the field had not come to accept training as essential. As Karpf stated in his study of training for social work:

There is still considerable doubt in the minds of most people as to whether social workers in general and case workers in particular need any special knowledge. . . . Nor is this limited to lay persons. In professional circles, too, among so-called professional social workers, including caseworkers, casework supervisors, and even executives, one still hears discussions on the merits of training versus experience.[46]

Opinion differed not only as to the validity of formalized training in the schools but also as to the content and emphasis of the training program. Part of this disagreement centered around the difficulty in defining social work. Tufts in his study of *Education and Training for Social Work* in 1923 reviewed the following possible methods of defining the field of social work:

1. The field defined as that of aiding certain disadvantaged classes.

2. The field defined by aim and process.

3. The field defined by historical approach.

4. The field defined by its relation to the various social institutions and to the social process.[47]

After weighing the pros and cons, Tufts leaned toward an operational definition, that is, viewing social work as that which the social worker does. In a sense, this merely represented a restatement of the problem, for social workers were doing many different things and in many different ways. It was perhaps another way of saying that the field had not progressed to the point where one could venture a generic definition that would be helpful rather than limiting. As Tufts wrote, "The moral would seem to be that the conception of the field of social work should above all be kept fluid in order to maintain in this profession at least an open mind toward humanity's changing needs and the best methods or agencies for meeting them." [48] Social work's main stock in trade during this period was casework. Little had been done in the majority of the schools in developing community organization, group work, administration and research. In fact, not until 1944 would the schools agree on the inclusion of eight basic areas in their curriculum: Psychiatry, group work, casework, community organization, research, public welfare, administration, and medicine.

Another interesting question raised by Tufts was whether preparation for training shall "be conceived as education or as training" and whether there should be a single standard of training?

Training suggests primarily the acquirement of a technique; it implies, in Professor Dewey's description, formation of habits with relatively little regard to the meaning of what is done. . . . Education, on the other hand, when distinguished from training, suggests rather an emphasis upon the full meaning of situations and experiences with which we deal. It suggests wide acquaintance with all aspects, and sensitiveness to all elements, of culture and life. It involves methods of observation and inquiry which are more or less rigidly exact according to the subject matter and the progress of science, but it emphasizes the consideration of wide ranges of relevant facts and values. It involves consideration of ends as well as means.[49]

The ideal was education rather than the mere teaching of techniques. Social work education by 1930 was beginning to accept this concept theoretically, but in actuality much of the teaching still fell into the category of training.

Tufts felt that just as social work was not yet ready for a generic definition, so it was not yet time for a single standard of training.

It may be that the ideally desirable plan would be a uniform standard of academic preparation and a uniform period in length of study such as now is approximately the case in the better schools of law, medicine, theology, engineering. But these other fields are older, and in the case of law and medicine people have become educated to pay such remuneration as will cover the expense of a long and thorough training. The public mind is not yet sufficiently convinced of the necessity of social work to guarantee any such scale of remuneration for the social worker as that which is recognized as necessary in law, medicine, and engineering. Social work is, perhaps, more nearly comparable with the professions of the ministry and of teaching, but these are notoriously unable to maintain anything like an equal standard for all candidates.[50]

He suggested, however, that all social workers be given a broad grounding in the biological, psychological, and social sciences, and in social philosophy, and that this be combined with "practical work." His recommendations were that the existing standard of the better schools be made a minimum for all social workers and that a broader, more fundamental, and thorough course be developed by a few schools as a new type. (These same questions were to be raised again in the Hollis and Taylor study in 1951.)

The study by Tufts has been quoted in detail because he was an outsider to social work looking at it with objectivity and with the yardstick of the experience of other professions. His recommendations concerning a double standard of training based on the level and type of task met with mixed reception. For social work was moving more rapidly toward professional education on a graduate level than had any of the older professions. The reason for this rapid move is an interesting subject for speculation. Is it because social work deals with a subject matter which demands greater maturity than the other professions and more intensive training? Is it because the experience of some segments of social work as part of a team with the older and more established professions has caused them to pattern themselves after these professions and to achieve their level as rapidly as possible? Is it the social worker's need for acceptance, both from the more established professions and the public? There is no question that certain types of social work demand maturity and intensive training. The question of whether this is true of all social work tasks can only be answered by a study of practice which is yet to be made.

The Social Work Profession

The concern with training was paralleled by a growing professionalization. The American Association of Medical Social Workers had a membership of approximately 1700 by 1930, the National Association of School Social Workers, a membership of approximately 275. The American Association of Psychiatric Social Workers, at first a branch of the medical group, but organized as a separate association in 1926, had a membership of 364; and the American Association of Social Workers, a membership of 5030. Despite this growth, however, less than 25 per cent of the paid social workers listed in the 1930 census were associated with the professional organizations. This in spite of the fact that until 1933 the requirements for membership in the AASW were based on length of service, not education, as a measure of competence. It is evident that a small nucleus was pushing the field toward higher professional standards and toward membership requirements which had a basis in education even though the educational requirements were such that only a comparative handful of new workers were obtaining the level of training demanded. Thus even with social work in its professional infancy, a bill was introduced into the California legislature in 1929 providing for certification through written and oral examination, with training in an approved school or three years of experience in social work. Although the bill was amended several times and failed to pass, it was a straw in the wind. It is significant that the drive seemed to come primarily from those segments of social work which were supplementing the work of other professions.

The absorption of social work in its methodology and professionalism during this postwar period, and its tendency to withdraw from the socioeconomic sphere is borne out by the cool reception given in 1924 to the report of an offshoot of the Committee on Standards of Labor and Living. This report delivered at the National Conference twelve years after the report of the original committee, was entitled "The Challenge to Social Work of the Changing Control in Industry." It called for a closer alliance of social work with labor and outlined the following five principles to govern the relationship:

1. Building up a political class party of the producers, committed to such economic reforms as now characterize the farmer-labor movements; namely, public control of natural resources and public utilities, public control of money and credit, preservation of civil rights, and reform of the judiciary.

2. Participation in the social, industrial, and business enterprises of organized labor, notably workers' education, labor journals, labor banks.

3. Participation in the organization of producers' and consumers' cooperative societies, both among farmers and industrial workers.

4. Aid in the organization of all workers with a direct relationship to function in the shop through workers' representation, and to various arrangements for increased working-class control.

5. Efforts toward greater international cooperation between labor and producing groups in the struggle against war and imperialism.[51]

The report, prepared by Roger Baldwin and concurred in by Frederic Almy, Eduard C. Lindeman, Ben M. Selekman, and

Mary Van Kleeck, was evidently too radical for social work in its then stage of development. Social work's conservatism was not to change until the depression, with the "rise of the 'rank-and-file' movement, reflecting sharp dissatisfaction on the part of a large section of social workers with what they considered the excessive timidity of the existing leadership, the crystallization of a radical approach to economic and political problems, a sense of urgency requiring heroic measures to prevent any recurrence of the mass misery with which social workers came into first-hand contact, and a conviction that a permanent working alliance must be cemented between social work and organized labor." [52] Then social work turned once again from its focus on the individual to the socioeconomic factors in his environment.

Public Welfare

Private social work was in the ascendancy from 1900 to the depression and represented the chief medium for furthering social welfare. By 1917, however, largely through the activities of the private agencies and their success in raising of relief standards, along with a growing interest in the problem on the part of political scientists and government officials, public welfare began to move out of the charities and corrections stage toward more modern concepts. Public welfare still remained the primary responsibility of the states and local communities, but progress was made in "actual re-organization, legislative and administrative development and technical study of programs and principles." [53] The Illinois Administrative Code, which had been enacted in 1917, represented the first move toward greater administrative control and the consolidation of the numerous state commissions and boards dealing with different aspects of social welfare. It marked a shift from boards of charities and corrections to state departments of public welfare. By the middle 1930's a majority of the states were to consolidate their numerous social welfare functions into a single major public welfare function. With greater administrative and fiscal power given to these new state departments, the experts began to replace the lay commissioners. There also began to be greater coordination of state and local activities, with a trend toward the use of the county as the administrative unit. Improved coordination on the state level stimulated better coordination of social welfare activities on the local level. State departments also increased their supervision over local private agencies.

On the federal scene, however, the pattern remained substantially the same. Welfare activities of a varying nature were being handled by some thirteen departments of the federal government. Two attempts were made in the 1920's to integrate these activities through the establishment of a federal Department of Education and Welfare. Both bills, however, were unsuccessful. The relationship of the federal government to state and local welfare also remained the same, with the states and local communities continuing to bear the heaviest proportion of the costs of ordinary public welfare activities. In spite of the exigencies of the time, Hoover reiterated his basic philosophy of rugged individualism in his Lincoln's Birthday address in 1931. Here he spelled out the principle of the local community and the state as the basis of self-government and warned against the danger of encroachment of power by the federal government.

The moment responsibilities of any community, particularly in economic and social questions, are shifted from any part of the nation to Washington, then that community has subjected itself to a remote bureaucracy with its minimum of understanding and of sympathy. It has lost a large part of its voice and its control of its own destiny. . . . Where people divest themselves of local government responsibilities they at once lay the foundation for the destruction of their liberties. . . .

Character is made in the community as well as in the individual by assuming responsibilities, not by escape from them. Carried to its logical extreme, all this shouldering of individual and community responsibility upon the Government can lead but to the superstate where every man becomes the servant of the State and real liberty is lost. . . .

There is an entirely different avenue by which we may both

resist this drift to centralized government and at the same time meet a multitude of problems. That is to strengthen in the Nation a sense and an organization of self-help and cooperation to solve as many problems as possible outside of government.[54]

With this as the prevailing philosophy during the regimes of Harding, Coolidge, and Hoover, it is not surprising that the advances made during this period were in the nature of greater efficiency and economy rather than in strengthening the basic philosophy and method of meeting welfare needs.

Although the federal government spent $752 million on its total public welfare program in 1928, only 4 per cent of this sum went to other than veteran programs. Of this $30 million, $11,500,000 went to Indian Affairs; $6,450,000 to maintenance of Federal correctional institutions; and $4,900,000 to the health and service program for merchant seamen. In brief, the federal government was doing little in the area of ordinary public welfare activities. On the state level, where the bulk of the responsibility for ordinary public welfare activities was being carried, the increase in per-capita welfare costs between 1915 and 1928 was minimal.

A functional analysis of the trend of state welfare costs per capita of total population shows that the aggregate of all state public welfare expenditures, expressed as a ratio of the total population, increased by 95 per cent between 1915 and 1928. Inasmuch as the index of the general price level, compiled by the Federal Reserve Bank of New York (used for this analysis), registered a rise of 73 per cent during this period, it is evident that the real increase in the per capita public welfare costs of state governments was comparatively slight. Of the three major functions, "charities," "hospitals," and "corrections," charities experienced the most rapid rate of expansion, per capita expenditures for this function being 157 per cent greater in 1928 than in 1915. Per capita expenditures for hospitals increased by 97 per cent while per capita correctional expenditures showed a growth of only 64 per cent, which was less than the percentage rise in the general price level.[55]

The increase in the local community for this period was larger, the total being 179 per cent. "Of the three major public welfare functions, hospitals showed the most rapid expansion of per capita costs, the increase between 1912 and 1928 amounting to 222 per cent. Charities [came] next with an increase of only 91 per cent." [56]

The nation was entering the greatest depression in its history with a public welfare vehicle that was being overhauled administratively but that, for all intents and purposes, was still the same one that had been constructed to meet the needs of dependent people in a simple economy. The power on which it was propelled still flowed from "the poor or pauper statutes which had remained practically unmodified from colonial days." The growing unemployment in 1927 and the emerging problems of relief raised a question in some quarters as to the adequacy of the vehicle. It was becoming evident that replacement with a more modern model rather than further repair was the answer. Although community chests were raising larger sums—297 chests raised $64 million in 1927—they were insufficient to meet even minimum welfare needs in these communities. Public welfare expenditures were increasing at a greater rate than private social welfare expenditures. Local and state public welfare expenditures, furthermore, were becoming inadequate to meet the growing needs on even a minimum basis.

In searching for a new vehicle clues were offered by several different types of developments during this period. The practice of transferring activities first undertaken by private efforts to public responsibility was a reality. By 1930 forty-seven states had enacted legislation providing for some form of public aid to children in their own homes. There was also evidence of a growing concern for public aid to the aged; by 1930 thirteen states had some form of plan in operation for aid to the aged. The methods of the private agencies, as well as some of the programs, were introduced into public settings. This practice began to break down the stereotype that the public program could deal only with mass problems and that it could not operate on a quality level. Another development was the increased experience with plans of social insurance.

Summary

The present pattern of services was emerging in every part of the field of social work. The movement was from a highly undifferentiated stage toward the establishment of agencies with specific functions. Social work began to spread out both under sectarian and community sponsorship. Its services were also invited by such host settings as the hospitals, the schools, and the courts. As the segments became more clearly defined, the patterns of national agencies and the machinery for coordinated financing and planning were established. Developments in the private field were of greater moment during this period than in the public, the primary concern in the public field being with administrative changes.

The body of knowledge and the theoretical framework of social work as we know it today took its shape and substance during this period. It drew on the various social sciences but began to lean heavily on one: the enlarging body of psychoanalytic knowledge. More specifically, the developments included a shift in emphasis from cause to function and a concentration on technique and method. In the development of casework, social work placed social relationships at the center of its approach. It sought to develop a better understanding of the relationship between worker and client and of the meaning of the relationship to both. Although social work strove to integrate the social and psychological aspects of social problems, when the impact of psychiatry had been felt it began to shift its attention from the family to the individual. With its new emphasis on mental health, social work moved to extend its boundaries beyond those of the economically disadvantaged.

As social work moved ahead in the development of its techniques and methods, its approach was affected by the character of the setting in which it was operating. Thus, there resulted specialization in terms of setting such as medical, psychiatric and school social work. Such specialization proceeded at a more rapid pace than did the definition of the common core.

Another major development was the growing use of the principle of insurance as a method for promoting human welfare. Workmen's Compensation and the Amended War Risk Insurance Act of 1917, with the emphasis on the cooperative responsibility of government, the employee, and the employer, pointed the way for later attacks on the problems of unemployment, health and medical care, and old age. It presaged a new role for public services.

The point of view in social work reflected that of the general society, namely, the sharp swing from the era of social reform at the turn of the century to the search for a return to "normalcy" after the war. In the period between 1900 and 1917 social workers had joined with other groups in helping to further the liberal programs of Theodore Roosevelt and Woodrow Wilson. Between the end of World War I and the Great Depression, social work felt the impact of the general disillusionment and the breakdown of values. The spirit of unity and the goal of making the world safe for democracy had given way to pettiness, partisanship, provinciality, and reaction. Social breakdown was rampant. Social work, with its new-found methods for helping the individual with problems of personality adjustment, came face to face with the problems of not only a changing individual but also a changing society. There no longer was the anchorage of stable social institutions for the individual; moral standards and social norms were adrift. Personality theory, which to some extent had been projected on the basis of the values of a stable society, was not fully adequate to meet the challenge of the times.

In this period social work became introspective and poured its energy into the further development of its methodology, its educational training, and its professionalization. In the conservative and reactionary atmosphere that prevailed, social work tended to ignore the signs which pointed toward the need for a new look in meeting the emerging mass problems. It had put aside its major interest in social reform and had become absorbed in function and technique as these related to the individual problem. The crying need for a social policy called for the use of a set of muscles which had become atrophied and, in the minds of some, "unprofessional."

6

THE GREAT

DEPRESSION

The Social Institution
and the Individual

(1929-1940)

THE HOUSE literally caved in with the Great Depression which followed the stock market crash in 1929. America was like the rat in the maze seeking the exit which would bring a solution to the problem. The path to new territories bore the sign, "Frontiers closed as of 1900." The path of planning—the interdependence road—had become a series of detours with private byways for various vested interests, all leading to dead-ends. The main highway—the Big Business Skyway—was the scene of increasing economic accidents, and people began to fear traveling on it. The government's prevailing approach of putting all its efforts into increasing traffic on this highway—the trickle-down theory—was to no avail. The great industrial giant had slowed down and threatened complete collapse.

The extent to which the economic machinery had broken down is evidenced by the change between 1929 and 1932 in the basic economic indices such as national income produced, national income paid out, and employment. National income produced dropped from $81 billion in 1929 to $40 billion in 1932. Production of goods and services had shrunk in value to less than one half. National income paid out dropped from $78.5 billion in 1929 to $49 billion in 1932. The employment index which had risen from the base of 100 in 1923-1925 to 106 in 1929, dropped to 66 in 1932, a decrease of approximately 40 per cent. By 1933 approximately one-fourth of the civilian labor force was unemployed. A further indication of the extent of the depression was that by 1934 approximately

20 million individuals were receiving relief from the federal government.

The conditions under which people existed during the height of the depression are described vividly in the hearings held before a committee of the Senate. The following is an abstract from Philadelphia:

Only the other day a case came to my attention in which a family of ten had just moved in with a family of five in a three-room apartment. However shocking that may be to the members of this committee, it is almost an everyday occurrence in our midst. Neighbors do take people in. They sleep on chairs, they sleep on the floor. There are conditions in Philadelphia that beggar description. There is scarcely a day that calls do not come to all our offices to find somehow a bed or a chair. The demand for boxes on which people can sit or stretch themselves is hardly to be believed.[1]

The state of the people is further reflected by the fact that during the height of the depression emigration exceeded immigration. "In the 1930's, the 'land of opportunity' actually suffered a net loss from emigrants going to Europe or elsewhere to repair their fortunes. In 1932, 35,329 immigrant aliens came in while 103,295 emigrant aliens departed."[2]

The birth rate for the white population decreased from 30 per thousand in 1930 to 18 per thousand in 1940. There was a continued increase in the percentage of the older groups, with the median age increasing from 26.4 in 1930 to 29 in 1940, and the proportion of persons 65 and over increasing from 5.4 in 1930 to 6.8 in 1940. The latter group was hard hit, for employers had begun to refuse to hire people over 50, and no provision had been made by government to protect their economic needs. The population increase in the nation from 1930 to 1940 was only 7.2 per cent less than one-half of that in any previous decade.

Economic insecurity during the depression was further aggravated by the change that had taken place in the pattern of family living. As pointed out by Clough:[3]

1. Close ties developed from working on common tasks as a

producer group were absent in the urban pattern of family living.

2. With the family dependent completely on wages for meeting the basic economic needs of food, clothing, and shelter, unemployment affected the total fabric of family living.

3. Urbanized living with its demands for more material things and more expensive recreation, and with the increased emphasis on installment buying, resulted in the average family living close to the margin and having little savings.

4. Urban family living did not provide the flexibility in matters of food, clothing, and shelter for absorbing additional dependents as was true in the rural pattern of family living.

5. With the increasing unemployability of the aged, the dependent aged were not too welcome in the homes of their relatives.

In brief, "The family obviously was deteriorating as an agency for alleviating the rigors of economic security. It was less willing, and the worker's family was less able, to support those who had suffered economic misfortune than it had been in earlier times." [4]

The welfare of the people was at a low ebb. The administration in power under the leadership of Herbert Hoover was hesitant to take any steps which might in its judgment subordinate individual enterprise to the common welfare. It failed to see that unless economic individualism could be reconciled with the general welfare, the ideals of democracy would be subverted.

The New Deal

Hoover went before the people in 1932 with his views and theory of government unaltered, but the people decided that it was time for a change and voted in the Democratic Party under the leadership of Franklin Delano Roosevelt. Roosevelt assumed the Presidency at a time when the entire world was in the throes of ideological conflict. Revolutionary socialism was a going concern in the U.S.S.R. and Communist parties were gaining strength in other nations. The various forms of evolutionary socialism were also making headway. Fascism, with its negation of democracy as a philosophy, was in power in Italy and Germany, and was gaining power in other countries.

The Roosevelt administration rejected both of these patterns of collectivism and proceeded to develop a pattern of economic and social planning within the traditional American framework. Private capitalism was not to be scrapped, but rather retooled the better to serve the aims of democracy. Individualism was still to remain as a basic concern, but not in terms of our early pioneer days. The concept of rugged individualism based on the economic philosophy of natural laws as stated by Smith, Ricardo, and Malthus, and reenforced by Social Darwinism with its emphasis on survival of the fittest, was replaced by a social concept more in line with an urban and industrial society. It emphasized interdependence as well as independence. In the same way that a relationship of dependence was undemocratic, so too was independence without an awareness of interdependence. The view of the least government as the best government gave way to a positive and active concern by government for the public welfare.

The role of government had been changing since the latter part of the nineteenth century, but the change became explicit and formalized during the New Deal. The government entered the economic arena actively, dealing with the following among other things: anti-trust suits to regulate competition; a system of social security; regulations for public utilities; provisions for collective bargaining between employers and employees; controls for the stock market; extension and protection of loans to industry, farmers, and home builders; farm controls and subsidies; protection of bank deposits; protection of the consumer through fair trade practices; protection and rehabilitation of natural resources; and public owned and operated projects. Frederick Lewis Allen describes two new political principles that emerged during this period:

One principle is that the fortunes of individual Americans are in-extricably interlocked; that we are "all in the same boat"; and that if any of us fall into deep trouble it is the job of the rest of us—not simply family and friends and neighbors, or even the local community, but the federal government itself if need be—to help them.

The other principle is that it is the job of the federal govern-ment, through whatever means, to see that there shall not be an-other Great Depression. Most of us want to keep as much economic liberty as possible for ourselves as individuals; most of us hate to see the powers of the federal government extended; but we realize that it is the only instrument on which we can rely, in a severe economic emergency, to provide us with a measure of security.[5]

The shift in attitude toward the role of government was reflected in the changes in interpretation of constitutional theo-ries on the part of the Supreme Court. In January 1936 the Court, in the case of the *United States* v. *Butler,* 297 U.S.1, held unconstitutional the first Agricultural Adjustment Act. The basic question involved was the right of the federal government to provide funds for "the general welfare." In March 1937 the Court began to show a marked shift in its legal philosophy. In a short span of three months—from March 29, 1937, to May 24, 1937—it reversed in ten important cases its attitude toward the power and role of the federal government. "Minimum wage legislation was upheld against a claim of 'freedom of con-tract.' . . . But more significant was the upholding of fed-eral regulation of manufacturing enterprises under the consti-tutional delegation of power over interstate commerce. . . . Next, the federal power to tax and spend for the general wel-fare was vindicated in cases upholding the Social Security pro-gram. Here was an abandonment of the philosophy of the But-ler case." [6]

The case of *Helvering* v. *Davis* (Supreme Court of the United States, 1937, 301 U.S. 619) was one of the important landmarks in establishing the validity of the Social Security program. It dealt with the old-age pension provisions of the act. The majority opinion, written by Justice Cardozo, spells out the changed pattern of needs, rights, and responsibilities:

Congress may spend money in aid of the "general welfare." Constitution, Art. I, section 8; United States v. Butler, 297 U.S. 1, 65. . . . There have been great statesmen in our history who have stood for other views. We will not resurrect the contest. It is now settled by decision. . . . Yet difficulties are left when the power is conceded. The line must still be drawn between one welfare and another, between particular and general. Where this shall be placed cannot be known through a formula in advance of the event. There is a middle ground or certainly a penumbra in which discretion is at large. The discretion, however, is not confided to the courts. The discretion belongs to Congress, unless the choice is clearly wrong, a display of arbitrary power, not an exercise of judgment. This is now familiar law. "When such a contention comes here we naturally require a showing that by no reasonable possibility can the challenged legislation fall within the wide range of discretion permitted to the Congress." United States v. Butler, supra, p. 67. . . . Nor is the concept of the general welfare static. Needs that were narrow or parochial a century ago may be interwoven in our day with the well-being of the Nation. What is critical or urgent changes with the times.

The purge of nation-wide calamity that began in 1929 has taught us many lessons. Not the least is the solidarity of interests that may once have seemed to be divided. Unemployment spreads from State to State, the hinterland now settled that in pioneer days gave an avenue of escape. . . . Spreading from State to State, unemployment is an ill not particular but general, which may be checked, if Congress so determines, by the resources of the Nation. . . . But the ill is all one, or at least not greatly different, whether men are thrown out of work because there is no longer work to do or because the disabilities of age make them incapable of doing it. Rescue becomes necessary irrespective of the cause. The hope behind this statute is to save men and women from the rigors of the poor house as well as from the haunting fear that such a lot awaits them when journey's end is near. . . .

The problem is plainly national in area and dimensions. Moreover, laws of the separate states cannot deal with it effectively. Congress, at least, had a basis for that belief. States and local governments are often lacking in the resources that are necessary to finance an adequate program of security for the aged. This is brought out with a wealth of illustration in recent studies of the problem. Apart from the failure of resources, states and local governments are at times reluctant to increase so heavily the burden of taxation to be borne by their residents for fear of placing themselves in a position of economic disadvantage as compared with neighbors or competitors. . . . A system of old age pensions has special dangers of its own, if put in force in one state and rejected in another. The existence of such a system is a bait to the needy and dependent elsewhere, encouraging them to migrate and seek a haven of repose. Only a power that is national can serve the interests of all.

Whether wisdom or unwisdom resides in the scheme of benefits set forth in Title II, it is not for us to say. The answer to such inquiries must come from Congress, not the courts. Counsel for respondent has recalled to us the virtues of self-reliance and frugality. There is a possibility, he says, that aid from a paternal government may sap those sturdy virtues and breed a race of weaklings. If Massachusetts so believes and shapes her laws in that conviction, must her breed of sons be changed, he asks, because some other philosophy of government finds favor in the halls of Congress? But the answer is not doubtful. One might ask with equal reason whether the system of protective tariffs is to be set aside at will in one state or another whenever local policy prefers the rule of laissez faire. The issue is a closed one. It was fought out long ago.

When money is spent to promote the general welfare, the concept of welfare or the opposite is shaped by Congress, not the states. So the concept not be arbitrary, the locality must yield. . . .[7]

The New Deal was an ideological revolution, a recognition of the fact that the goals of democracy are dependent on more than economic forces. The main themes of democracy—respect for personal worth, equal opportunity for all, and personal freedom—were seen to be inextricably interwoven with political and social as well as economic forces.

An ideological revolution of such magnitude does not spring into being overnight. It was being hammered out over many decades with many interwoven strands of influence. One of these strands was the effort of social work to counteract the injustices and problems growing out of industrialization. The social reform group in social work had made an important contribution to the program of the progressives in the era of

Theodore Roosevelt. Their influence, both educationally and politically, was to be even more fully felt in the period of the New Deal. As Schlesinger reports:

Hull-House, Henry Street, the Consumers' League, and the other organizations educated a whole generation in social responsibility. Henry Morgenthau, Jr., Herbert Lehman, and Adolf A. Berle, Jr., all worked at Henry Street; Frances Perkins, Gerard Swope, and Charles A. Beard at Hull-House (where John Dewey was an early member of the board of trustees); Sidney Hillman at both Hull-House and Henry Street; Joseph B. Eastman at Robert A. Wood's South End House in Boston; an Iowa boy coming east from Grinnell College in 1912 went to work at Christadora House on the lower East Side of New York; his name, Harry Hopkins. Through Belle Moskowitz the social work ethos infected Alfred E. Smith; through Frances Perkins and others, Robert F. Wagner; through Eleanor Roosevelt, active in the Women's Trade Union League and a friend of Florence Kelley's and Lillian Wald's, Franklin D. Roosevelt.

And for all the appearance of innocence and defenselessness the social workers' apparatus wielded power. "One could not overestimate," observed Wagner, "the central part played by social workers in bringing before their representatives in Congress and state legislatures the present and insistent problems of modern-day life." The subtle and persistent saintliness of the social workers was in the end more deadly than all the bluster of business. Theirs was the implacability of gentleness.[8]

Economic individualists had seen welfare as merely a by-product of economic activity. They had set personal freedom at the core and had failed to understand that if people were not competing on equal terms liberty could become license for the stronger to take advantage of the weaker, and personal worth could become secondary to personal greed and success. By 1932 it was clear that the law of the marketplace could not long remain free in an economy where "one half of all corporate enterprise was in the hands of just two hundred companies." If people came first in a democracy and the purpose of its institutions was to further individual and collective welfare, the economic institutions must also be guided by moral judgments. The citizen in a democracy had a right and a responsibility to determine the goals he desired from the economic process as well as from the political and social aspects of his life. In brief, the New Deal encompassed democracy as a whole, with its political, economic, and social aspects closely interwoven. It recognized that the welfare of all the people could be achieved only if government took an active role, through legislation and planning, in bringing about a better balance among the interests of the worker, the farmer, the consumer, and the industrialist. The New Deal's philosophy was not that of the Marxists or the Socialists but that of the "liberal capitalist economists." Capitalism could survive in a democracy if government would buttress the economy "with a strong pillar of government investment, with active enforcement of anti-monopoly laws, with the regulation of industries which are deemed to affect the public interest," [9] with protective rules for collective bargaining, with greater responsibility for price and wage levels, with a program to abolish substandard housing, and with protection of the citizen through social insurance against unemployment, ill-health, and old-age.

New Deal Programs with Special Meaning for Social Work

If we view social welfare in the broad sense, that is, as involving social policy in a program of prevention, then the entire scope of the New Deal has significance for the goals of social work. For our purpose, however, a review of those aspects directly related to social work will be adequate. The program of the New Deal is often referred to as the three R's—Relief, Recovery, and Reform.

RELIEF

The first task of the new administration was to alleviate conditions of suffering, to provide the wherewithal for meeting the basic needs of food, clothing, and shelter for millions of unemployed. In the early stages direct relief was stepped up. It included cash relief subsidies, and purchase and distribution of surplus food and clothing. Through the FERA, established in May, 1933, half a billion dollars were appropriated for direct emergency relief to states and to local communities. The FERA eventually disbursed over $3 billion. Local agencies administered expenditures but the FERA exerted an important influence on standards.

An extensive work relief program soon followed. This program had a threefold purpose: work for the unemployed, to restore man's belief in himself by providing the opportunity to be self-supporting; help to the consumer rather than just to the producer, to stimulate industry; and, to bolster the whole economy, economic reforms which the states could not afford to subsidize. The first such program was the National Recovery Act in June 1933 which provided for a comprehensive system of public works. Under the authority of this act Congress established a Public Works Administration to coordinate the system of public works. Through this program useful public works such as dams and bridges were undertaken in the various states. The necessary funds for these projects were loaned to the state and local governments by the federal government. Over four million men were given jobs ranging from clerical work to construction. It was under the PWA that the first federal low rent housing and slum clearance project was launched. In April 1935 the federal program was expanded when by executive order of the President the Works Progress Administration (later the Works Project Administration) was established. The WPA was intended primarily to provide employment for those in need of relief through work relief projects which would have long-range value to the country. These projects utilized the skilled and white collar workers as well as the unskilled laborers. Through this program approximately $5 billion were spent on building thousands of miles of roads, public parks, airports, schools, post offices, and other public buildings. It also provided work opportunity for those in the arts through the Federal Art Project, the Federal Writers' Project, and the Federal Theatre Project.

THE TVA

One of the most controversial projects created by the administration was the Tennessee Valley Authority, established by an Act of Congress on May 18, 1933. More than an emergency measure, the act embodied a concept of long-time social planning on the part of the federal government. The project had as its purposes flood control, land reclamation, improved river navigation, production of nitrates for national defense, and generation of hydroelectric power for sale to municipalities and cooperatives. The geographical region involved included about 49,000 square miles of seven Southeastern states. The project area had a population of approximately 2.5 million people.

There were two questions about the project: on the one hand, the attitude of the utility companies toward the right of government in what they considered to be their domain; and on the other, the attitude of the population of the region toward a project of social planning.

The mountaineers of the Tennessee Valley, individualists of the pioneer type, influenced hardly at all by the growth of our industrial and urban civilization, would seem to be the most unpromising subjects for social planning. . . . The project assumes that by a tour de force the industrial revolution which elsewhere in the United States required two or three generations will here be telescoped into four or five years and in that time mountaineers with their intense individualistic traditions and attitudes will become completely adjusted to the power age and modern technology.[10]

The TVA administrators approached the project with a concern for the customs and attitudes of the inhabitants, and through a sound process of involving the local population in the planning they accomplished what looked like the impossible. The TVA has become known the world over as a feat not merely in physical and economic engineering but also in human engineering.

The private utility companies, in the meantime, fought this venture through the courts. Their suit against the government was carried to the Supreme Court. But on January 3, 1938, the Supreme Court upheld the right of the government to make loans to municipal light plants; and on February 17, 1938, it declared the governmental sale of power to be constitutional. These were momentous decisions for a nation that had in previous years denied such a role for government, and a defeat for a powerful group that in previous years had enjoyed a favored and influential position with government.

HOUSING

The depression revealed that a third of the nation were not only ill-fed and ill-clothed but also ill-housed, living in substandard dwellings and in slums. As a first step, the Home Owners Loan Act was passed in June, 1933. Through this act emergency mortgage credit was extended to distressed home owners. Between June, 1933, and June, 1936, when the lending operations were discontinued, the HOLC had refinanced mortgages in all but 72 of the country's 3072 counties. In June, 1934 Congress passed the National Housing Act, which created a Federal Housing Administration. The purpose of the FHA was to provide assurance to approved lending institutions against losses on secured and unsecured loans for repairs and improvements and loans secured by first mortgage on residential property. On August 21, 1937, Congress took a more permanent step to meet the problems of the nonhomeowners in the low-income level. A slum-clearance and low-rent housing program with federal aid was being carried on as part of the PWA program. The United States Housing Act was passed by Congress establishing a permanent United States Housing Authority within the Department of the Interior. The purpose of the USHA was to establish a long-term program of federal aid to state and local governments for slum clearance and housing for families of lowest income.

HEALTH

Concern for the one-third of the nation living below decent standards also was expressed in the field of health. Surgeon-General Parran reported that "the one-third of our population ill-fed, ill-housed, ill-clothed also is ill provided with the opportunity for health and life. Illness among persons on relief is 57 per cent higher than among those in comfortable circumstances. The case rate of chronic illness among those on relief is 87 per cent higher than among those with comfortable incomes." [11] This group, which had the greatest need for medical care, was receiving less than the higher economic groups. Another group hard hit was those wage earners who could provide the basic needs of food, clothing, shelter, and occasional medical and dental services for their families, but were in no position to meet an emergency illness of some duration necessitating expensive medical or hospital care.

There was also a lag in the nation's program of preventing disease. The nation was spending an infinitesimal amount on its public health program as compared with other services. A study in 1932 revealed that exclusive of hospitalization, a total of $115 million was being spent as follows: federal, $5 million; state, $14 million; local communities, $69 million; and voluntary agencies, $27 million. Furthermore less than one fifth of the nation's 3072 counties had a full-time program of health supervision, and less than one fourth of the local health departments were operating under accepted standards. The Social Security Act provided for expansion of the public health program. Under Title V "authority was granted for an appropriation to the Children's Bureau to extend maternal and child health activities and to provide for the welfare of crippled children." Title VI authorized "an annual appropriation to the Public Health Service not to exceed $8 million for the purpose of assisting states, counties, health districts, etc., in the establishment and maintenance of adequate health services, including the training of personnel, for state and local health work." The act also provided an appropriation for research and administrative activities, the Public Health Service to receive an annual appropriation not to exceed $2 million for the program.

Plans were also initiated for a more comprehensive national program of health. Several of the government departments were dealing with some phase of health services. An interdepartmental committee to coordinate the health and welfare activities of the federal government was organized "in order that the full benefits of the various federal programs under the Act's provisions might reach with minimum delay and maximum effectiveness the individual men, women, and children for whose aid and service the program was brought into existence." The Interdepartmental Committee to Coordinate Health and Welfare Activities sponsored a conference on national health in July, 1938. The conference explored such major problems as the care of the medically needy, a general program of medical care, and the expansion of hospital services. Also discussed was a further expansion of the maternal and child health program, and a program of insurance against the loss of wages during illness.

Two major recommendations resulted from the conference. The first projected a ten-year program of federal grants-in-aid to tackle the following: implementation of programs of maternal and child care, industrial hygiene, and mental hygiene; a concentrated program against cancer, pneumonia, malaria, tuberculosis, and venereal diseases; construction of hospitals in unserved areas; and a program of care for the medically needy. It was estimated that at the end of ten years when the program would be in full operation the annual cost would be $850 million. The plan recommended that half of the cost be met by the federal government, and the other half by the state and local governments. The second recommendation dealt with insurance against the loss of wages during sickness. The conference did not recommend a specific plan for meeting the problem but suggested that "temporary disability insurance can perhaps be established along lines analogous to unemployment compensation; permanent disability insurance may be developed through the system of old age insurance."

The findings of the conference served as the basis for the Wagner Health Bill introduced into Congress as an amendment to the Social Security Act on February 28, 1939. The bill provided for federal grants-in-aid to states as an incentive for a program of health to meet the needs of the total population. It proposed a three-year budget of $98,250,000, to be expanded as necessary, to assist the states in building and developing public health services, in maintaining needed medical facilities, and in providing for the prevention and control of disease. It also took an initial step toward health insurance by providing cash benefits for wages lost during illness.

PROGRAMS FOR YOUTH

The youth of the nation—the 16-25 age group—were hard hit by the depression. Their problem was not only unemployment but also loss of morale and social breakdown. "Thousands of youth were roaming the country as destitute young tramps. High schools in almost every community were swamped with sudden increases in enrollment at a time when school taxes often remained unpaid and school budgets were being drastically cut. No one knew exactly what was happening to the millions of oncoming youth who were unable to remain in school, yet it was obvious that they were not moving smoothly into employment." [12] The American Youth Commission reported that by 1935 over 4 million of the youth 16-24 years of age who were out of school were unemployed.

An emergency conservation program was established in March, 1933, for youth between the ages of 17 and 23. In June, 1937 by an act of Congress it became the Civilian Conservation Corps. Its purpose was to furnish temporary employment and to rehabilitate forests and soil. Enrollees were selected by the public assistance authorities of the various states. Part of their pay went to their families. Over 2.5 million young men, including a number of unemployed war veterans, were served through this program. The value of the program in maintaining and developing natural resources "has been officially estimated to be in excess of $1,500,000,000." [13] The value in salvaging human resources cannot be estimated in dollars and cents. The following analysis of the group, however, provides a good picture of the needs that were being met:

The enrollees come predominantly from a low-income family background, whether urban or rural, and their records at the time of entering camp indicate many deficiencies in the care, education, and training they have previously received. The typical enrollee has completed a little more than eight grades of school in the course of ten to eleven years of school attendance. A considerable number of the enrollees have not progressed in literacy beyond the fourth grade level, although others have been graduated from high school, and a few have attended college. Important segments of the CCC youth population include the 20 per cent of enrollees with foreign-born parents, the 10 per cent who are Negroes, and the 37 per cent from broken homes. About 70 per cent have had no significant work experience before entering camp, and most of the others have had only a few months of previous employment.[14]

A leisure-time educational program was provided, with most of the enrollees spending several hours a week in pursuing vocational and academic subjects. Although conservation of natural resources was the main objective, high priority was given to the welfare and training of the enrollee.

In 1935 another youth program, the National Youth Administration, was added for those who wanted to remain at home and for needy students in the high schools, colleges, and universities. The NYA, which started as a junior WPA, provided part-time employment for more than 1,750,000 out-of-school young people, plus student work programs through which more than 1,800,000 needy youth in schools and colleges were assisted.

Both the CCC and the NYA programs were transferred to the Federal Security Agency in 1939, but were run as separate projects. The American Youth Commission Report recommended a "consolidation of the CCC and the NYA into a single youth work project administration." They also recommended that there be special youth programs in any future periods of unemployment that necessitated a public works program. But by the time of their report, America was at war again, and the slack of one aspect of the program, assistance to college and university students, had been absorbed temporarily through the G.I. Bill.

SOCIAL SECURITY

Relief alone was not enough to assuage the economic insecurity growing out of the Great Depression. In other countries faced with the same problem the solution was being sought through an economic revolution, through Socialist, Communist, and Fascist forms of government. The solution required something beyond the usual pattern of helping those suffering from economic misfortune. Aid through the family, the local community, and the state was inadequate. It had to become the responsibility and the job of the federal government. The government faced the challenge and on August 14, 1935, passed the Social Security Act.

A plan of compulsory insurance for all under government sponsorship had already been developed in Germany in the 1880's. Rapid industrialization and urbanization—and a fear of a growing Socialist movement—had motivated Chancellor Otto von Bismarck to launch the program, which included coverage for old age, health, and workmen's compensation. Other countries followed Germany's lead slowly. Thus it was not until 1911 that England added a program of sickness insurance, and not until 1928 that France had adopted a comprehensive system of social insurance. In brief, the development in the United States was long overdue. A trend in the direction of welfare laws for the aged and the unemployed had begun in some of the more progressive states at an earlier date. Between 1923 and 1934 twenty-eight states had adopted old-age assistance laws. Workmen's compensation, a form of social insurance, had been introduced in 1912, and by 1920 all but eight states had enacted compensation acts. It took the pressure of the Great Depression, however, for the United States to develop a comprehensive program of social insurance. The reasons for the slower development were that "ample job opportunities, resulting from the extraordinary economic expansion of the country, a tradition of self-reliance, the high development of private insurance, and a wide application of local poor relief meant that the pressure for governmental measures to reduce economic insecurity was not particularly insistent." [15]

The original act provided the following: (1) A national old-age insurance system, to be financed by a tax on the payrolls of eligible employers, the tax to be shared equally between employers and employees. In 1939 the survivorship feature was added. (2) A federal-state unemployment insurance system, to be financed by a federal tax on payrolls. When and if the state developed an unemployment insurance system, credit for 90 per cent of the tax paid to the state system could be offset against the federal tax. This was in essence a device to encourage or force states to adopt a program, for if they did not the tax money went automatically to the federal government. (3) Federal grants-in-aid to the states for old-age assistance, aid to dependent children, and aid to the blind, and for the development of services to promote maternal and child health, medical care for crippled children, child welfare, public health, and the vocational rehabilitation of disabled persons. The act authorized federal grants-in-aid to the states setting up approved old-age assistance plans, in an amount equivalent to 50 per cent of the payment up to thirty dollars per month. In the case of mother's aid the act authorized an annual appropriation of $24,750,000 for the purpose of adding one federal dollar to every two dollars spent by the state. Except for old-age insurance, which was a federal program, the provisions of the act were based on the principle of federal-state cooperation and dependent on the action taken by the states. All states adopted unemployment acts shortly after the federal enactment.

The Social Security plan as formulated was based on income, and was referred to as an "income insurance" system.

While a person is earning, contributions are made by or on behalf of him to a fund, with the understanding that when his earnings are interrupted by causes such as death, injury, unemployment or old age, a substantial proportion of his average former earnings will be paid to him or his dependents. . . . The sole test for getting benefits, once the individual is so "insured," is the loss of earnings due to one of the specified events. As long as a man is drawing his regular income, our present insurance system is not concerned with him, even if he is in financial distress because of, say, the large size of his family or the impact of heavy medical expenses.[16]

The assistance aspect of the act was to provide for those categories of people who were not and could not become income producers because of physical disabilities or broken homes, individuals in need and not eligible for the social insurance program, and individuals with substandard income even though employed. Eligibility for assistance was to be determined by a means test. Amounts to be paid, unlike those of the insurance program, were related to need rather than to a formula of accumulated insurance assets.

The plan was in many respects a compromise and represented a beginning rather than a comprehensive system of social insurance. In its initial form, various groups—farm and domestic employees, independent contractors, the self-employed, public employees, employees of charitable and educational institutions, self-employed professional men, and farm owners and operators—were excluded from old-age insurance coverage. Coverage for unemployment insurance was even more limited, with about a third of the workers excluded, and there was no provision for long-term unemployment. Poor health was neglected as a major factor of financial distress, and no protection was provided in the event of temporary or permanent disability from causes unconnected with work. The funds provided for special welfare services under the vocational rehabilitation program and under the maternal and child health and child welfare programs were inadequate. The assistance program, dependent as it was on a matching formula, meant that people in the less affluent states would have their needs met at a lower level.

The Social Security Act had special significance for social welfare services in rural areas. The highly developed network of services under private auspices in urban areas did not have its counterpart in the rural communities. Of the private national welfare programs only the American Red Cross had penetrated the rural areas on an extensive basis. Their programs in these areas, however, were limited. On the public side, the United States Department of Agriculture, through its extension services, carried on a well-developed program of adult education. The County Extension Agents included in their programs extensive recreational services for boys and girls through the 4-H Clubs.

The Social Security Act provided that any state wishing to cooperate was required to make the services of the federal-state categorical assistance program available to all groups and sections. This necessitated an extension of much-needed public welfare service activities in behalf of older people in need, dependent children, and the needy blind in all units of the state. In the area of old age and survivors' insurance, although farm workers were not to be included until the 1950 amendments, a considerable number of farm residents had some credits because of employment other than agricultural.

The provisions in the act authorizing the federal-state child welfare services also extended child-welfare programs to rural areas. They made possible the employment of full-time child-welfare workers in large enough numbers to create an impact; the development of programs in maternal and child health; and the extension and improvement of services to crippled children.

Social Work in the Depression

Social work brought to the depression attitudes and methods developed in the period between World War I and the Great Depression. The heavy involvement with Freud's teachings and the climate of reaction after World War I had pushed social reform and social action into the background. By 1931, however, social workers had begun to raise their voices, and to recognize that private charity was not the answer to problems such as unemployment, hunger, substandard housing, inadequate medical care, and low wages. The sums raised by community chests were insufficient to meet even minimum welfare needs in the communities. Public welfare expenditures were increasing at a greater rate than private social welfare expenditures. For example, in 1931 between 70 and 80 per cent of all the relief spent in the nation came from public tax funds. Furthermore, even with the increase in public funds on a local and state level, welfare expenditures were proving inadequate to the growing needs. Federal participation was essential, and social work through its professional organization, the AASW, began to make a study of how such a new pattern of operation could best be accomplished.

Probably the most dramatic activity of the Association was its work with the Costigan-LaFollette Committee of the United States Senate in the early years of the Great Depression. Under the leadership of its Committee on Government and Social Work, it arranged for notable hearings, presenting data and recommendations on the need and manner of federal participation in the care of the unemployed. Although up to 1933 these recommendations failed of passage, they did establish the structure on which the relations between federal and state authorities could develop, and laid much of the groundwork for the legislation passed in the first term of President Roosevelt.[17]

Social work was again showing its flexibility and responding to the changing economic, political, and social climate. The new approach represented a major change in the thinking of social work, which at this time was still steeped in privately sponsored services. It meant for social work a reorientation of its views about philosophy and goals, method, education, and function. Would expansion of the publicly sponsored services threaten the future of the private agency? Would it threaten the political and social philosophy held by many of the board members of the private agencies? Was it a question of either-or, or was a concept of both-and possible? Could the newly developed methodology with its emphasis on the individual and his psychological problems be applied to mass problems stemming from the breakdown of social institutions? If the public agencies were to take over major responsibilities for relief, what was to be the function of the private agencies, especially the family welfare agencies? With the large number of untrained workers being recruited to man the public services, what was to happen to the standards established by the professional organizations and the schools of social work? These among others were the problems which faced the shapers of policy in the 1930's.

The Relationship of the Public and Private Agencies

In social work, as in the community in general, there were those who saw an emergency role for public services, but refused to grant them permanent status. They tended to regard the new developments growing out of the depression as stopgaps that would be abandoned once the crisis was over, rather than as the beginnings of a new era in social welfare services. For them it was as if social work had laid aside its tools to help the nation fight a disaster, but once the disaster was under control, like the returning soldier, social work would pick up again where it had left off.

At the other extreme were those who with the advent of the new public programs no longer saw any role for the private voluntary services. This group pointed to the decrease in the growth of private expenditures during the 1930's as a sign of the beginning of the demise of private social services. They were able to point out that in the period of temporary recovery, between 1933 and 1937, national income rose from $44.9 billion to $69 billion—an increase of 53.7 per cent—whereas in the same period chest income rose from $52.5 million to $54.7 million—an increase of only 4.8 per cent. They also stressed that the expenditures of the private agencies represented a constantly decreasing share of the total expenditures for welfare programs in the community. In 1929, in 116 urban communities reporting to the Russell Sage Foundation on welfare expenditures, 24.2 per cent of the funds spent on relief had come from private sources; in 1938 these same communities reported that private funds accounted for only 0.7 per cent of the total expenditures for relief.

Perhaps the largest group in the social work community stood between these extremes. It was their opinion that social work was going through a transition that called, not for a substitution of the new for the old, but rather for an integration of the two with the roles of the public and private services more clearly defined. They saw a new role for the private agencies as leaders in research, setting standards, and pioneering. They felt that once the field was able to interpret this role, support would be forthcoming from the public. In brief, the future of private social work depended on its ability to meet the challenge of the changing social scene, to see itself within a new Gestalt in the community's efforts to meet the needs of all the people, rather than as an isolated attempt to defend its accrued vested interests. This meant among other things critical self-examination, redefinition of objectives, reformulation of programs, and cooperative endeavors with all groups in the community interested in furthering human welfare.

Redefinition of Function and Method

The problems of the redefinition of function, however, differed for the various fields. The impact of the newly developed public programs was greatest in the family-welfare field which had been handling relief. In the child-care field the public programs were not far advanced and it was more a question of looking to the future than an immediate problem. The trend of the public services, however, was discernible, and the child-care field began to recognize the need for reviewing its objectives. With the provisions for the aged in the social security program, homes for the aged were faced with new conditions. Some of them began to change to institutions for the chronically ill. Others began to see themselves as boarding homes for independent pensioners who could now make a choice about their place of residence in old age.

In the field of recreation and informal education the problem was complex. Most of these agencies were interested not only in services but also in particular ideologies. These ideologies could not be catered to in a public program, for many of them had a religious base. They were not adverse to an expanding public program to meet the needs of the total community, but they were jealous of their role in fulfilling a special need which they felt was important to the democratic philosophy of cultural pluralism. In brief, their function was already defined. Those agencies that did not have an ideological core, however, had more difficulty in differentiating their programs from those sponsored by the public agencies. In community organization the shrinking budgets first led to studies emphasizing coordination for efficiency and economy. It was an effort at planning within a framework of frozen budgets rather than an emphasis on needs to be met. As the financial situation began to adjust and the public programs became more explicit, the councils of social agencies began to move toward a broader frame of reference and to involve the community in their effort to overcome duplication and to achieve planning around unmet needs.

The Family Welfare Agency

In order to understand fully the impact of the public services on the family welfare field, it is useful to remember the effect of psychiatry on casework. Prior to the depression psychiatric social workers had functioned primarily in clinical settings. These new specialists, Bertha Reynolds[18] points out, worked with the economically secure, were isolated from their colleagues, and out of touch with the public and the community. This resulted in a gap between those caseworkers in the family agencies involved in environmental adjustment and those in the clinics who were doing therapeutic work. The depression, however, scrambled the picture. Because of lack of funds many clinics closed. Psychiatric workers began to move back into the then mainstream of social work, namely, the family agency. Many workers from the family agencies in turn went to the newly evolving public agencies. The private agencies with their meager budgets had little to offer in the way of environmental help and found it necessary to become skilled in the art of listening. They discovered that their listening helped the client. Furthermore, they found that many clients preferred public relief because in its new interpretation it reflected a right rather than charity. These developments meant that the family agency, the fountainhead of casework, had to review its purpose, program, and method.

In terms of method the top-down authoritative approach of earlier days was still prevalent. At first the new psychiatry was utilized as a way of overcoming the resistance of the client to having his welfare needs attended to without his collaboration. Slowly, however, the realization grew that the integration of psychoanalytic learnings with casework represented a basic change in the method and philosophy of casework. Relationship, its meaning and use to both the client and the worker, became the central consideration. Psychoanalytic knowledge was utilized to understand these relationships and to develop techniques for dealing with them. The new philosophy involved such concepts as helping people to help themselves; participation of the client in decision making; beginning where the client is and proceeding at a meaningful pace; and focusing on the psychodynamics underlying the individual's stated problem. Basic to the approach was the attitude of the worker toward the client and the ability of the worker to keep his own needs and biases in the background. Virginia Robinson defined the approach as follows: "The case work relationship is a reciprocal relationship in which the case worker must accept herself and the other equally, in which all of her attitudes toward the client would be such that she would be content to be at the other end of such a relationship herself." [19]

As the method became clarified problems of purpose and services arose. In the earlier days casework had been primarily a social service delivered through and controlled by specific agency policies. In a sense the worker had been an agent for the agency. With the new emphasis on the individual the focus shifted to the worker-client rather than the agency-client relationship. Rigid agency policies were regarded as a deterrent to the flexibility needed by the worker. The problem loomed especially large in the public agency, where policies were determined by law and had to be adhered to rather rigidly. An attempt was made to resolve this dilemma by theorizing that relief was a tool in a rehabilitative process rather than a service in itself. Grace Marcus[20] pointed up the problem by posing a series of questions. Was the caseworker merely using the client's need of money to attempt to save him from something else? Were we assuming that because clients were in need of relief they were also in need of rehabilitation? If these personality problems were universal (i.e., not necessarily tied up with economic need) why should relief clients be singled out for treatment? Is it our traditional benevolence that makes us want to compensate the poor for their poverty by ridding them of problems the rest of the populace may retain at their will? Was casework in imitating therapy, forgetting that psychoanalysis had not evolved around relief-giving situations and therefore could not be taken over lock, stock, and barrel?

Although the problem was most acute in the public setting there were some who felt that in the private agency, too, casework had become too closely identified with therapy. It was their opinion that the casework agency was becoming nothing more than socialized therapy, a housing arrangement for individual therapists. Their view was expressed as follows:

The resulting tendency of social workers to rest upon the authority, even to utilize the supervision, of this more firmly grounded, better trained, legally sanctioned profession (psychiatry), in order to fill what seems to be a void in their own, has been the source of much confusion as to what, if anything, is indigenous to social casework. It has often blinded both agencies and workers to the nature and potential value of their own task.[21]

This group felt that the essential nature of casework was to be found in "the human beings' problem in taking help." They sought in the theories of Rank, at first a disciple of Freud and later a "modified" Freudian, a psychology and philosophy of helping that could "be used independently of therapy." In applying the Rankian teachings they shifted the emphasis from the role of the worker in assuming "responsibility for determining and meeting the need of each individual client" to the "importance of the social agency and its particular function as a determinant of the case work process." This group, which is now known as the functional school in social work, made "agency in use" the central focus of their approach. As one of their leaders stated:

. . . It was only when we realized that it is the function and structure of the social agency that differentiates the helping that belongs to social casework from the helping found in therapy, that we were finally freed from the necessity to confuse the two modes of helping and could concentrate on learning to use with skill the particular process for which we are responsible.[22]

This deviation was not merely an attempt to redefine function but also an attack on method. It is not to be confused with functionalism in the philosophical sense, with its stress on activity and process as against structure and setting, which had already been accepted in the field in general.

Emphasis on function had emerged early in the 1920's with the expansion of welfare fields and with the studies of function made in the child welfare and the medical social work fields; it was implied in the historic 1929 report of the Milford Conference which promulgated the principle that process in social casework and the equipment of the worker should be basically the same for all fields; it was accelerated by the growth and spread of the child guidance movements, in the expansion of the American Red Cross during World War I, and in the shifts of emphasis in the public services during the first quarter of the century; and it was given added impetus through greater participation of the federal government in welfare services after 1930.[23]

Most of the field did not turn to the functional school in their search for definition, but rather went on to refine their diagnostic approach as it applied to the nonrelief problems of the client. Some seized upon the difficulty of applying the social casework method in the public setting as the basis for differentiating function, seeing the client as coming to the private agency with psychological problems that could be dealt with apart from economic ones. A natural corollary of this development was the introduction of experiments in charging fees for service. With the growing emphasis on problems of adjustment and with the effort to keep the child in his own home or in a foster home, a trend developed to merge family and other casework services to avoid overlapping of services to the same family.

Child Care

Between 1900 and 1920 there had been a revived interest in foster home placements as opposed to the use of institutions. The heightened emphasis on the importance of family life appearing after the turn of the century and made explicit by the Conference on the Care of Dependent Children in 1909 had a marked effect on the future trends in child care. From then on, increasing efforts were made to keep the child in his own home; and for those who needed a new environment, the foster home was preferred to the institution because it provided a home atmosphere. Institutions tried to meet the challenge by giving up their large facilities in urban communities and developing cottage units in suburban and rural settings. Cottages were organized on a family basis with a wide age range, and with a couple to serve as parent substitutes for the children.

The social welfare program in the 1930's provided further persuasion for keeping the dependent child in the home or in a foster home. As a result, institutions found themselves with a decrease in children under 10 years of age and a considerable increase in the age group over 10. Part of the reason for the increase in the older age group was that the institutions had begun to deal with children needing therapy. Foster-home experience had shown that some children required specialized treatment and supervision before they were ready for placement with a family. The religious provisions for foster-home placement existing in some states, and the growing recognition of the need for specialized treatment services in the institutions, made the reallocation of function in the private child-care field comparatively easy. The religious factor was influential, for as Thurston points out one of the chief motivations for the original private orphan asylums had been to give children care under religious auspices, and save them for their parents' religious faith, whatever it might be—Catholic, Protestant, or Jewish.[24] The function of specialized treatment was unfolding but the institutions needed much retooling to qualify for this task. The majority of them had no trained caseworkers on the staff; some had persons designated as caseworkers, but their education was limited to high school or some undergraduate work.

Group Work

Ideological differences had tended to keep the informal-educational and recreational agencies isolated. The crisis of the depression, however, was sufficiently intense to cause them to lay aside their basic interest in difference in order to combat common problems. One of these problems was the growing lack of financial support from the public. Many of the agencies had expanded their physical facilities during the false prosperity before the depression and found themselves not only without adequate operating funds but also with insurmountable mortgage responsibilities. Since competition for funds between the agencies was not yielding results they formed a united front to interpret their work to the public. This necessitated abstracting what they had in common in the way of goals and methods. The increasing number of community surveys emphasizing coordination for efficiency and economy also helped to point up what the agencies had in common in the way of goals, method, and program. Another factor which helped to bring about "togetherness" was the expanding public program and the growing use of staff provided through the WPA and NYA projects. The addition of these workers to the staffs of private agencies permitted an expansion of program and enabled the agencies to better meet the recreational and informal educational needs of the unemployed youth and adults who came to them for help morning, noon, and evening.

As in other fields clarification of function was a concern. Hendry, in an analysis of the papers presented at the Group Work Section of the National Conference of Social Work between 1935 and 1940 dealing with social planning, observed that "in terms of larger aspects of social planning it is seen that more discussion is directed to an attempt to differentiate between the functions of private and public agencies than to an effort to appraise inequalities in opportunities and resources for play, recreation, and informal education." [25] He then proceeded to spell out a cooperative relationship between private and public agencies.

Impartial analysis demonstrates beyond a doubt that any absolute differentiation in the functions of voluntary, private agencies and official, public agencies is impossible. Functions are relative to particular situations in both time and space. Each is capable of performing identical functions and neither enjoys a monopoly of excellence in performance. Each is needed in a democracy, and as governmental services are enlarged and extended, far from reducing the need for vital voluntary non-governmental agencies, the importance of strengthening such agencies and of creating new ones is actually increased.[26]

Although this statement reflected intention rather than actual practice at this time, efforts were being made on the level of the local communities as well as the nation to clarify the roles of private and public agencies through joint planning bodies. The Education-Recreation Council organized in 1933 consisted of the leading national agencies in the leisure-time field and the federal agencies dealing with similar problems. One of its chief purposes was to exchange information and study common problems.

Out of this mutual effort and search for similarities among the agencies came stimulation for the evolving method of group work. By 1935 a Group Work Section was added to the National Conference of Social Work. In 1936 the American

Association for the Study of Group Work was formed. The association devoted itself to such problems as: group work in relation to social needs and objectives; group work as a method and process; meeting personality needs through a guided group process; the role of the leader in the group work process; professional training for group work; program development in group work; group work and community planning; and social action. By 1939 fourteen of the schools in the American Association of Schools of Social Work were offering courses in group work. Group work was moving from the early concepts of character building to a conception of method and process for furthering the adjustment and development of the individual and preparing him for citizenship in a democracy. Thus, group work began to draw more closely to social work, and to explore the relationship of casework and group work.

Group work had drawn many of its ideas about social relations from sociology and cultural anthropology, about method from progressive education, and about program from recreation. Casework, on the other hand, had drawn its ideas principally from psychiatry. In one of the classic articles on the relationship of casework and group work and the contributions they could make to each other, Coyle[27] saw the learnings in casework as helping to sharpen the sensitivity of the group worker to the "personal needs or personal maladjustments" of the individual, a "better understanding of family relationships and of the early life of the child," "a greater realization of the therapeutic possibilities of group experience," and "the technical matter of record keeping." Group work's potential contribution to casework was "to enhance the case worker's understanding of the place and function of group life outside the family—both in its relation to individual development and in its function in society," "to stimulate an increased interest in education and the enrichment of life," to develop a better understanding of the importance to our democratic society of individual identification with political and economic as well as recreational groups, and to add to the body of knowledge for enriching group life for all. Group work, with its diverse body of knowledge, could well have been the channel through which the tendency in social work to emphasize one dimension, the psychological, might have been broadened to include the learnings of the social sciences. Unfortunately the social sciences were just beginning to pull themselves out of a highly individualistic era, and furthermore, there were not enough leaders and teachers in the group work field sufficiently oriented in the social sciences to serve as a bridge. As group work drew more closely into the social work family, with casework playing the parent role, it tended to become more influenced than influencing.

By 1940 the trend of group work toward emphasis on problems of individual adjustment and away from helping people become involved in social change was in the making. The following observations by Johns on group work's practices are pertinent:

> Relating young people to social change is apparently difficult to accomplish. The close identification of agency financing with conservative community interests, combined with the problem of discovering specific enterprises in which young people can participate and which contribute toward needed social change, makes participation far less effective than Grace Coyle's challenging Pugsley Award paper suggests may some day be possible.[28]

> In one Eastern city, 538 persons, many of them active in group work programs have been identified as already revealing personality difficulties. Two functions for agencies doing group work are suggested: (1) early recognition by staff and volunteer workers of incipient personality problems and quick referral for proper social treatment through well-established social work channels; and (2) treatment as an important part of the total social work program of service for some problem cases.[29]

In the social work schools group workers like caseworkers were being prepared more for professional practice than for professional responsibilities. They were becoming skillful in the diagnosis and treatment of those individual and group problems which the worker meets in day-to-day practice, but they were not being prepared to speak with knowledge and understanding of the wider social issues involved, or with authority on possible courses of action and development for society as a whole.

Community Organization

Community chests and councils of social agencies, with the impetus received from the experience with War Chests in World War I, had greatly expanded in number and function. By 1921 McClean had "cited thirteen different functions of councils actually in operation, such as passing on new projects, reorganization of old agencies, abandonment or combination of existing agencies, improvement in relationship between agencies, advice to agencies on publicity and advancement of standards." [30] By the time of the Great Depression most large urban communities had some form of community welfare council that could provide a center for community-wide planning. The economic events of the day were making it clear that to tackle problems of social disorganization one must go beyond the bounds of the social agencies, that a community consisted of more than just its social agencies. As Steiner put it:

Community disorganization includes far more than the problem of ill-coordinated social agencies. In fact, the more serious aspects of disorganization are frequently found in connection with economic, political, educational, and religious institutions of the community. . . . As long as we give a minimum of attention to the problem of regulating industry in the interests of community welfare, it is useless to expect a community council to accomplish the far reaching results that its supporters frequently claim for it. If community organization is the way out it must be sufficiently inclusive to deal with the fundamental forces that are making for disorganization.[31]

As the councils moved from their immediate concern with coordination for greater economy toward a broader concept of social planning around unmet needs, the method and place of the survey as a tool in community organization began to take on new meaning. New value was being given to fact finding as a basis for evaluating the various programs and seeing them in relation to the community as a whole. Agency-centeredness began to give way in some areas to community-centeredness in interpreting the findings. There was growing awareness that the success of a study depended on involving, from the very beginning, individuals and groups with an interest and stake in community welfare. In a sense, fact finding was being regarded as a tool in affecting attitudes, attitudes which in the final analysis would determine the action to be taken on recommendations.

The New Deal climate was conducive to planning. Thus one finds not only a heightened activity by the existing organizations but also the appearance of several new planning organizations on the national scene. The Council of Jewish Federations and Welfare Funds was established in 1932. Its purpose was to help organize community resources to meet local, regional, national, and overseas Jewish needs. In 1935 the American Planning and Civic Association, based on individual membership, was organized for the purpose of educating the American people to the virtues of local, state, regional, and national planning for the best use of physical and human resources. Other organizations which came into being during this period were the Council of Seamen's Agencies (1932), the Council of State Governments (1933), National Association of Housing Officials (1933), the American Society of Planning Officials (1934), the National Catholic Youth Council (1937), Coordinating Councils, Inc., (1938), the American Society for Public Administration (1939), and the Jewish Occupational Council (1939).

Community organization as a field was expanding, but as a method and process in social work it had not yet taken its place alongside casework and group work in the social work family. A course in community was taught at the schools of social work as one of the requirements of the minimum curriculum agreed upon in 1932 by the Association of Schools of Social Work, but few schools attempted to build a specialization in community organization. The first real endeavor to spell out community organization as a method and a process was at the National Conference in 1939, when Robert Lane[32] delivered a report on the scope and method of community organization. The following are the main points outlined in the report:

1. That the term "community organization" is used to refer to a process, and, as is often the case in other professions, to refer also to a field.
2. That the process of organizing a community, or some parts of it, goes on outside, as well as inside, the general area of social work.
3. That within the area of social work, the process of community organization is carried on by some organizations as a primary function . . . and by other organizations as a secondary function.
4. That within the area of social work the process of community organization is carried on at the local, state, and national levels, and between such levels.
5. That organizations whose primary function is the practice of community organization do not, as a rule, offer help directly to clients.

The publication of the report stimulated an evolving interest in a theoretical basis for community organization within the framework of social work. The following observation, which appeared in the *Newsletter* of the American Association for the Study of Community Organization—formed in 1946—indicates the significance of the report for the future trend in community organization:

In some respects it performed a service for community organization practitioners and students comparable to that performed for case workers by "Social Case Work—Generic and Specific" ten years earlier. The report stresses the generic nature and the pervasive quality of the process of community organization as contrasted with its various specialties; it provides a working description and analysis of the process and it marks the growth in professional self-consciousness on the part of social workers representing a wide range of thinking, experience and practise in respect of community organization.[33]

Research in Social Work

With the entrance of the federal government into the social welfare area, gathering of information about social conditions became important for formulating legislation and planning programs. Federal agencies like the FERA, the WPA, the NYA, and so forth, were responsible for a large number of social surveys. The private agencies had also turned to the social survey as a tool for finding answers to their problems.

The focus on budgetary problems and the concern for personnel practices which emerged during the Depression resulted in a new area of research in social work, namely, research in administrative problems. The Cleveland Health Council conducted a study in 1929 entitled, "A Time Study of Public Health Nursing and Clinic Services for the University Public Health Nursing District." It was one of the first attempts to apply cost accounting methods to administrative problems in social work. Studies in personnel were also introduced, covering matters such as job specifications, recruitment, and salaries. A monumental study in this area was conducted by the Los Angeles Community Welfare Federation in 1936. The study dealt with "Class Specifications for All Positions in Agencies and Institutions Receiving Support from the Los Angeles Community Welfare Federation."

Social Work Education

Social work education up to the 1930's had been geared primarily toward private social work, with the one outstanding exception of the School of Social Service Administration at the University of Chicago. "Faculty and student research there, having as an objective the improvement of social welfare services, had already provided a rich source of scholarly materials setting forth the principles of public welfare administration and presenting descriptive and critical studies of a larger number of programs in both private and public agencies." [34] With the entrance of government into the social welfare field on a large scale there was an immediate need for a large number of workers. The schools of social work rose to the emergency and cooperated with the FERA in a program of training institutes and short special courses. It was not an easy task, for most schools had not developed an adequate curriculum in public welfare, administration, and community organization, all essential to carrying out the new program. Furthermore, the curriculum dealing with the individual had to be adapted to use in a legally defined setting. The limitations of time, the lack of adequate field work placements for the large number of students, and the absence of a tested curriculum made the task difficult.

Although social work education rose to the emergency, there is some question as to whether it understood the full meaning of the times. Thousands of new workers had entered the field without any training in social work beyond the in-service programs of the agencies or the short-term courses of the schools. Few of these workers met the standards of the graduate program as projected by the schools and, in fact, few were eligible for membership in the professional organizations. The existing channels in social work evidently did not meet the needs of this new development, for in 1930 a new organization, the American Public Welfare Association, was formed to develop and maintain sound principles and effective administration of public welfare services; provide technical, consultant, and advisory services to legislative and administrative authorities and to public welfare officials; act as a clearing house for exchange of thought and experience in the public welfare field; and promote the development of methods of training public welfare personnel. If the times had been regarded not as an emergency but as the beginning of a new era in social welfare policy and services, then some reappraisal might have been made of the original plans that called for placing professional education for public welfare on a graduate level within the framework of pre-1935 social work. It was full steam ahead, however, and in 1937 the Association of Schools of Social Work voted to place all professional education on a graduate level as of January 1, 1940. Not enough thought was given to the fact that with more and more workers entering the field with only undergraduate education increased attention had to be paid to the role of the undergraduate schools in training for social work. As might be expected, the demand created by the large number of public jobs that did not require graduate training resulted in the introduction of many undergraduate programs for the training of social workers operating outside existing social work channels. Most of these programs emanated from sociology departments in land-grant colleges. The growth of such training programs during this period is evidenced by the fact that thirty-four of these institutions were to form an association in 1942 known as the National Association of Schools of Social Administration.

The Social Worker and Reform

Although social work was expressing growing concern for environmental problems, it was still inclined to lose sight of the importance of the social institutions themselves and to think of society and its group structure merely as the place where the individual works out his emotional problems. Coyle makes the following interesting observation:

I have come upon two attitudes occasionally among the case workers of my acquaintance. The first is a tendency to regard affiliations primarily from the viewpoint of the emotional effect upon the client. If the client can work off the hostility produced by facing a destitute old age through joining a Townsend club, the social effects of increasing the strength of the Townsend movement are no great concern of the social worker. . . . Psychiatry and case work have much to contribute in unraveling the tangled skein of motivations always present in social movements. It is not enough, however, to regard these movements wholly as clues to the emotional life of the participants. Whatever their psychological origin they also must be viewed sociologically in terms of their social consequences.

Another attitude which I have come upon occasionally does

recognize the social implications of group membership but tends to judge them conventionally. We do not hesitate to refer our clients to their church or to a nearby settlement if they need recreation. But we do not show the same freedom in recognizing the value of their relation to controversial organizations, such as unions, political parties, youth movements or pressure groups for legislative purposes.[35]

But already in 1937, when Coyle was writing, the depression had challenged this approach, for mass problems had necessitated an attack on environmental causes through a broad legislative program affecting all of the basic social institutions.

Mass movement for social reform in the European countries had been carried out through political parties or political pressure groups. Social work in those countries had not been as directly concerned with social policy as in the United States. The New Deal in a sense meant that for the first time in our history a political party had made social welfare policy its concern on a comprehensive scale. For some social workers the New Deal development meant that the responsibility for social policy was no longer theirs and that they could now return to the approach which they had laid aside temporarily to help in the emergency, namely, work with the individual and the family on problems of emotional adjustment and development.

Other workers, however, interpreted the experience of the thirties as proof of the fact that economic forces were at the root of the problems with which social work dealt, and that social work could make its best contribution through a close identification with those groups in the society working toward economic, political, and social change. For them the New Deal represented only a first step in the process of change necessary to accomplish economic security for all the people. This group believed that the private social work agency had to rethink its role in the light of the full meaning of the ideological revolution. They could no longer view themselves in narrow philanthropic terms, as agencies for the less fortunate by the more fortunate. In the same way that the public agency belonged to the people as a tax-supported institution, so the private agency as a community-supported institution in a democracy belonged to them. The increase in the number of small givers and the pattern of employee giving to the community chests were pointed to as examples of a new development. The boards of directors, therefore, were not to regard the agencies as belonging to them but rather to see themselves as social trustees for the people. An important responsibility of the professional was to guide the boards of directors toward an understanding of one of the primary goals of social work, i.e., to help the people provide for themselves services which they understood, needed, and wanted. This in turn meant involving the people more and more in the formulation of policies in such basic areas as administration, personnel practices, and program. The professional was not merely an employee of the board. He was also a representative of the peoples' needs, interests, and rights, and had the responsibility of protecting these in relation to the board's social trusteeship. In identifying with the interests of the people and viewing the boards as not necessarily representing these same interests, the social workers saw their own economic security tied up with an employer-employee relationship similar to that in industry.

A third group, accepting the fact that social work must do its share in working toward continued social reorganization, began to draw a distinction between what could be done on the job and what could be done by workers as individual citizens and through their professional groups. This view was expressed as follows:

The dependence of social work either upon large givers or upon a large group of small givers or tax-payers makes it unlikely that it will promote fundamental reorganization, especially of our economic institutions, though it may modify certain social institutions. It is especially true that social agencies as such are limited by this dependence, though this does not preclude all action of this sort by certain agencies. . . . Social workers are prevented in many cases from taking an active part in movements for social reorganization by such conditions as: a) absorption in problems of the individual; b) absorption in administrative and technical detail; c) unfavorable reactions to certain groups working for social reorganization; and d) a lack of knowledge of social and economic conditions and a social philosophy. Any contribution to social reorganization by social work will depend largely on social workers as individuals or professional groups.[36]

This dichotomous approach reflected the realities of the American scene more closely than did the approach of the more militant group. It assumed that social work could not move too far beyond existing political, economic, and social canons if it was to survive. The extent of contribution to social reorganization was directly proportional to the distance you traveled from the lay control of social work. Some things could be done within the agency setting, more could be done in the professional organizations, and most could be done as individual citizens. In a sense this group was also proceeding on the premise of the conflict of interests between the boards and the goals of social work but resorted to a method of gradual change rather than drawing the battle lines sharply with the agency as the field of battle.

The Rank and File Movement

The professional groups, especially the AASW, had been active not only on the legislative front but also in the area of personnel practices. Its Division on Employment Practises began to formulate a code of personnel practices, and published in *The Compass,* the AASW organ, for July 1935 a tentative procedure for considering grievances. The statement affirmed the association's belief "that employment in social work should be on a contractual basis, and recommended that chapters, upon request, investigate instances of dismissal or changes in status for considerations other than professional competence, and employment practises so inadequate as to jeopardize professional performance." The May 1935 report of the Personnel Practise Committee of the New York Chapter had made a similar suggestion and had also dealt with such additional personnel problems as criticisms and grievances; appeal from executive decisions; freedom of speech; dismissals; staff members' organizations; collective bargaining; salaries; hours; leaves of absence; working conditions; selection of personnel; and workmen's compensation. It was felt by many practitioners, however, that the efforts were too limited and too slow. Their grievances with the association included "incomplete participation in chapter activities, the failure of chapters to express an opinion on important social issues, the failure of chapters to stop salary cuts, and the domination of chapters by executives." As a result, rank and file practitioner groups began to emerge in the AASW chapters located in such large urban areas as New York, Chicago, and St. Louis.

Rank and file groups had also emerged in other areas of social work. These groups held a conference in Pittsburgh in February 1935 and promulgated the Pittsburgh platform which outlined their views on "social welfare, professional and personnel practises." The platform proposed the following:

Social Welfare—support of a program of genuine social insurance; the improvement of relief standards; the development of an adequate work program; federal aid for the so-called normal social services; cooperative action with other workers' groups and with professional associations in their demands for adequate relief and security measures; support of measures to guarantee freedom of organization and collective bargaining; and support of national measures to guarantee civil liberties.

Professional Standards—more opportunities for free training; and a re-evaluation of the content and direction of education for social work.

Personnel Practices—mandatory yearly increases; equal remuneration for equal work; a shorter work week; full compensation for overtime; adequate housing and working conditions; abolition of clerical quotas; reduction of case loads; leaves of absence for illness, maternity and study; the elimination of the use of volunteer workers for work normally performed by persons on a salary basis; the hiring of all employees on the sole qualification of merit; civil service status for public agency workers; and workmen's compensation.[37]

The strength of the rank and file movement during this period is further reflected by the launching in December 1934 of the magazine *Social Work Today*. It regarded itself as the organ of the rank and file workers in social agencies throughout the country, and devoted itself to a discussion of the current issues in social work. Although a magazine with a militant point of view more in line with the thinking of the second group described above, it became a forum for social workers from all three groups.

Trade Unionism

The professional associations had done a good job in helping to develop standards of professional practice and in representing social work in the legislative arena, but their very purpose and structure limited action in a period of rapid change. Their method was primarily that of education and affecting public opinion in general rather than action around specific situations. The rank and file movement seeking a more effective instrument for carrying out their objectives began to move rapidly toward a conception of trade unionism in social work. The mass needs of the period; the coming into the field of a large number of untrained workers with little identification with the professional character of social work; and the task of working directly with the "millions of unemployed and their families" on a mass and routine basis; all were changing the "character" of social work.

In a sense the trained social worker experienced just what the industrial worker experiences when a new machine reduces a craft to a routine job. The new type of social worker was often an unemployed recruit from another vocation. The insecurity of past unemployment, combined with uncertainties in the relief program of the present, led these social workers increasingly to feel an identity with their clients. A rank-and-file movement resulted which developed a program of economic protection for individual social workers, based upon the policy of making common cause with the labor movement in what had been called in 1924 the task of "furnishing the dynamics for an industrial democracy." Their ranks were reinforced by the group who had organized earlier within the American Association of Social Workers as "practitioners," distinguishing themselves from supervisors and upper executives.[38]

The climate for trade unionism was a propitious one. Labor's strength, sharply sapped by the impact of the depression, turned to government for help in their cause. This time, unlike previous periods, they found a friendly ear. The Norris-LaGuardia Act in 1932 outlawed the yellow-dog contract and injunctions by the federal courts in labor disputes. The National Industrial Recovery Act in 1933 established the right of collective bargaining. When the act was declared unconstitutional, the Wagner Act (the National Labor Relations Act) was passed by Congress in 1935.

It provided to the American Labor movement now, for the first time in its history, a federal statute guaranteeing the right to organize and engage in collective bargaining witout hostile interference by employers. "Unfair labor practices" were defined, and employers were forbidden to engage in them. The National Labor Relations Board was set up to see that the law was obeyed.[39]

Another advance for labor was the enactment of the Fair Labor Standards Act on June 23, 1938. The act, which applied to interstate industries, put a floor under wages, a ceiling over hours of work, and an end to child labor in those industries. Its immediate effect was an increase in wages for 750,000 workers and a decrease in the hours of work for 1.5 million workers, located, in the main, in the Southeast.

Labor's ranks, which had declined to 2,887,000 in 1932, rose to nearly 9 million by 1940. As in other areas the times also had their effects in the labor movement. The craft form of unionism predominant in the AFL was being challenged as inadequate for the rapidly developing mass industries like steel and automobiles. A group in the AFL formed a Committee for Industrial Organization to pursue a vertical form of unionism. It was their thesis that since industry had grown more organized and more powerful, and methods of work had become so mechanized and dependent upon other work, the old craft unionism had become outmoded as a means of protecting workers in mass industries, and as a channel through which labor could act directly and in mass. As the committee moved ahead with its efforts, the members ran into jurisdictional disputes with the strong craft unions in the AFL and were suspended from the union. In 1938 they founded a new union, the Congress of Industrial Unions. By 1940 they claimed a membership of 3,625,000, approximately 600,000 less than the AFL.

It was to the CIO that the first major organized effort in trade unionism in social work turned for affiliation. There had been some earlier independent affiliation of social workers with trade unions in the public field. The American Federation of Government Employees, organized in 1932, and the American Federation of State, County, and Municipal Employees, organized in 1936, both affiliates of the AFL, included in their membership social workers employed in government agencies. In 1937 several national unions with sizable numbers of social work members emerged. In the public field there were the State, County, and Municipal Workers of America, and the United Federal Workers of America, which merged in 1946 to form the United Public Workers of America. In the private field there was the United Office and Professional Workers containing within it a National Social Service Division to coordinate the work of the locals of the Social Service Employees Union. All three groups affiliated with the new CIO. A Joint Committee of Trade Unions in Social Work was formed to coordinate the efforts of the three groups, particularly in connection with their programs at the National and State Conferences of Social Work.

The unions soon became a vibrant force in all areas of social work. They devoted themselves not only to matters of social welfare and personnel but also to a program of partisan political activity. Progressive candidates for public office were endorsed and actively supported. It was not long, however, before the question arose as to whether or not there was an inherent conflict between a trade-union and a professional approach. This was especially pertinent in two areas: the methods of handling employer-employee conflict when the machinery of collective bargaining broke down, and the role of social work organizations in matters of international politics. In regard to the first, many social workers felt that because they were dealing wtih boards of nonprofit institutions or agents of tax-supported ones, rather than with owners or managers as industry, the traditional weapon of the union—the strike—would not directly affect the material interests of these groups. Furthermore, from a philosophical point of view, the client would inevitably suffer most from any prolonged strike. Some felt that work stoppages, demonstrations, and picketing should be utilized only when the client's welfare was at stake. The other side argued that without economic security the professional could not do an adequate job. For them sound professional practices were difficult without sound employment practices; the necessary professional development and the ability to serve the client adequately were contingent on economic security for the worker; and independence and maturity in relationships were enhanced by the experience of collective bargaining.

In regard to international politics the unions were reflecting the growing storm on the horizon of the nation in general. America was on the brink of World War II and had some momentous decisions to make. Isolation versus international participation and responsibility was again rearing its head. Because of the Nazi atrocities and the fear that Hitler would conquer the world, sentiment was moving in the direction of participation. Some of the union members were against participation, claiming that it was a "capitalist" rather than a "people's war." They were strong enough to have this point of view voted as policy, and there resulted an exodus from the union of a number of members who felt deeply about the issue. The full impact of the schism was not tested because with Germany's surprise attack on the USSR the conflict centering around America's war policy dissolved.

Reaction Sets In

By the end of 1938 the early glow of the New Deal had begun to lose some of its lustre. As the nation showed signs of recovery, those interests that had submerged their differences during the height of the crisis began to clamor for a return to business as usual. It mattered little to them that there were still about 11 million unemployed. In January 1939, when the President presented his request for an appropriation of $2,266,-165,000 for recovery and security, they were successful in cutting $150 million from the WPA budget. The President fought back, declaring that "for more than six years it has been the definite policy of the President and the Congress that needy persons, out of work, should not be allowed to starve; that it was the obligation of the federal government to give work to those able to work." The President's leadership, the pressure from the unemployed, labor, and the liberals, succeeded in having $100 million of the cut restored in April of 1939. At about this time, however, developments on the international front began to receive priority on the attention of the Administration.

Events had been moving rapidly in the world in the thirties, but America had played only a minor or negative role in dealing with them. The feeling of having been tricked into World War I by the economic interests was still prevalent, and had created a strong isolationist movement in the country. With partial blinders on our international spectacles we watched the rapid move of events toward World War II. In 1935 the Fascist government of Italy under Benito Mussolini attacked Ethiopia. The League of Nations, without the active participation of the United States, was weak and could apply only ineffectual economic sanctions. It showed its inability to contain the rising tides of war. Fascism was on the march. A rising Socialist movement in Austria was falling victim to a growing Fascist movement in the country. When Hitler began his march to conquest he was able to take over Austria without firing a shot.

In 1936 civil war broke out in Spain. It represented the revolt of the most reactionary elements in Spain under the leadership of Franco against a democratically and legally elected government. Franco, with aid from Germany and Italy, was successful in overthrowing the government (which in turn was receiving aid from the USSR), and establishing a Fascist dictatorship. America, attempting to stay neutral, put an embargo on arms to either side in 1937. It was a sham neutrality, however, for we were still selling arms to Germany and Italy who in turn were making them available to Franco.

On the other side of the world Japan began its march to conquest with the invasion of Manchuria in 1937. The League of Nations was again powerless. Economic sanctions with the full cooperation of the United States might have stemmed the tide, but again we remained neutral. Our foreign policy was in conflict. Originally the USSR, which had been recognized by the United States in 1933, seventeen years after its establishment, was regarded as a potential buffer against a rapidly growing Japan. By 1937, however, strong forces in the nation viewed Japan as a buffer against a rapidly growing Soviet Union.

Hitler followed his bloodless conquest of Austria with a similar conquest of Czechoslovakia when England and France, hoping to avoid war, appeased Germany and deserted their ally. With Hitler's invasion of Poland in 1939 it became clear that Hitler could not be appeased and England and France decided to make a stand. In this country neutrality had begun to give way to a program of helping the allies in every way short of war. America rapidly became the arsenal of democracy, the hope of the free world for survival.

One of the early tests of America's sympathies was its reaction to the emerging refugee problem. During the depression the number of immigrants had fallen below the legal quota, with only 699,375 entering the country for permanent residence between 1930 and 1939. But the rising Fascist tide in Europe made it necessary for thousands of individuals to seek refuge from political and religious persecution. Many of them turned to America.

Since most of the refugees seeking asylum in the United States were from the countries with the smaller quotas, the problem was acute. Furthermore, the strong isolationist feeling found a channel of expression in Congress in 1939 through a series of anti-alien measures which threatened to put an end even to the limited immigration. There were, however, a number of groups deeply interested in the refugee problem who were mindful of America's humanitarian and democratic traditions and sense of responsibility. In October 1934 the National Coordinating Committee for Aid to Refugees and Emigrants Coming from Germany was formed to coordinate the work of these groups. In the meantime on the international level the Evian conference on the refugee problem was held. As an outgrowth of this conference the Intergovernmental Committee on Refugees was organized with thirty-six nations participating. The United States took a leading role and with Britain pledged funds for operating costs. Interpretation of the quota laws became more sympathetic and in 1938-1939, for the first time since the restrictive laws were invoked, the German quota to the United States was filled. Furthermore, in 1939 it became possible for 185,333 refugees from all countries to enter the United States on the basis of temporary visas.

By 1939 the problem had grown too large for the National Coordinating Committee to handle within its original purpose. An over-all operating agency was needed to handle the many problems of migration, resettlement, relief, family and medical care, social and cultural adjustment, and employment. The National Refugee Service, Inc., was organized in June 1939 and recruited a large staff of trained social workers to cope with the expanding demands. Other major organizations which continued to operate in the field were the American Friends Service Committee, the Committee for Catholic Refugees, and the American Committee for Christian Refugees.

Unfinished Business

Between the beginning of World War II in September 1939 and the entrance of the United States in December 1941 the economy began to swing into full gear again. The wheels of the New Deal in turn began to slow down leaving much in the way of unfinished business. A new crisis had arisen demanding priority in the consideration of the nation. The real test of the permanence of the changes which had taken place in the thirties was to be postponed until a future date. There were already signs by the end of 1938 that the process of change would not be achieved without further conflict between the conflicting interests. The unity prevalent in the early days of the New Deal was giving way to deep cleavages and sharp differences of opinion around economic, political, and social problems. Since the test was yet to come, it may be helpful to review some of the unfinished business.

Labor

Labor had made important gains, but on the debit side there were still 23 states which had not enacted minimum wage legislation; 30 states had not legally established the eight-hour working day; 26 states still permitted legally a work week in excess of 48 hours; and 28 states did not provide protection under their workmen's compensation programs against occupational diseases.

Housing

The program of slum-clearance and low-cost publicly-sponsored housing had gotten off to a good start. In the short period of operation, however, it had just begun to scratch the surface of the problem.

In the fall of 1939, just as World War II broke out, the

Congress was considering a bill which would have doubled the bonding power of the USHA, thus making possible another $800 million worth of low-cost housing. The bill passed the Senate, but the foes of public housing, taking advantage of the impending war climate, were able to sidetrack the bill in the House. Permanent long-range planning for public housing began to give way to a program of defense housing under new auspices. Defense housing was essential, but many feared that it would be utilized by the opponents of public housing to push the USHA program into the background and eventually to kill it completely.

Health

First steps toward an expanded public health program had been initiated in the Social Security Act. The program to assist the states made it possible to improve standards. In the words of the Surgeon General, "It has been possible to allot a preponderance of federal funds to those states and communities with the most meager financial resources but with the most urgent health problems. It has been possible to insist upon qualified public health personnel. The number of counties under the direction of whole-time health officers has been increased by 96 percent." [40]

Further steps toward a more comprehensive National Health Program, including some aspects of insurance, were blocked by strong opposition of the conservative forces led by a militant American Medical Association. The various studies and conferences sponsored by the government on health during this period, however, were making some impact. In 1933 the American Medical Association had opposed any form of insurance program for medical care, including those projects under private auspices. "By 1939 insurance as a device to spread the economic risk of illness ceased to be an issue. The hospitals had for several years supported insurance plans pertaining to hospitalization, and the American Medical Association recognized them and began to direct attention to medical plans along similar lines." [41] The issue for the AMA in 1939 was not the use of insurance systems to cover some aspects of the medical program but a comprehensive insurance system "covering the nation." It opposed such a plan even under private sponsorship:

The attempt to place the many facets of a health program in one bill was regarded by some as poor strategy, for it aligned in opposition many who were not against certain aspects of the measure. For example, there were many social workers who thought that the tripartite plan of administration, including as it did the Children's Bureau, the United States Public Health Service, and the Social Security Board, was too complicated to be operated successfully. The American Hospital Association was interested and positive about several aspects of the bill but dissatisfied with the section on hospitals. The AMA was against the insurance features but favored the centralization of governmental health programs under one agency. The proponents of insurance regarded the bill as weak and ineffectual, for it did not propose compulsory insurance. With the division of opinion so great the bill was killed in committee after the President withdrew his support in December 1939, giving as his reason that the program would be "too costly." Future progress seemed to demand dealing separately, at first, with some of the features of a National Health Program before attempting a more integrated and comprehensive plan.

Youth

The programs sponsored for youth through the CCC and the NYA were providing employment for approximately 550,000 young people. Another 400,000 were being kept in high school, college, and university through part-time jobs under the NYA program. In other words, about 1 million of the approximately 4.5 million unemployed youth between the ages of 16 and 25 were being served. With 600,000 of this age group being added to the labor supply annually, and the absorption capacity of the labor market still below par, the problems of youth continued to be enormous. The inadequacy of the school programs was also pointed up during this period. Some 50 per cent of youth in the country were not going beyond the ninth grade, and 70 per cent were not completing high school. There were reasons other than the educational program for this record, but the lack of adequate facilities, poor teaching, and unrealistic educational content also bore their share of responsibility. Furthermore, with so large a percentage not going on to college the school programs were doing little to equip youth for jobs. The youth of the nation were being emotionally and morally scarred during this period and it is not surprising to find that although they represented one out of six in the normal population, they numbered one out of four of the criminal population.

World War II was to solve the problems of this age group temporarily, for they were no longer a drain on the society but a much needed part of manpower. It is rather sad that during periods of depression we have too many in this age group while in periods of war there are not enough.

Work Relief

The three work relief programs—CCC, NYA, and WPA— represented a new approach to handling problems of relief during a depression. Aside from the economic aspects of increasing consumer purchasing power, the rehabilitation and morale aspects represented an immeasurable contribution to the human side of life so important in a democracy. From an economic standpoint it is interesting to observe that the curtailment of WPA rolls from 3 million in the first part of 1936 to less than 1.5 million in the latter part of 1937 is regarded by some as responsible for the recession that set in in 1937-1938. Although these programs, because of lack of experience and because of the speed with which they had to be put into operation, had many aspects which could be open to valid criticism, there is no doubt that they represent an important potential tool for helping to meet unemployment problems in a recession. Permanent full employment within our economic structure in a nonwar economy may be more of a hope than a reality. From 1938 to our economic involvement in World War II there were between 11 and 12 million unemployed, which lead some economists to predict that our economic system would continue to grow at a slower tempo than in the previous 150 years. This meant that even after the nation moved out of the depression, from 6 to 7 million people could remain jobless. Dr. Alvin Hansen saw as the cause of this development the declining birthrate, which meant the loss of the greatest stimulus to investment. It was his opinion that investments would thenceforth be tied up primarily to technological progress which occurs in spurts, necessitating the creation of economic props to meet the lulls between periods of technological advance.

It looked as though the government meter which had been hastily rigged during the worst of the depression doldrums would have to be converted into a fixed auxiliary engine. The old free enterprise system would have to settle for a partner—an unwanted but necessary partner—in the shape of a permanent stream of government spending to keep the economy moving steadily on ahead. The era of self-directed, self-powered capitalism had come to an end; a new era of state-controlled capitalism was beginning.[42]

The war intervened before the full effects of this aspect of the New Deal program could be tested, but it should be borne in mind that during the war there would be a steady stream of government spending, and government would become the largest consumer of production.

Social Security

The Social Security Act represented one of the greatest achievements of the New Deal. Although the Act was approved in August 1935, it did not really become effective as a security measure until 1938, for it took this length of time for the states to enact their unemployment insurance laws and for the Social

Security Board to approve state old-age pensions laws. In 1939 the act was further improved and strengthened by the adoption of amendments recommended by the Advisory Council on Social Security and the Social Security Board, which advanced the date of benefit payments from January 1942 to January 1940, increased markedly the size of benefits to be paid in the early years of the program, and added a provision for annuities for elderly wives, widows, orphans, and other dependents of insured workers.

Other recommendations of the Advisory Council, however, were not put into effect. Congress turned down the important amendment which would have expanded old-age insurance coverage to include farm laborers, domestic workers, and employees in nonprofit, religious, charitable, or educational agencies. In the area of unemployment insurance, the early experience tended to show that those with greatest need—the part-time, the irregular, and the marginal salaried workers—either did not qualify for unemployment benefits, or received inadequate amounts for brief periods. It revealed the need for including "provisions for benefits for those partially employed, a shorter waiting period, a longer benefit period, a higher minimum benefit, more adequate benefits, and a re-examination of the eligibility and disqualification provisions of the states." The lack of integration of the social insurance plans with the relief and assistance programs created hardship for a substantial segment of the population. Federal responsibility for relief had decreased between 1933 and 1939, and the determination of standards was left to the progressiveness and resources of the various states. This lead to the recommendation that the system of federal grants-in-aid be modified to provide a system of variation based on the economic capacity of each state. Such a provision would help the poorer states and result in an immediate increase in the average monthly grant.

The Social Security Act represented an excellent step toward a comprehensive program of social insurance. Based as it was, however, on a plan of income insurance, it left to the states—with assistance through a grants-in-aid program for old age, dependent children, the blind, and the totally disabled— responsibility for those who for various reasons could never become income earners or who were marginal salaried workers. Furthermore the plan did not take into account the need of those who although employed had difficulty in making both ends meet because of the size of family or heavy medical expense. There were no provisions for nonoccupational sickness and disability, insurance against total permanent disability, or long-term unemployment. The latter was explained:

. . . by the general conviction that the kind of unemployment which spreads over years during a depression is beyond the realm of insurance altogether. . . . This excuse for omitting unlimited unemployment does not quite end the matter, however. We still find that, during periods of high employment, as many as 50% of the beneficiaries in 19 states exhaust their temporary benefits before being re-employed. . . . It suggests that many states could well consider extending the duration of their benefits at least enough to ensure that the job for which the program is designed is really accomplished.[43]

All in all a new era in American life had arisen. Deeply rooted political, economic and humanitarian individualism had given way to the acceptance of government as a tool in furthering the welfare of the nation. Thus one of the important goals of the social-work leaders in the social reform movement was being realized. Social workers as individuals and through their organized bodies made important contributions to the new concepts of social planning. Some segments of social work also went so far as to seek common ground with other groups in the community who shared similar broad objectives, such as the trade union movement. The social work agencies, however, varied in their zeal for, and interpretation of, the new era. Some made honest attempts to change with the times, rethinking their functions and retooling their services. Others remained passive and went through a process of accommodation. A third group, and perhaps the largest number, could not get their feet and minds out of the past, and attempted to proceed as if "this too shall pass." The war brought temporary relief and a postponement of the full meaning of the era until a later date.

7

NEW FRONTIERS, NEW METHODS, NEW UNITY

(1941-1945)

ALTHOUGH America did not enter the shooting war until the attack on Pearl Harbor by the Japanese on December 7, 1941, it had chosen sides and entered the fray spiritually at an earlier date. In his report to Congress in 1941, at the beginning of his third term, President Roosevelt stated, "Every realist knows that the democratic way of life is at this moment being assailed in every part of the world. . . . I find it, unhappily, necessary to report that the future and safety of our country and of our democracy are everywhere involved." In this speech to Congress he outlined the now famous four freedoms—freedom of speech and expression, freedom of religion, freedom from want, and freedom from fear—and called for a program of all-out production to help put a stop to the steady advances being made by the dictator nations. There followed in rapid succession three major steps to help the side of democracy and to prepare the nation for the eventuality of war. In March the program of Lend-Lease was put into effect authorizing the production of essential war materials for all nations whose defense was considered necessary for American security. In May the President asked Congress to back a program for the production of 50,000 planes. Many months before—in September, 1940—the Selective Service Act had been passed.

Unemployment, the key problem of the thirties, faded into the background. Labor scarcity now became the problem. By 1944 there were 17.5 million more people working and in the armed forces than there had been in 1940. In fact, the ranks of the unemployed were not large enough to meet the need. The additional manpower came from the normal growth of the population, employment of older men, entrance of women into industry on a large scale, and the hiring of young people of school age not formerly seeking employment. The economy was transformed as government became the largest consumer of production. By 1944 the government was purchasing $96.5 billion worth of goods and services as compared with $13.1 billion in 1939, or 45 per cent of the total spending in 1944 as compared with 14 per cent in 1939.

Mobilizing for War

Retooling the nation for the war effort brought dislocations that necessitated planning that went beyond even the efforts in the preceding period of crisis. By October 1942 the government had organized new bodies to handle the problems of production and labor. The War Production Board, created in January 1942, had the responsibility of assaying total needs, both civilian and military, and developing a plan for establishing priorities, allocating scarce materials, and controlling distribution. The Office of Price Administration, established in August, 1941, was given broader power in January 1942, and was responsible for controlling prices and wages to prevent the inflation that might result from the increase in purchasing power at a time of decreasing supplies of civilian consumer goods. Prices were frozen as of March 1942, but a mistake was made in exempting agriculture until it reached 110 per cent of parity. This provision resulted in an increase in food prices and a corresponding demand for wage increases. In October 1942 a more stringent law was enacted freezing wages and setting a ceiling on farm prices at parity. A National War Labor Board had already been created to adjudicate problems between management and labor, both of whom had agreed to set aside the usual methods of handling their differences.

Two agencies had been created at an earlier date to coordinate the nation's efforts in civilian defense and private and public services for health and welfare. The Office of Civilian Defense, established in May 1941, had according to the executive order of the President the following purposes: "To assure effective coordination of Federal relations with State and local governments . . . in respect to measures for adequate protection of the civilian population in emergency periods, to facilitate constructive civilian participation in the defense program and to sustain national morale. . . ." The second agency, the Office of Defense Health and Welfare Services, was created in September 1941 within the Federal Security Agency and with the administrator of the FSA as the director. The purposes of the ODHWS as outlined in the handbook issued by the Office of Emergency Management were as follows:

The ODHWS serves as the center for coordination of health and welfare services available through Federal and other agencies, both public and private, to meet the needs of localities arising from the defense program and for the coordination of such services for the nation as a whole during the emergency.

The Office makes available to States and localities . . . the services of health and welfare specialists to assist in the planning and execution of State and local programs. . . .

It is further the policy of the Office . . . to work with and through the State and local Defense Councils and other appropriate State and local agencies and, in this connection, to cooperate with the Office of Civilian Defense in its relationships with State and local groups. . . .

Both agencies were confronted with a herculean and often overlapping task of community organization and planning.

The full impact of the war can best be seen in its effect on the people. President Roosevelt in his message to the White House Conference on Children in a Democracy in 1939-1940 had proclaimed that, "the success of democratic institutions is measured, not by extent of territory, financial power, machines or armaments, but by the desires, the hopes, and the deeplying satisfactions of the individual men, women and children who make up its citizenship." At the same time he had expressed his concern about the children of the unemployed; other children without adequate shelter, food, or clothing because of the poverty of their parents; children of migratory families; children of minority groups; children living beyond the reach of medical service or lacking medical service because their parents could not pay for it; children not in school or attending schools poorly equipped to meet their needs; and children outside the reach of religious influences. He was actually reviewing the health, welfare, and education problems of the nation in terms of its children. These needs, extensive as they were, paled into insignificance when compared to the needs growing out of the war situation.

The retooling of industry brought temporary unemployment in some sections of the nation. The expansion of plants and the development of new ones in remote areas, and the sudden concentration of large numbers of military trainees in camps adjacent to small towns, all created large migrations. Boom towns sprang up lacking the fundamental necessities of shelter, sanitation, health, educational, and recreational facilities. Over-burdened industrial communities found their facilities taxed beyond the maximum. The shortage of doctors, nurses, teachers, and social workers created by the needs of the military added to the burden.

The movement to the large industrial centers and the boom towns included many members of the minority groups. In the thirties there had already been a general migration of Negroes from the South to the large industrial centers in the North, with a net loss to the South of nearly 1.5 million colored persons. There had also been a movement in the South from the rural areas to the cities. The additional migration during the war found the already overcrowded segregated neighborhoods in Southern and Northern cities unable to absorb the newcomers. The attempt to extend the boundaries of these areas in communities faced with a general housing shortage created additional tensions, and these were further aggravated by overcrowded transportation, recreational, and educational facilities. Before America entered the war there had been a large number of groups, sympathetic to the racial program of the Nazis, who were attempting to rekindle old prejudices and race hatred. Many of them now continued their programs under new banners. All of these conditions, added to the general wartime strain, led to open conflict in riots between Negroes and whites, such as the one in Detroit in 1943. The Japanese, especially on the West Coast, were also victims of racial tension. Although two thirds of the 110,000 of Japanese lineage were American citizens—the other third was forbidden citizenship—they were deprived of all civil rights and placed in internment centers. The singling out of this group of loyal Americans intensified interracial hostilities.

The family unit was being challenged to a greater extent than ever before. Family life was disrupted daily through the mobilization of men for military services, and of both men and women for production services. Four million women were engaged in war industries by 1943, and the number continued to increase. This meant less family life and a corresponding decrease in the supervision of children. Between 1940 and 1946 divorces increased from 264,000 to 610,000 annually; and the number of children born out of wedlock increased from 71 per 10,000 to 127 per 10,000. The impact was most drastic on the adolescents, whose dislocation replaced the youth problem of the thirties as a major concern. The sudden loosening of those close family ties so essential to the formation of attitudes was a hardship for children of all ages; on the adolescent, who at this stage is experimenting with emancipation from parental control, the effect was critical.

The school, another important institution in the development of social attitudes, was also dislocated. With emphasis on gearing the manpower and resources of the schools to the needs of the armed forces, there was a corresponding de-emphasis of the subjects dealing with human values. In some communities school terms were shortened and the school day compressed, so that the children could be released to work in fields, stores, and factories. Furthermore, the curtailment of budgets and the loss of personnel resulted in overworked teachers who found little time or patience for catering to the emotional problems of youth.

Many high school students left before graduation to take jobs in the factories. A report by the National Child Labor Committee in September 1942 reported that approximately 4 million children were employed during the summer in agriculture and industry, and that at least 3 million were employed at the beginning of the new school term, of whom 75,000 were under 16. High wages and numerous opportunities to earn money opened up to the young many avenues of experience for which they were not prepared. They found themselves with greater personal and economic freedom but without the inner stability or maturity necessary to utilize this freedom. There was a general shift in human values, often growing out of a confused interpretation of patriotism and resulting in sanction for aggressive behavior in the case of boys and promiscuous behavior in the case of girls. Human values were being further threatened by the uncertainty of the future and the tendency to regard life as cheap in view of the large number of lives being lost on the battlefield. A report on crime in New York City during this period showed a decrease in offenses against property, but an increase in attacks against people.

The rate of juvenile delinquency rose markedly. In a report to Congress on April 6, 1943, J. Edgar Hoover, Director of the Federal Bureau of Investigation, revealed the alarming increase in juvenile crime throughout the nation. He stated that "prostitution by girls under 21 had increased 64.8% as compared with last year, other sex crimes by girls 104.7%; that arrests of males under 21 had gone up 17.1%, and rape 10.6%." After analyzing some of the causes, he went on to say that "we of the adult generation have not any right to excuse this condition which these figures reflect on the grounds of war. If we do, it means that the postwar is going to be worse than the war."

Social Work in World War II

Shelby Harrison,[1] President of the National Conference of Social Work when war was declared, outlined a threefold task for social work. The first front was the development of direct services in the immediate war program. These included services centering around the soldier and his family, such as assistance to Selective Service and the armed forces in determining facts about dependency, special services of a counseling, recreational, and legal nature to men in the armed forces, interpreting to the men and their families their rights under the Soldiers and Sailors Civil Relief Act and the National Life Insurance Act, and rehabilitation services for the returning veterans; active cooperation in the civil defense program; and services to the boom towns and other communities disorganized by war. The second front was the continuation of the day-to-day services which had become an integral part of our democratic fabric. The third front, on which he felt social work had a vital contribution to make, was the broad field of postwar reconstruction. Let us examine the efforts of social work, both public and private, in all three of these areas.

Direct Services in the War Program

Although no specific provision was made in the Selective Service Law for the use of social workers, the social work profession offered its services immediately. The use of social workers varied from state to state. The time factor was such, Woodward pointed out, that it was impractical to have all potential 1-A registrants interviewed by social workers. "In some communities trained social workers were made available to local boards to make investigations of certain men selected by the board. In some boards the social workers had access to the questionnaires of all registrants who were being considered for 1-A classification and could thus select additional men who might need investigation." [2]

The record of rejection because of nervous and mental diseases and disorders indicated the importance of such service. Of the 9,220,000 men called up for examination by the local Selective Service boards, 702,000 (7.6 per cent) were rejected because of mental or nervous disorders. Of 60,000 men inducted between November 1, 1940, and November 30, 1942, who were later discharged for special disabilities, 32 per cent were discharged because of mental or nervous disorders. In several communities sensitive to the meaning of rejection for the draftee special projects were set up to help him discuss his feelings and to direct him to community resources for help. The rejectees represented a large group, for besides the million turned down for educational inadequacy, or for mental and emotional difficulties, there were several million rejected for purely physical reasons. The conditions of poverty and want during the depression were showing their effects, and it was important that these victims receive the benefit of community services to prevent the problems from multiplying.

Through the efforts of the Wartime Committee on Social Work Personnel, the official body for all social work organizations in their dealings with the major federal bureaus, psychiatric social workers were given a professional classification in the armed services. This was followed later by a classification for commissioned officers. By the end of the war there were over a thousand enlisted and commissioned men and women in the social welfare program of the armed services. Military psychiatric social work, which began early in 1942, dealt with the problems of soldiers who were having difficulty in adjusting to their military duties. It was an interesting experience for social workers in that the setting and purpose necessitated many adaptations of the usual approach. The social worker had to accept the conditions and the limitations of the "army community" in handling problems of the individual. Interviewing had to be focused on the immediate problem and had to be done in very short periods of time. Recording had to be at a minimum. Group counseling or group therapy began to emerge as a method of dealing with the large numbers in a military setting. The lessons of the war experience, especially in group therapy, were to be helpful for the long-range program of casework.

One of the most difficult tasks was to interpret emotional problems to the nonprofessional staff in a positive and effective way. In general, armed services personnel were not too receptive to psychiatric interpretations of disability and tended to regard such disability cases as "goldbricking." It was difficult for them to understand that an individual who was functioning adequately in civilian life could be upset emotionally by the military experience.

The Red Cross, through its home services division, had the primary responsibility for assisting the serviceman or ex-serviceman and his family to meet the needs that arose from the man's service in the armed forces. The various chapter committees on home service provided for communication and information between the serviceman and his family; information on family situations for the military and naval authorities in cases where requests for furlough, discharge, or clemency had to be decided; claims services; and family service involving financial and other problems. If the home service committee did not have the necessary resources for dealing with the problem, referrals were made to other agencies.

Family welfare societies in many communities extended their regular services to make special facilities available to families of servicemen. Cooperative agreements were drawn up by the American Red Cross with the Family Welfare Association of America, with the Office of Defense Health and Welfare Services, and with the American Public Welfare Association. In these agreements the basic responsibility of the Government for the relief of persons in need of basic maintenance was recognized, as was the designation of the American Red Cross by the Army and the Navy as the official agency to render service to the men in the armed forces and to their families. It was agreed that there must be full use of resources of all organizations.[3]

Special services of a recreational and counseling nature for the men in the armed forces were carried out through the Red Cross and the United Service Organizations. The Red Cross through its military and naval service division provided recreational and counseling services in military and naval posts, stations, camps, and hospitals, both at home and overseas. One of their major projects was the overseas club. In all there were some 530 such Red Cross clubs located overseas. Each club provided lodging facilities, a snack bar, reading rooms, game rooms, and a restaurant, and was staffed by specially trained Red Cross workers. Another major project was the work in the hospitals, where recreational programs had to be adapted to the physical and emotional condition of the patients.

The Red Cross in expanding its program during the war was fulfilling its Congressional charter obligations, which empowered it "to act in matters of voluntary relief and in accord with the military and naval authorities as a medium of communication between the people of the United States of America and their Army and Navy." The United Service Organizations on the other hand was a new agency created by the special war-born needs of members of the armed forces and workers in defense industries.

When war came, communities near camps found their services quite inadequate to the new needs thrust upon them. Leaders in national, voluntary agencies believed that cooperatively planned, jointly administered, yet differentiated services would be possible. After conferences with governmental officials, the National Jewish Welfare Board, the National Catholic Community Service, the National Travelers Aid Association, the Salvation Army, the National Council of the Young Men's Christian Associations, and the National Board of the Young Women's Christian Association formed the USO.[4]

Two of these organizations, the YMCA and the JWB, had been involved in a program for men in the armed services since 1917. The YWCA and the Salvation Army had participated in such services during World War I. The National Catholic Community Service was a new organization created in 1940 for the specific purpose of meeting the social, personal, cultural, educational, and religious interests of service men and women.

The USO, which viewed itself as a coordinating mechanism for its six constituent members in this specialized program, was incorporated in February 1941, and by June it had launched a fund-raising campaign to put the plan into operation. At first facilities were rented, but with the passage of the Lanham Act in September 1941, providing $155 million for developing roads, sewerage, schools, clinics, and recreational facilities in areas near military camps and defense industries, the USO was able to arrange with the government to utilize some of these funds for the erection of USO club buildings. The work with government through the ODHWS (which later became the Office of Community War Services) involved not only the development of facilities but also the important matter of broad community planning. This experiment in the cooperation of private agencies on a national scale with government threw new light on the controversies of the thirties concerning the function of public and private agencies. Some social workers saw in this collaboration a potential new pattern "for the meeting of needs where resources are limited."

The USO program involved more than recreational activities. It attempted to deal with the total needs of the men and women in the armed services, army and navy nurses, wives of servicemen, and industrial workers. Since many of the 3000 USO operations were in communities without adequate social welfare services, the staffs found themselves involved in a generic social work task necessitating casework, group work, and community organization skills. Besides the USO clubs, of which 178 were located overseas—in Alaska, Newfoundland, Bermuda, the Caribbean, the Panama Canal Zone, and Hawaii—there were services to the troops in transit, a mobile service division for the men on maneuvers, and the USO camp shows which covered the fighting fronts as well as the camps. The program was carried out by a large professional staff of varied backgrounds and literally millions of volunteers.

Just as the Red Cross program in World War I had brought social work services to many individuals and communities for the first time, so too the USO was broadening the frontiers of social work in the nation. It exposed many individuals to their first experience with an organized recreational program and with counseling services. On the national level it represented a step forward in interagency cooperation, and in the cooperation of private agencies with government. A major contribution was also made on the local level. In the larger communities in which social agencies and community planning machinery existed, the experience provided stimulation and guidance for expanding services to meet the special needs of the men in the armed forces from the pre-induction period to the return to the community. The interest in being of service during the war also helped to uncover new resources in local leadership and finance for social work. The impact on communities that had little in the way of health and welfare services was of great value to the long-range program. Some communities were having their first experience in helping to provide social services, and the result was the organization of permanent services for the community. For many the war experience represented the first contact with trained workers and a planned approach to community problems.

With interest concentrated on the men in uniform the needs of an important though ununiformed group, the merchant seamen, was at first neglected. Their task of delivering war materials to all parts of the globe was hazardous and the casualty rate was high.

Until the United Seamen's Service was established in September, 1942, merchant seamen were "stepchildren" of the war. When their ships returned after delivering essential war material, the men landed in war swollen ports. There, no matter how much money they had in their pockets, they were usually unable to find overnight accommodations. Some even had to sleep in hallways and noisome flophouses. The recreational services open to uniformed men were not available to them because they wore no uniforms.[5]

The USS was the result of the combined efforts of the government, the ship operators, the ship builders, and the maritime unions.

The task of the USS was not easy, for it involved the development of facilities and the recruitment of a professional staff for operations over the six continents. Its program, furthermore, had to be all-inclusive, with such varied services as medical, residential, welfare, recreational, entertainment, and aid to prisoners of war and to families of seamen. The medical program that was developed jointly by the Recruitment and Manning Organization of the War Shipping Administration, a government agency, and the USS was comprehensive. It included "repatriation, examination and consultation, treatment, overseas medical care, medical social work, medical studies, health education, sanitary inspection of USS hotels and clubs, and liaison." Special attention was given to psychiatric ailments, for the hazardous task of the merchant seamen was creating a high rate of emotional problems. One half of the medical staff had specialized training in psychiatry, and the rest centers were medically staffed entirely by psychiatrists. There was close cooperation between the medical division and the personal service division of USS. Personal services dealing with general welfare needs were rendered in all of the 115 facilities that the USS was operating on the six continents. The twenty personal service units in the United States, staffed by professional social workers, gave 70,108 services to 37,404 seamen and their families in 1943 alone.

The war community services of the OCD and the ODHWS, directed specifically toward defense communities, were another cooperative effort on the part of national agencies. Cooperation did not come easily at first. The ODHWS had organized committees of specialists in the fields of health and medical care, family security, nutrition, recreation, social protection, and community organization. It channeled its program through the twelve Security Board regions with the regional director of the Social Security Board designated as regional director of Defense Health and Welfare Services. The OCD, on the other hand, in assisting states and local communities to coordinate civilian defense activities, had established its regional offices in areas coinciding with Army Corps Areas. The difference in the pattern of operation coupled with an overlap of interests and functions led to some conflict at first. The ODH-WS from its previous experience of federal-state-local relationships operated primarily through the states to the local community. The OCD, on the other hand, went directly to the local communities, organizing thousands of civilian defense councils without the necessary state machinery for dealing with them. An attempt was made to clarify the areas of functional conflict by allocating to the ODHWS the province of social needs of a long-standing nature, and to OCD the needs of a temporary and emergency nature. The line between the two, however, was often thin. Trial and error brought better communication between the two organizations, and a cooperative pattern of operation developed.

The civilian defense program, as Lyman Ford[6] points out, had many positive aspects for the long-range program of social welfare. It brought many new people into community endeavors; for the first time it involved local government as such in planning for health and welfare; it stimulated and furthered the development of centralized bureaus for recruiting, training, and placing volunteers; it pointed the way to new units for community organization such as the block, the neighborhood, and areas larger than the official community; it broadened the base of community planning; and it aided in the development of state machinery for community organization in which state welfare conferences, state charities associations, and public welfare and health departments had been interested for some time.

Basic Social Work Services

There was frequently little distinction between these special wartime services and the second front of social work dealing with regular day-to-day services. In many respects the dichotomy was false, for there were really no longer any normal services as contrasted with wartime ones. The entire nation in one way or another was affected by the war. The basic social needs that always exist were still there, but they had taken on new forms and proportions because the ordinary channels for meeting these needs were closed. The disruption of family life, the entrance of women into industry on a large scale, the increase in divorces and in the number of unwed mothers, the rising rate of juvenile delinquency, and the myriad emotional problems arising from the fear of losing loved ones in the service provided a more than average load for casework services. The question of jurisdiction—that is, decision whether a case belonged to the Red Cross, because it concerned the family of a serviceman, or to the family welfare agency—was of less importance than the question of how to provide necessary services.

With the entrance of women into industry, as well as of newcomers unfamiliar with community facilities, management found itself plagued with absenteeism, which interfered with production schedules. It soon came to recognize that it was dealing with problems of human relations that needed special handling. Counseling programs were established by many of the larger industries, based on the pioneer experience of such companies as Macy's, Metropolitan Life Insurance, and Western Electric. Caseworkers were employed by some of these industries and by the federal agencies, most of which had also introduced a program of employee counseling. One of the major responsibilities of the employee counselor was to help the worker make better use of community resources, and to work with the community in helping to develop new resources.

Many of the activities of the group work agencies took on the coloring of the wartime effort. Three major developments, from the long-range point of view, were the introduction of day-care programs for the children of working mothers; work with the adolescent, including the juvenile delinquent; and further experimentation in the relations of casework and group work, including group therapy.

The war pointed up the fact that only a small fraction of adolescent youth was being reached by the youth-serving agencies, and the fact that often those who were not being reached were in greater need of the services than those who were affiliated. The agencies learned that in order to attract the adolescent they had to consult him in planning their programs in order to meet his needs realistically. The endeavors of the youth-serving agencies, however, were not sufficient to cope with the growing problems. There was a need to interpret to both the government and the people the importance of youth work and services in wartime, so that greater resources could be made available. One development in this direction was the formation of the Associated Youth Serving Organizations in 1943 consisting of the following national agencies: Boys' Clubs of America, YWCA, YMCA, Camp Fire Girls, Girl Scouts, National Federation of Settlements, and the Jewish Welfare Board. The purpose of the association was to work together on such problems as "interpretation of youth needs and youth services; local planning and action for youth needs; relations with federal government agencies and bureaus; planning for special groups—Negro youth, rural youth, etc.; relations with other groups—schools, churches, labor, etc.; and post war needs of youth."

The difficulty the agencies were having in coping with the increase in juvenile delinquency brought the realization that they were dealing with problems of multiple causation, which had to be dealt with through a multiple approach. Group work by itself was no panacea. The problems involved individual and community factors as well as group ones. Group workers began to see the need of moving beyond the confines of their four walls and their agency-centered programs out into the community. They also saw the need for greater knowledge in handling the individual and began to cooperate on a large scale with casework agencies in exploring further the relations between casework and group work. An outstanding experiment in cooperation was the one at Bronx House in New York, in collaboration with the Jewish Board of Guardians. This involved the use of a caseworker on the staff of the settlement house on a part-time basis. The caseworker was loaned by the JBG and continued her relationship with both agencies. Out of these experiments came a clearer understanding of the role of both types of workers, a refinement of referral procedures, and a better understanding of the areas of responsibility of both types of agencies as they worked with the same individual and his family.

There were many important developments in the area of community planning and coordination, among which were the efforts to deal with interracial problems, the experience of the National War Fund, and the greater involvement of labor in the social welfare programs of the community.

The interracial issue is a good example of a social problem which had existed for years but took on special shape and proportions during the war. The fight against discrimination had been long and arduous, with many voluntary agencies—over 125 national agencies—working in some aspect of race relations, but government had done little in the way of establishing agencies and programs to further the civil rights laws that were on the books. A major move early in the war was the creation of the Fair Employment Practices Committee by executive order to serve as a wartime federal body to safeguard the employment rights of minority workers in plants handling government contracts. By 1945 permanent state committees against discrimination were established in New York, Massachusetts, and New Jersey. Two other states, Wisconsin and Indiana, enacted fair employment legislation, but without the enforcement power that existed in the other three states. The wartime race riots and the impetus from developments on the federal and state levels led to the creation of official agencies in some thirty-one municipalities. These varied in their pattern of sponsorship, form of organization, and effectiveness.

The voluntary agencies in the meantime had stepped up their efforts to improve race relations. In 1944 the American Council on Race Relations was established "to help bring about full participation of all citizens in all aspects of American life; and to assure equal rights and equal opportunities for all racial, religious, and national groups." The council, operating through three divisions—community services, information service, and clearing house—cooperated with both government and voluntary national agencies in developing programs of race relations. Out of this total effort there began to emerge a greater interest in research on intergroup relations and in the development of techniques to deal with the basic factors of race relations. These techniques involved work with individuals, groups, and communities. The social scientists became interested and began to assemble all available knowledge and to move into programs of action research. Social work with its experience in casework, group work, and community organization had much to offer in these undertakings and also much to gain, for some of the hypotheses under which it operated were being put to a research test for the first time. This was especially true in community organization with its intensified focus on intergroup relations.

The chest pattern of fund raising was expanded during the war with the creation of the National War Fund in 1942, a community chest on a national basis. This move was stimulated by numerous national appeals launched for wartime projects. Through the National War Fund, operating in turn through state war funds, thousands of new workers and contributors joined the ranks of federated financing. Every county in the country was involved, thus bringing the experience of joint fund raising to many areas for the first time. As these new areas developed machinery for the wartime appeals they began to include funds for local services, an important step toward long-range federated financing and community planning. Many of these new ventures were to continue after the war. The following from a speech by the director of the North Carolina State War Fund shows the impact of wartime federated financing on long-range efforts toward community organization:

It has been said recently that the emphasis on community organization today is fast moving and chaotic, that if we do not move with it, its dynamic evolution will leave us behind. To take the State of North Carolina for an example, there exists in respect to community organization at this moment more concern and activity—vocal and otherwise—than ever before in the state's history. . . .

Recently, local USO Committees from a network of ten cities and towns met in Farmville, N.C. It was apparent, as the real community leaders told their stories, that they were thinking not only of their immediate responsibilities for war services, but also of the need for an immediate beginning in providing similar services for the children, the young people, the men and women who live in their communities. That was as convincing demonstration as could have been provided of the "fast-moving" grass roots emphasis on community organization. It emphasized not only ways in which the state war fund could help these communities to realize their new ambitions, but how much it has already contributed toward this exciting development.[7]

The experience with the National War Fund not only brought federated financing to new areas but also threw light on the potentialities of larger units of organization such as the state and the county. An outstanding example was the State of Michigan.

The Michigan Community Chest and Councils Association petitioned the Michigan United War Fund, Inc., to take the necessary steps to provide in Michigan a year-round service to the individual communities and areas in community organization; to explore the relationship of intrastate social welfare agencies; to institute proper training for community organization and federated financing in chest and non-chest areas; to develop state-wide educational programs; and to provide special services related to campaigns, standards and techniques, and techniques in the fields of community organization, federated financing, and welfare services.[8]

Wartime also saw the trade unions participating in health and welfare programs to a greater extent than ever before. Labor had in the past been suspicious and mistrustful of social work—and frequently with good reason. The workers had felt that the agencies were on the side of management, and their feelings were often justified by the refusal of private agencies to provided relief to needy workers' families during periods of strikes. On the other hand, workers had often been compelled to contribute to welfare campaigns as employees, although the company received credit for the contributions. Management had also utilized their "so-called welfare workers" at times to "spy on employees and report on union organization." During the depression, however, labor and social work had grown closer together as they recognized that their goals and concerns had much in common.

In 1938 the AFL had established the Labor League for Human Rights to serve as their vehicle for cooperating with welfare organizations in promoting health, welfare, recreation, and fund raising, and in 1941 the league organized the United Nations Relief Committee to raise funds from among its members for relief of war victims. In the same year the CIO created the National CIO War Relief Committee—renamed in 1945 the National CIO Community Services Committee—to carry out a similar function among its constituents. Between the two unions large sums of money were raised and both the National War Fund and the Red Cross, who included employee giving in their campaigns, saw the need for gaining labor's cooperation.

Both unions were approached in the spring of 1942 by a committee of Community Chests and Councils, Inc., and asked to join forces with the National War Fund. The unions, in the prevalent spirit of unity, accepted the invitation and coordinated their fund raising within the National War Fund from the fall of 1942 until the end of the war. They also worked out a plan for cooperating with the Red Cross in its annual appeal for funds. The interest in joint fund raising soon led to a growing desire to participate in policy making and social planning on the local and state as well as national levels. A joint committee of the two unions and the Community Chests and Councils, Inc., explored the problem; and in May 1943 a "Memorandum on Relations with Organized Labor," outlining the objective and the principles of labor's participation in areas of program and planning, was issued. In September 1943 the three organizations sent their constituents "A Joint Suggestion for Labor Participation." These developments represented a great step forward in broadening the base of agency boards, and in making agencies more representative of community interests. The positive attitude of labor toward participation was expressed by Philip Murray, President of the CIO, in a statement in December 1944:

Three years ago CIO was represented on no more than 90 boards of social agencies. Today more than 4,000 men and women of CIO sit on the policy-making boards as well as on the administrative and budget committees of hundreds of national, state and local social service organizations. We have both voice and vote in the National War Fund, American Red Cross, Community Chests and Councils, many allied war relief societies, and many all-time social service agencies, nationally and locally, which deal with important health and welfare problems. Through the establishment of labor participation and community service committees and through the promotion of the union counseling program by CIO councils and unions, the committee (National CIO War Relief Committee) has developed not only better relationships between community agencies and CIO but has created a better understanding in the community of our problems and needs. These problems and needs, while great in wartime, will be as great or greater during the immediate period of demobilization and reconversion.[9]

In the November issue of the same *Newsletter* there appeared a statement made by Ralph Blanchard, Executive Director of Community Chests and Councils, Inc., expressing as follows the attitude of the private agencies toward the broader participation of labor in matters of program and social planning: "Chests and Councils welcome this great new partner in the social planning field just as they welcome the great work which has been done and is being done in campaigns."

The unions also became interested in developing ways in which their membership could make better use of existing community health and welfare services. Company-operated counseling services were regarded with mistrust, but the unions saw the need and value of making available to their members the services in which they had become partners. Under the leadership of the Michigan State CIO Education Department and the United Auto Workers War Policy Division the plan of union counseling was developed early in 1944. The plan involved training a selected group of rank-and-file workers with the cooperation of the council of social agencies in interviewing techniques, knowledge of community resources, and referral procedures. The function of the union counselor was not to provide services or engage in treatment, but to help the workers understand the need for the various services and the existence of community resources to meet this need, and to refer them to the appropriate agencies. The plan was adopted in many communities with appropriate modifications.

The emerging pattern of union-community cooperation had significance as well for the problem of public versus private services. The philosophy of the progressive trade unions—many of them leaders in these new developments—had emphasized public rather than private welfare services during the thirties. They were now seeing the need for both.

Perhaps the greatest impact of the war on the second front of social work, that is, its permanent services, was the growing recognition of interdependence. The major crisis projected us into the future and demanded a maturity that went beyond that of day-to-day experience. As a result, vested interests gave way to a better understanding of interdependence. The real test, however, would come only when the crisis was terminated. Those who drew a sharp line between "normal" services and emergency developments, and failed to see their interrelationship, would try to return to "business as usual." Others, however, would gain perspective from the crisis experience. Fortunately, it is not possible without a drastic change in the structure of our society to go back all the way, for the experience, if sufficiently intensive and extensive, leaves a residue which inevitably affects future action.

Postwar Reconstruction

The third front of social work—the broad field of postwar reconstruction—was approached before the war had ended, proving again that one of the strengths of civilized man is his ability even in periods of danger and disaster to plan for the future. Under the leadership of President Roosevelt (who unfortunately did not live to see the fruits of his efforts), Winston Churchill, and Joseph Stalin, the groundwork for the United Nations was launched as early as January 1, 1942. On that date the twenty-six nations fighting the Axis Powers "pledged to unite for victory and win a peace based on the terms of the Atlantic Charter." In 1943 these nations joined by eighteen others established the United Nations Relief and Rehabilitation Administration (UNRRA), agreed on the continuation of the Intergovernmental Committee on Refugees (IGC), and made plans for immediate postwar relief through the American and British armies and the necessary arrangements for relief to be provided by the numerous voluntary agencies in the field.

The war was leaving a devastating toll of death and destruction in its wake. Families were separated, homes destroyed, and the bare necessities of food, clothing, and shelter were no longer available for millions of people in war-torn areas because of the disruption of agriculture, industry, and social services. UNRRA projected a program of providing basic supplies, technical health, welfare, industrial, and agricultural rehabilitation services, and work with displaced persons. Funds were made available by all uninvaded nations in the group, who pledged 1 per cent of their national incomes for a specified year. The United States up to June 30, 1946, contributed 73 per cent of the total fund of $3,662,910,000, and the United Kingdom 17 per cent. Both of these nations also provided approximately 70 per cent of the total UNRRA administrative and operating staff, which at the peak of the program comprised a total of 12,876 persons. There were many complications of an economic, political, and social nature, but all told, the accomplishments in all phases of the program were tremendous.

By the end of June, 1946, a total of nearly 13,000,000 tons of desperately needed food, clothing, textiles, shoes, medical supplies, industrial and agricultural rehabilitation supplies and equipment, ranging from baby bottles to locomotives, had been shipped to fourteen receiving countries. . . . Health work done by UNRRA doctors in various countries is largely credited with the prevention of any really major postwar epidemic anywhere in the world. . . .

In all fields one of UNRRA's most significant contributions has been in the training of indigenous personnel. This has been done through lectures, seminars, on-the-job supervision, and through the UNRRA fellowship program by which selected personnel from various countries were permitted to study health, welfare, industrial, and agricultural programs and methods in other countries. . . . The number of displaced persons being cared for by UNRRA . . . as of May 31, 1946, were: Germany 750,000, of whom 6,400 were unaccompanied and orphaned children; Austria, 45,000; and Italy, 28,000. . . . UNRRA has aided the United States, British, and French military authorities not only in the operation of camps but also in the repatriation of displaced persons desiring to return to their homelands.[10]

A number of voluntary agencies in the United States had overseas programs. In 1943 they established the American Council of Voluntary Agencies for Foreign Service, Inc., which included sixty-two organizations by October 1946, "to promote joint program planning and coordination of national voluntary agency activities on foreign relief and rehabilitation." The council served as the channel for its constituent members in their relations with the programs of the United Nations Relief and Rehabilitation Administration, the Intergovernmental Committee on Refugees, and the United States military forces. Overseas agencies were required to register with and be certified by the President's War Relief Control Board—this provision did not apply to the American Red Cross—and by 1945 some ninety organizations were registered.

From the outbreak of the war in September, 1939, through the six years ending December 31, 1945, the organizations registered with the President's War Relief Control Board collected and distributed funds and supplies to the total value of $464,191,775. Of this, $265,303,441 consisted of money contributed through the National War Fund, the United Jewish Appeal for Refugees, Overseas Needs and Palestine, and various smaller independent solicitations, and $198,888,334 consisted of contributed supplies. . . . Between September, 1939, and June, 1946, foreign relief provided by the American Red Cross totaled more than $170,000,000, of which Great Britain received some $35,000,000, the Union of Soviet Socialist Republics and France approximately $25,000,000 each, and Italy and China approximately $10,000,000 each.[11]

Although the Germans did not surrender until May 7, 1945, and the Japanese did not formally give up until September 2, 1945, the plan to create a permanent international machinery was already launched. An historic meeting of delegates from fifty anti-Axis nations was opened in San Francisco, in April 1945 to draw up a charter for a permanent United Nations organization. The plan of organization included a Security Council, a General Assembly, an International Court of Justice, a secretariat, a Trusteeship Council, and an Economic and Social Council. The Security Council was to be made up of representatives of eleven member nations, five of which—the United States, Great Britain, the Union of Soviet Socialist Republics, France, and China—were to have permanent seats, and its primary function was the enforcement of the peace. The General Assembly provided a forum for debating world issues and for developing recommendations for action. The function of the International Court was to handle legal disputes, and the Trusteeship Council had as its responsibility the administration of "non-self-governing territories."

Of special interest to social workers was the establishment of the Economic and Social Council whose stated purpose was to provide "international machinery for the promotion and social advancement of all peoples." One of the chief functions of the council was to coordinate the many agencies—some old and some new—dealing with the related problems of social welfare. Among the agencies involved were the World Health Organization, the International Labor Office, the United Nations International Children's Emergency Fund, and the International Refugee Organization. The council was to function in many respects like a council of social agencies, including in its program such activities as coordination, fact-finding, exchange of experience and information, and recommendations for action to the member nations and to the General Assembly as a whole. Recommendations to the council on social questions and measures needed in the social field were to be the responsibility of a social commission made up of representatives of eighteen nations elected by the Security Council.

The climate for international cooperation had been established through the many collaborative efforts of the Allied nations during the war. The United States, under the leadership of Harry S. Truman, who had succeeded to the Presidency upon the death of Franklin Delano Roosevelt on April 12, 1944, was receptive to the plan. It was ratified by the United States Senate in July 1945, and by January 1946 the United Nations had started to operate.

The problems of international postwar reconstruction, although of a unique scale and nature, had counterparts on our national scene. As might have been expected, the rapidly expanding social welfare program under public auspices in the thirties had virtually come to a standstill with the advent of war. The National Resources Planning Board had begun a study of public-aid policies in 1939. The report, entitled *Security, Work, and Relief Policies* and representing three years of careful study, had been presented to Congress by President Roosevelt on March 10, 1943. Along with it was a second report entitled *National Resources Development Report for 1943*, which dealt with plans for a transition from a war to a peace economy in a way that would insure the maintenance of full employment. The two reports complemented each other, the latter dealing as it did with full employment, and the former with the "problem of insuring freedom from want." The report on transition from war to peace recommended an orderly and gradual removal of wartime rationing and price controls. Since the maintenance of full employment necessitated an expanding economy, the report further recommended that this could be achieved only through the cooperation of government and private enterprise. This meant a continuation of the philosophy and pattern established by the New Deal, with government taking leadership in planning and maintaining a role in the control of private enterprise. The report dealing with security, work, and relief policies included a detailed analysis of the problem based on the experience of the thirties, and series of recommendations which urged the government to:

provide real jobs for those whom private industry cannot employ; provide necessary work and training for young people if they should not find jobs on completing their education; take steps to extend the benefits of existing social insurance programs to as large a proportion of the populaton as possible, including enactment of permanent and temporary disability insurance; develop a comprehensive general public assistance system to care for needy people regardless of their age, sex, or place of residence; and, examine the social services which have a preventive and constructive character and plan for their expansion where this is needed.[12]

Some people felt that President Roosevelt had been playing politics and laying the groundwork for the 1944 campaign in presenting these reports at the height of the war period. Others, however, saw his action as reflecting a comprehensive understanding of the total war effort. Military victory did not necessarily mean a democratic victory. War was not an isolated phenomenon, but rather an exaggerated phase of a problem of long standing—the lag of economic and social democracy behind political democracy. The defeat of the Axis represented the dissolution of an immediate threat to the democratic way of life, but it did not in itself solve the problems of poverty, unemployment, substandard housing, ill-health, racial prejudice, and crime that made antidemocratic forms of government possible in other countries. Concern with our internal affairs was an integral part of the fight against totalitarianism, for many of these problems would be with us in an exaggerated form in the postwar period unless we planned in advance to meet them.

Action on the Social Security recommendations was not to come until 1950. Some steps were taken, however, toward an orderly reintegration of the returning veterans into the economic and social life of the nation. The government provided for veterans to draw unemployment compensation while seeking employment; enacted the G.I. Bill for those who wished to complete their education; and established a system of bank loans guaranteed at a low rate of interest for those who wished to purchase homes or to go into business for themselves. Other benefits described in the pamphlet *Your Rights and Benefits,* published by the Retraining and Reemployment Administration of the Office of War Mobilization, were mustering-out pay, insurance, employment service, hospital care, pensions, death gratuities, and allotments and allowances. Such government agencies as Selective Service, the United States Employment Service, the United States Civil Service Commission, and the Veterans Administration were authorized to provide special services. In many states legislation was enacted to provide help to the returning servicemen.

The private voluntary agencies also devoted their efforts to aiding in the reintegration of the approximately 12 million men and women in the armed services. A National Committee on Service to Veterans was formed to give leadership to the planning and coordinating of services. In a pamphlet entitled *Community Services for Veterans* the committee outlined the types of services which might be rendered. These included "counselling on personal or family problems, information, assistance with claims filing and claims prosecution, financial assistance whether disabled or able bodied and financial assistance for dependents, hospital, medical and follow-up care, psychiatric and follow-up care vocational rehabilitation, job training, employment service, unemployment compensation, education, assistance with insurance, help with reassembling the family, guardianship service, home or business loans, and other types of planning." The same pamphlet recommended a central planning body in each community, with the following functions.

1. To be the central clearing-house for all ideas and projects concerning the welfare of the returning veteran to the end that every organization and individual may make the maximum contribution without harmful duplication of effort.

2. To gather and make available the facts about the number of veterans returning to the community and their potential needs.

3. To determine the adequacy of direct service facilities to meet the needs of the veteran; plan and stimulate community action for the provisions of additional services where neces-

sary; and act as the medium through which organizations rendering services arrive at satisfactory working agreements.

4. To determine whether or not there is a need for an information service center and determine the auspices under which it should be administered.

5. To carry on a program of public interpretation and information regarding the veteran and his proper reception by the community.

6. To act as the official liaison with state and national veterans planning bodies.

The Meaning of the War Experience for Social Work

In World War II social work showed great ability and flexibility in mobilizing its resources to help defeat the Axis powers. The period was significant for social work; the growing status of the profession was made evident by the recognition accorded to it, along with other professions, by the military and the government. In the general atmosphere of unity and cooperation, social work began to pull itself together internally. It also expanded its activities on the international scene, and into new fields. The size of the social work force was enlarged to meet increased demands for service. The war experience also necessitated new approaches which, in turn, brought new insights and skills. Many of the questions about objectives and philosophy which had arisen during the thirties had to be re-examined.

The work of the Wartime Committee on Social Work Personnel had significance beyond attaining professional classification for social workers in the military and government services. The experience of all the professional groups in social work operating through a joint committee laid the groundwork for a growing interest in a single over-all professional organization. In order to interpret social work to the military it was necessary for the various groups to explore what they had in common rather than to emphasize their differences. They had to find common ground in answering such basic questions as, Who is a qualified social worker? and What kind of training makes a person qualified? The joint approach led to a greater interest on the part of the professional groups in a better integration of social work education.

Social work also made strides in the field of practice. Thus during World War II private agencies entered into a closer relationship with each other and with government in such efforts as the United Service Organizations, the American War Community Services, the National Committee on Services to Veterans, the National War Fund, and the Associated Youth Serving Agencies. The relationship of private and public agencies on all levels was also seen in the larger perspective of the common good.

Social workers had participated in international programs prior to the war through the various American agencies which had overseas programs or participated in international organizations, but never on the scale or in the form demanded by World War II. Besides establishing the use by government of trained social workers as technical consultants in helping other countries develop their social welfare services, the war brought social workers of many nations closer together than ever before. An International Conference on Social Work had already been organized in 1926 for the purpose of bringing "social workers together from all countries in order to cooperate in improvement of the methods of social work and its development throughout the World." Conferences had been held in Paris in 1928, Frankfort in 1932, and London in 1936. The next conference, which was to be held in the United States in 1950, would show the results of the war experience in the magnitude of the group and its interest in seeking common ground.

The war saw the social work skills of casework, group work, and community organization utilized not only in many communities formerly untouched by professional services but also in new settings such as the military and all its branches, industry, and the trade unions. Perhaps even more important was the large number of individuals who through experience with the USO, the Red Cross, and the psychiatric program in the armed services had come into contact with organized social work for the first time. This meant that more of the general public would have an understanding of social work services, and would perhaps make use of them.

The military was a large human laboratory. It not only provided opportunity for psychiatric practice but also gave the psychiatrist, the psychologist, and the social worker a chance to communicate with each other and to work together. As might be expected, a great deal of new knowledge was obtained about special types of cases, which would be applicable in civilian life. The size of the operation, furthermore, demanded new ways of cutting down the traditional detailed case histories, paperwork, and constant supervision, problems which casework was to face in the not too distant future as waiting lists of people seeking help grew. Menninger pointed to several major lessons from the war experience which were to have a bearing on future trends in social work. The experience in the military, he observed, pointed up the inadequacies of the psychiatric resources and programs in civilian life.

The rapid building of so large an army and the necessity of adjustment to life in the basic training camp, in combat, and in isolated, barren stations have called attention to the high incidence of psychiatric problems. According to testimony before the Health Committee of the Senate 1,400,000 men have been rejected because of some type of neuropsychiatric difficulty. This is evidence that similar problems must exist in civilian life.[13]

It was quite evident that more would have to be done in civilian life to meet growing psychiatric needs and that methods would have to be developed that permitted dealing with larger numbers than was possible through individual psychotherapy. Prior to the war group psychotherapy had been developed in work with children but was not utilized to any degree with adults. Menninger saw the experience in the armed services with group psychotherapy as having good potentialities for the civilian scene, and saw a role for the social worker in such a treatment program. He pointed out that social workers in the Army had a wide opportunity to participate in a program of prevention and in an active treatment program, in both of which they were concerned with groups of individuals; and that the practice of group psychotherapy was far more extensive than individual psychotherapy, and that in many instances the social worker had the major responsibility for it.[14]

If the problem in civilian life was to be dealt with adequately, however, the job involved more than an improvement in, or expansion of, methods of treatment. The answer had to be found in a program of prevention, in a greater concern for the causes of emotional breakdown. In this connection, Menninger[15] indicated that psychiatry in the army, perhaps even more noticeably than in civilian life, showed an increasing trend toward a social orientation rather than merely an individual diagnosis and treatment. In the army the psychiatric program had to be geared to the over-all objectives of a well-functioning unit with good morale. This meant that the problems of the individual could not be isolated from those of the group, and that the psychiatrist had to become involved with such environmental factors as selection and assignment, training methods and living conditions, leadership, and other factors that determined the adjustment of a soldier to his job.

A similar concern was being expressed by the social scientists as they became involved in research for action on the day-to-day problems of the war. In sociology the work of Emile Durkheim, with its emphasis on cultural values and social role, was being rediscovered. Durkheim, seeking for a regulating power in man which would serve the same function for emotional desires as the organism does for physical desires, hypothesized that since there was nothing within the individual which could set the necessary limits on his activities, the regulating force must be external, that is, a moral force. Society and the groups that constituted it played the role of the moderator. When society broke down or was involved in sudden and rapid changes the individual was left without a necessary guiding and authoritative force and the individual turned to asocial patterns of behavior. Within this general formulation social scientists like Merton, Kluckhohn, Linton, and Parsons proceeded toward a systematic approach to such basic problems as cultural value orientations, cultural values and social roles, age and sex determinants in the social structure, group membership, group processes, and value conflicts.

In experimental psychology Kurt Lewin, following the emphasis of the Gestalt school as contrasted with the individualistic stress, set out to clarify and apply holistic theories as they pertained to the fields of personality and social behavior. Lewin saw the group as a dynamic whole with properties of its own:

Groups are sociological wholes, the unity of these sociological wholes can be defined operationally in the same way as a unity of any other dynamic whole, namely by the interdependence of its parts. Such a definition takes mysticism out of the group conception and brings the problem down to a thoroughly empirical and testable basis. At the same time it means a full recognition of the fact that the properties of a social group, such as its organization, its stability, its goals, are something different from the organization, the stability and the goals of the individuals in it.[16]

Lewin and his followers tackled such problems as the effect of different types of leadership on group attitudes; the processes by which an individual adopts or comes to oppose the ideology and styles of living predominant in his social climate; the forces that make him belong to certain groups; and the forces that determine his social status and security within these groups.

New vistas of knowledge pertaining to personality and social behavior were opening up. By the end of the war this knowledge began to seep slowly into the social work curriculum. There is always a time lag of approximately a generation "for the new discoveries and techniques of one science to become a part of the regular working equipment of other sciences."

Social work, deeply imbedded in psychiatry, which might be regarded more as an art of healing than as a social science, was perhaps especially resistant to change. The experience in the war, however, indicated that psychiatry, too, was feeling the impact of the new developments. Since social work theory had borrowed heavily from psychiatry, the speed with which psychiatry was able to move ahead would in a large measure determine the rate with which social work would overcome the time lag.

The social work force had grown to 72,528 by 1940, according to the census report. World War II saw a further expansion of paid workers recruited for the numerous wartime services. It is estimated that the social work force totaled approximately 100,000 at the height of this period. Many of the workers were recruited from related fields, and not all of them were to remain in social work permanently. As a result of the continued increase, social work was facing a problem which had already become evident in the thirties. The standards in social work were moving ahead rapidly, with an increasing recognition of graduate training in an accredited school of social work as the basic requirement for professional standing. But although the total enrollment of students in accredited schools had risen rapidly in the thirties, by 1942 the schools began to show a sharp drop not only in the enrollment of men but also of women. The total drop from 1941 to 1942 was 13 per cent, with men accounting for 43 per cent of it. Social work was again faced with a growth in the number of workers who did not meet the ever-increasing level of standards being set by the professional organizations. As of 1940 the membership of the AASW, the largest professional organization of social workers, still totaled only 10,602. One of the reasons for the increased enrollment in the thirties had been the acceleration program in cooperation with the FERA training project in 1934-1935, providing financial aid to approximately 1000 workers. During World War II, however, there was no comparable program of financial aid, and acceleration consisted primarily in enabling the student to save about one half a year through provisions for advance credit for experience, and the use of the quarter plan, which included a summer quarter and also made possible admission at four different periods in a given year. The war experience made it evident that if social work was to keep pace with the desirable increase in standards, social work education would need greater subsidization.

What of social work objectives and philosophy during the war period? The test of the extent to which the heightened concern with social reform and social policy in the thirties had been permanently integrated into the fabric of social work thinking was interrupted by the war. In an atmosphere of war psychology a positive attitude toward extension of Social Security and other social measures of a permanent nature could not be expected. There were straws in the wind, however, that indicated a regression from the progress made in the thirties.

For one thing the expansion of the role of public welfare agencies in the total fabric of the welfare program on the local and state levels, which had been confidently looked for, did not materialize. The American Public Welfare Association, at its conference in December 1941, had expressed the conviction that public welfare agencies should and would expand their function beyond that of meeting normal needs during the war effort. Many of their members saw a potential role of "broad leadership in the entire field of welfare," including responsibility for planning in cooperation with other groups in all areas of the projected wartime health and welfare services. The private agencies, however, found that the wartime programs provided an opportunity to regain some of the vigor which they had lost during the thirties and to resume the role of leadership. A pattern of relationship between public and private agencies was becoming apparent, but the question of equal partnership was far from settled.

In social work education, where the reflection of new trends should have been apparent, there was a noticeable lag in the preparation of students for a role in public welfare services. An open poll taken by the National Conference of Social Work in 1945, included this question: Does professional social work training adquately prepare students to function with ease within the framework of law in the public welfare field? The replies from the rank and file of the sample "indicated by 59% that they did not believe their training had equipped them to function 'easily within the framework of law.' " [17] Without proper stimulation, including interpretation of the importance of public services and adequate preparation for them, there was some danger that these services would be placed on a lower hierarchical level, thus causing students to shun them. This in turn would affect the attitude of equality of partnership in meeting the health and welfare needs of the nation. Above all, this default indicated that the new directions developed in the thirties had not been fully integrated into the fabric of social work thinking.

In the broader area of social reform and social policy, the opinion poll referred to above asked two relevant questions. The first was whether a limited form of social action would strengthen the National Conference or divide it into warring camps. Limited action was defined to mean "the official public announcement by the Conference of principles which social workers endorse in regard to public policy or social legislation; the official announcement being based upon a two-thirds majority vote at the annual business session.[18] The results on even this limited approach were so divided that no decision was reached by the conference. The second question sought to discover the basis on which conference members made their decisions on important public issues, and used the Wagner-Murray-Dingell bill relating to health as a testing point. The question asked was: "Had they read the section of the Wagner-Murray-Dingell bill relating to health; or any of five publications which were listed which might throw light on the question?" [19] The results showed that "three fourths had read the section of the Wagner bill, but only 36% had read the Statement of Principles of a Nationwide Health Program. . . . More than 57 percent of those less widely read found themselves unable to express any opinion. The record stands with 27.7 percent for the Wagner-Murray-Dingell bill as written; 34.5 percent for a bill rewritten in the light of the Principles of a Nationwide Health Program; and 37.6 percent unable to express an opinion." [20]

Again, turning to social work education as a barometer, one finds that social reform and social action were not being given the same attention as the courses in methods of treatment and remediation. In a study of "Social Action and Professional Education" made in 1944 by Marion Hathway, it was evident that matters of social reform and social policy were being dealt with only around the fringe of the total curriculum rather than as an integral part of it. This led Hathway to make the following observation:

A fair analysis of the role of the profession of social work in the war period will reveal two things: first, that where specific services which can be performed by civilian social workers have been identified, the demand for competent professional personnel has been without precedent; and secondly, that where questions of broad policy in the development of social services to meet the needs of a nation at war and in the postwar period have been considered, their contribution has been a limited one. The social worker's entire preparation for professional service should be oriented to this dual responsibility, and schools should undertake to produce students—equipped with knowledge of the economic and political framework in which social work functions, a conviction to face its implications, and skill to move ahead.[21]

The real test was to come in the postwar period. A reactionary political, economic, and social climate could bring a repetition of the experience in 1919, with social work again becoming introspective and removing itself from responsibility in the areas of social legislation and social policy. There was hope, however, that the experience of two major wars and a major depression would militate against any attempt to turn back the clock.

8

AFTER

WORLD WAR II

Self-Examination and

Evaluation

(1946—)

Postwar Reconstruction

Wเ ITH THE SURRENDER of Germany on May 7, 1945, and of Japan on September 2 of the same year, the United States began to turn its attention to the numerous problems that emerged as the aftermath of a long and costly war. The unity forged in fighting the common enemy soon gave way to internal dissension on the political, economic, and social fronts. The administration, under the leadership of President Truman, attempted to pursue the New Deal philosophy in meeting the problems of reconversion to a civilian economy. One of the immediate concerns was the reabsorption into civilian life of the millions of men and women in the armed services, who were being demobilized rapidly. The New Deal economists had recommended that all the safeguards used during the war to curb inflation be maintained to prevent the spiraling of prices before the economy could be transformed to peace production. An opposing group, on the other hand, under the leadership of Senator Robert A. Taft of Ohio, favored a reduction in income taxes, a curbing of the powers of labor, and the abolishment of price controls. With the Congressional elections of 1946 just around the corner, the program soon became enmeshed in the pressures of politics. The administration, acting more out of political expediency than consistent New Deal economics, ordered the removal of most rationing immediately following the termination of the war, maintaining only price controls.

The two opposing economic theories were at work again, the one favoring controls and planning until civilian production could meet the huge demand for consumer goods, the other favoring the removal of all obstacles to allow the economy to work out its solution through the "natural laws of the market."

Political necessities had to some extent compromised the planned approach. Despite price controls, the black market was actually inflating the prices of many essential goods. Furthermore, the reduction of working hours to a 40-hour week meant a loss in take-home pay for a large number of workers. Strikes for higher wages soon broke out in the key industries, but industry refused to meet these demands without permission from the Office of Price Administration to raise prices. After numerous attempts through fact-finding boards to solve the problem without destroying the structure of price controls, the administration, fearing the effect prolonged strikes might have on the reconversion program, yielded to the demands of industry for an increase in prices to cover the increase in wages. The inflationary spiral was soon underway. The OPA could not remain effective under these conditions, and when in June 1946 it came up for renewal the original structure was so emasculated that the President vetoed the bill. The nation continued for six weeks without a program of price controls, and by the end of this period the administration felt that it was too late to try to stem the tide.

The price index of goods in the consumer budget, which had been 128.4 in 1945, rose to 159.2 in 1947, almost all the increase occurring in the latter half of 1946. Another boost sent it to 171.2 in 1948. This index is based on 100 for the average of the pre-war years 1935-1939. The nation, therefore, came out of the war with a cost of living in 1945 somewhat less than 30 per cent above that of the previous peace, and then within three years allowed it to jump to 70 percent above.[1]

The Republicans captured both houses of Congress in the 1946 election. They immediately enacted legislation to reduce the income tax and to curb the powers of labor. The Taft-Hartley Act, referred to by labor as the "slave labor" act, was passed over the veto of President Truman. The act, attempting to balance the powers given to labor under the National Labor Relations Act, defined and forbade unfair labor practices. It also banned the closed shop, provided for a sixty day "cooling-off" period before strikes could be called, and made it mandatory that the officers of unions file affidavits declaring that they were not Communists.

The move to reconvert the economy to a peacetime basis was interrupted in the meantime by a new phenomenon, the Cold War. In an attempt to stop Communist expansion, the Truman Doctrine was enunciated; it offered economic and military aid to nations threatened by Communism (in practice, Greece and Turkey). This was followed in 1947 by the Marshall Plan, which was aimed at providing economic assistance to European nations to help them reestablish their economies and provide for the basic needs of their people.

The question was raised as to whether these moves did not rightly belong within the United Nations, but the administration contended that the United Nations was not yet in a position to handle a problem of this urgency. The Cold War forced the government to continue spending vast sums of money, and produced a combination of a high level of prosperity, high taxes, and high prices. It probably also accounted for the failure of the predicted unemployment crisis to materialize. It was becoming clear that there was not to be a return to "normal," that the present situation represented the new norm for a long time to come. By 1950 the cold war had become hot again with the outbreak of hostilities in Korea. This new crisis gave rise to a speculative boom in the United States accompanied by an additional 5 per cent boost in the already high cost of living. The only shred left of a wartime plan of control of the economy was modified rent control. An attempt was made to work out some semblance of planning through the Office of Defense Mobilization, but it was not effective. On February 28, 1951, the United Labor Policy Committee withdrew its support from the program and issued a scathing statement in which it accused "big business" of dominating the program, freezing out workers and consumers, and imposing upon the plain people. Some of the significant observations were: (1) "The road is greased for higher prices"; (2) "The present wage formula will act like a vise on the aspirations of Americans for decent living standards and equality of sacrifice in the defense effort"; (3) "Rents are climbing steadily upwards, while effective rent control legislation lags in Congress"; and (4) "An unbalanced tax program which would place its heaviest burdens on the lower income groups is in the process of enactment." [2]

Although there had been a sharp difference of opinion in Congress concerning the reduction of income taxes, the powers of labor, and price controls, there was sufficient agreement in 1950 to expand the program of social insurance. Improvements were made. "Coverage of the federal old age and survivors' insurance system was increased from approximately 35,000,000 workers in an average week to approximately 45,000,000. The most important new groups included on a compulsory basis were domestic workers who work twenty-four days or more in a calendar quarter for the same employer, regularly employed farm workers, businessmen, and certain other groups of self-employed not engaged in agriculture." [3] Coverage was extended to the Virgin Islands, and opportunity was offered Puerto Rico to join the plan. Coverage was also extended on a voluntary basis to workers in such nonprofit organizations as schools, churches, hospitals, and social agencies. Eligibility requirements were liberalized, making it possible for an individual to qualify by being in covered employment one half the time from January 1, 1951, to the date of retirement or of death. A supplemental benefit was provided for dependent husbands as well as wives, and dependent widowers as well as widows. The formula for benefits was revised upwards.

In 1952 a divided Republican party, after a bitter convention struggle, was successful in forming a coalition of diverse groups under the leadership of General Dwight D. Eisenhower. Korea, communism, corruption, and states rights were the main issues. General Eisenhower won the election over Adlai Stevenson by a large electoral vote, cracking even the traditionally "solid" South. His victory brought to an end twenty years of continuous rule by the Democrats.

Uppermost in the minds of social workers—most of them apparently backers of Adlai Stevenson—was the question of what would happen to the New Deal and Fair Deal philosophies under which the vast social welfare program had emerged. Although the test of the permanence of this ideological revolution had necessarily been postponed by the war, it is important to keep in mind that the drive for social reform had actually lost its momentum by the middle of 1938. In fact, the last major successful measure of the New Deal type had been the Wages and Hours Law passed by Congress in that year. With the easing of the economic situation, the industrialists had begun to rebel openly against the philosophy of the New Deal, and there had been a sufficient change in the constituency of Congress in the 1938 election to provide the base for an anti-New Deal coalition. Although during the war there was at least a simulated truce on the ideological front, the conservative coalition had been consolidating for its postwar fight against the New Deal philosophy. "To make sure that the future of America would be shaped without benefit of New Deal planning, the Senate killed the National Resources Planning Board. Instead it created its own Postwar Planning Committee, vigilantly headed by George and Vandenberg, which was determined to stamp 'conservative' on every postwar policy." [4]

There was valid reason for the social workers' concern, for President Eisenhower had earlier expressed his philosophy of social security thus: "In these times we hear so much of security, security, for everything we do. . . . I should think that the best example of it would be a man serving a lifetime in a federal prison." It quickly became evident, however, that the new political principles and social policies that had emerged during the depression, emphasizing government's responsibility for the welfare of the people, were here to stay and that it was no longer a question of reversing them, but rather of changing the attitude with which they were applied. President Eisenhower reflected this view in his first State of the Union message. "In a modern industrial society," he said, "banishment of destitution and cushioning the shock of personal disaster on the individual are proper concerns of all levels of government, including the federal government. This is especially true where remedy and prevention alike are beyond the individual's capacity."

A notable accomplishment was the expansion of the Social Security Act in 1954, with coverage extended to 10 million more individuals and benefits increased for hundreds of thousands of others already in the plan. In its final form the bill provided coverage for about 3.6 million farm operators; about 2 million farm employees—600,000 less than recommended by the President—and for accountants, architects, engineers, and funeral directors. Clergymen and Christian Science practitioners were given an individual option to join the plan. Other groups to whom coverage was extended include about 150,000 Federal workers not covered by any other pension system; 250,000 household domestics; 100,000 industrial employees working at home; and 50,000 fishermen. The plan also provided an opportunity for about 3.5 million state and local employees, exclusive of police and firemen, to join if their employers agreed and if a majority in a government unit voted for it. Other provisions in the new law were:

1. It raised payments to all retired workers [covered by the system] by at least $5.00 a month. It also raised—by $13.50 a month for retired workers and by $31.25 a month for families— the former ceiling on payments. People becoming eligible in the future would also receive higher payments, including increases that result from raising from $3,600 to $4,200 the maximum wage base on which the amount of their benefit checks is determined.

2. The law eliminated the four or five lowest years of earning from the computation of the old age and survivors insurance checks of workers who would retire later. This provision was of great importance to many people whose years of unusually low earnings—for reasons of unemployment, illness, or otherwise— would sharply reduce their benefits.

3. All retired workers under the program were permitted

to earn more without forfeiting OASI checks. The amount of exempt earnings was increased to $1,200 a year, and this annual exemption was applied equally to wage earners and self-employed workers.

4. The Act preserved the benefit rights, under Old Age and Survivors Insurance, of those workers regularly covered under the program who become totally disabled for long and indefinite periods.[5]

In August 1956 the bill was further amended to lower from 65 to 62 the age at which women would draw old-age and survivors insurance benefits; and to make totally disabled workers eligible for cash payments at the age of 50—on the same formula as benefits were available to retired workers at 65. Thus about 250,000 disabled workers became eligible for payments averaging about $75 a month, beginning in July 1957. In order to finance these changes, payroll taxes were raised by about $850 million annually, starting January 1, 1957. The levies were fixed by the bill at 0.25 per cent each for employers and employees and 0.37 per cent for the self-employed. Beginning in July 1957 widows became eligible for full benefits at 62. Working women retiring at 62 were eligible for 80 per cent of the monthly benefits otherwise payable at 65. Wives of retired workers would draw 75 per cent of the full benefits. The developments proved that social security had become an integral part of our economic structure and no longer belonged in partisan politics.

Yet in both the Eighty-Third and Eighty-Fourth Congresses little or no progress was made on such important social issues as school construction, health plans, liberalization of the refugee program, housing, and civil rights. As The New York Times reported: "in general the more liberal of the President's proposals have suffered; the more conservative have everywhere prevailed." [6] It seems that "apart from manifestations like social security, which have become so built into our structure that no one thinks of suggesting their elimination, we live under what might be described as a reluctant or emergency variety of Welfare State." [7] As a nation we have always been able to rationalize the emergency concept of the welfare state; but we tend to forget that the previous decades—including as they did a major depression and two World Wars—represented forty years of emergency living. It does not take much crystal gazing to see that the present state of affairs, with its alternating cold war and hot war and its growing arms race also represents a period of instability which might well continue for several decades. In periods of this kind, government cannot default in its responsibility toward the total national interest and security. This in turn calls for planning in many areas.

Although loath to accept a major role for government in expanding the social welfare program, the Eisenhower administration did not hesitate to follow the New Deal pattern in guiding the national economy.

It is surely one of the great paradoxes of recent American political history that the Republicans, who bitterly condemned the New and Fair Deals for almost a generation, and who particularly opposed the idea of a major role for government in guiding the national economy, should have swallowed the basic tinkering techniques of the past and not even attempted to repeal a single New Deal measure. If anything, they manipulated the Government's influences over the economy with even more skill than the Democrats. While they would not dream of admitting to the label of Keynesians—after the late British economist whose name is associated with a large governmental role in the economy—Lord Keynes himself would have been delighted at their performance. Their record in dealing with the stubborn post-war inflationary trends has been brilliant.[8]

The economic record for the four years from 1952 to 1956 was impressive[9] (see the table on the facing page).

The question may be raised as to whether expanded social welfare services are needed when the standard of living is rising.[10] If the criterion of need is economic dependency alone, then perhaps the answer is no. If, however, one takes stock of the myriad social and emotional problems confronting the nation, the answer must be different. As a nation we enjoy the highest standard of living in the world today. On the other side of the ledger, however, is a troubling share of social welfare problems.

	June 1952	June 1956
Civilian employment	62,600,000	66,500,000
Unemployment	1,800,000	2,900,000
Average weekly hours	40.5	40.1
Average weekly earnings	$66.83	$79.40
Farm net income (first-quarter annual rate)	$14,700,000,000	$11,500,000,000
Industrial production (1947–49 = 100)	118	141
Business expenditure, new plants and equipment (second quarter)	$6,800,000,000	$9,100,000,000
New construction activity	$3,000,000,000	$4,000,000,000
Wholesale prices (1947–49 = 100)	111.2	114.2
Consumer prices (May) (1947–49 = 100)	113.0	115.4
Retail sales	$13,800,000,000	$16,600,000,000
Personal income (annual rate in May)	$268,000,000,000	$323,000,000,000
Gross national product (first quarter annual rate)	$338,000,000,000	$403,000,000,000
Population	157,000,000	168,000,000

Social Welfare Problems

Economic

The Mid-Century White House Conference on Children and Youth reported that one out of five mothers with children under 18 works outside the home, and that most of them do so in order to earn a living. Women now represent approximately one third of the labor force, and the number of employed married women now exceeds the number of single women at work.

At midcentury about 20 per cent of the American people

were living in low-income families. As Frederick Lewis Allen[11] makes clear: "These people are not 'the masses'; they are not a proletariat. They are rather, a great number of very widely scattered people who for one reason or another are out of luck, such as small businessmen whose ventures have foundered; farmers who have had a bad year or series of years; lone widows, deserted wives and children; migratory laborers; workers of marginal ability, and invalids and defectives." This group are least adequately covered by insurance plans and have least access to financial resources. They represent not merely an economic problem but also a social problem.

America is continuing to increase its productive capacity and the machine is continuing to replace the human. The mass production method, first introduced in the automobile industry, continues to set new horizons for the productive capacities of the nation. Automation, referred to by some as the Second Industrial Revolution, is already coming around the corner. Like previous technological change, it can bring not only increased leisure but also technological unemployment.

Automation means great gains in efficiency and the demand for new skills. But what about those whose old skills are no longer wanted? A vast retraining program will be necessary if a large slice of the labor force is not to be abandoned. Some less privileged workers may suffer severely unless close attention is paid to their relocation. For example: low seniority Negroes and southern whites who have just recently found a semi-skilled foothold in industry may find themselves squeezed out. Retraining and upgrading for many of them will be either difficult or costly, and their alternatives—a bleak return to subsistence farming or lowpaid jobs as servants, dishwashers, night watchmen, common laborers etc. (and even here, opportunity is declining).[12]

Man is increasingly able to produce more in a shorter period of time, but as yet does not have any guarantee of his share in the increased productivity or security. If anything, increased productivity may, without adequate planning for its distribution and consumption, make his economic position more hazardous and his insecurities greater. More leisure is not automatically and in itself a blessing. In fact, leisure without adequate resources for using it and without sufficient economic security to enjoy it can add to the mental health problem of the nation.

Health

There was a 19 per cent decline in the mortality rate between 1937 and 1954 due primarily to advances in medicine and to more and better medical care." But the increased span of life has brought with it an increase in illnesses among the older age group and in the number of the chronically disabled. The handling of the medical problems of these groups involves social as well as medical care. Although resources for medical care have increased, their distribution throughout the nation is uneven. The Mid-Century White House Conference on Children and Youth reported that children in the five lowest states were receiving less than half the medical care of children in the five highest states; that the proportion for dental care was one seventh; and that one out of four counties in the nation was without a fulltime public health nurse in rural areas. The report of the President's Commission on the Health Needs of the Nation pointed up how large and important the unmet needs still were. The report recommended that present federal expenditures for health should be more than doubled and proposed in addition federal expenditures of approximately $1 billion, apart from the recommended grants to the states to make facilities available to fight tuberculosis, mental disease, and chronic illness facilities available to the entire population.[13]

The picture of mental health is not so clearly focused, for the statistics are more difficult to define and analyze. There have been sufficient clues in recent years, however, to suggest the magnitude of the problem. In World War II one out of every eight draftees was rejected because of personality or mental difficulties. It is estimated that one out of every twelve persons in the nation will spend some part of his life in a mental hospital. At present slightly over 50 per cent of all available hospital beds are occupied by mental patients. Other indices are the significant rise in the numbers of problem drinkers, chronic alcoholics, and narcotic addicts. The number of serious crimes has also increased. Add to these facts the number of children between the ages of 7 and 17 brought to juvenile courts each year, and the problem appears acute. The toll of divorces and annulments, although lower than during the war period, still approaches 400,000 annually. Approximately one out of every seven marriages ends in divorce. "Yet divorce is only one index of family disorganization. Almost 2,000,000 married persons are separated—temporarily or permanently—because of marital discord. And surveys reveal that one-fifth or one-sixth of all couples living together think of themselves as unhappy and that an equal number can report only 'medium happiness.' " [14]

It is estimated that to meet current needs mental hospital facilities must be approximately doubled, and that community clinics, both full- and part-time, must be tripled. Psychiatric services for schools, colleges, courts, and prisons are woefully inadequate. The total force of psychiatrists, psychiatric social workers, clinical psychologists, and psychiatric nurses does not even begin to approximate the number needed to deal with the mental health problems affecting a minimum of 15 million citizens. The amount of money being spent under government and private sponsorship for research in mental health is infinitesimal compared with the sums being spent on cancer, heart disease, and so forth. Although prevention would involve work with children, not a single state has adequate psychiatric clinic service for children, and some states have almost no service.

Recently there has been a trend to move adult as well as young patients from the institutions back into the community. "With modern treatment methods, from 40 to 60 per cent of schizophrenic patients can be helped . . . with maximum intensive therapy. The Topeka State Hospital in Kansas has been able to discharge 80 per cent of its patients as improved or recovered within the first year. As a result of new drugs, such as reserpine and thorazine, New York State reports a 19 per cent increase in discharges from its state mental hospitals and expects a net drop in admissions." [15] New problems, however, are being created. A great deal of work has to be done to prepare communities to accept these people and to provide resources for a new adjustment to jobs and family life.

Demographic

There has been a steady increase in the population with a growth of 13 million—from 157 million to 170 million—between June 1952 and June 1956. Most marked are the increases at both extremes of the population curve—that is, the very young and the very old. The educational, recreational, health, and housing resources of the nation are not geared to help meet the changing pattern of family life created by the shift in age distribution. Although economic provisions for the aged have increased, provisions for their many social problems are not adequate. With the breakdown of the kinship structure in American life and the emphasis on the "nuclear" family, the problems of the aged have multiplied.

Children have the duty to build their own careers, and set up their own households—with a corresponding right to independence. They leave one by one until the older couple is finally left alone—'with no one left to respect them, for them to have responsibility for or have authority over.' . . . At this point, all of the things that happen to old people become very much more tragic. If the spouse should die, the widow or widower is not generally expected to move in with the married child. If he does it occasions much strain on both sides. If the older worker is retired—and until recently, this has been early and abrupt, he has no clear claim to support from his children. Should he be subject to disabling illness or debilitation, the same emancipation from children becomes an even more difficult load to bear. In this system, parenthood in retrospect becomes for many not old-age insurance, but a sacrificial duty, a thankless task.[16]

Another significant demographic factor is the shift from large metropolitan areas to Suburbia. It is too early to tell whether suburban living will bring greater stability to family living and whether social breakdown (crime, delinquency, mental disease, and so forth) will decrease.

It does seem likely, however, that on balance, the suburbs are setting a pattern for a newer family form. The evidence seems to indicate that the fringe area family, compared to the central city family, tends to be somewhat larger, attaches more positive value to children and becomes more important in the daily routine of its members. The parents not only try to take their child-rearing cues from medicine and psychology; they may also try to supervise the education and recreation as well as courtship of their children more closely than is possible in the central city. They may participate more actively in community organizations. The greater financial resources required may be one reason why the fringe family also seems to approve more of employment for mothers, especially when the children are 12 years old or more. These tendencies seem to contribute to family solidarity.[17]

At the same time social welfare services have been concentrated primarily in the large metropolitan areas, and there is a lag in the necessary services in many suburban areas.

The movement to Suburbia has involved primarily middle-class groups. They are being replaced in the metropolitan areas by lower economic groups—frequently those who are victims of discrimination—who are compelled to live in blighted slum areas and are left with a need for housing and increased social services. The nonwhite population is more mobile than the white and is seeking liberation in the large metropolitan areas. For example, the 1950 census showed that the nonwhite population more than doubled in the large metropolitan areas of California and Michigan, and increased more than 50 per cent in New York and Illinois. The push for housing beyond the imposed ghettos is bringing with it increased racial tensions.

Education

There is concern about inadequate school facilities and lack of properly trained teachers to meet the expanding educational needs of the nation. A survey of school building needs, made by the United States Office of Education at the request of Congress, reported that to bring present facilities up to standard and that to construct the necessary new facilities would cost $10.7 billion. Funds are also needed for additional teachers, and for special programs such as those for handicapped children and for the children of working mothers. "There is a current deficit of 340,000 schoolrooms and 58,000 qualified teachers according to one estimate, in the face of a million-a-year increase in the School population each year until about 1965. It is estimated that 10 per cent of the nation's children are having to use makeshift and improvised school quarters even now." [18] The school program proposed by the Eisenhower administration is regarded as inadequate by most educators. Furthermore, school legislation has become snarled in the segregation controversy, and it may not be possible to put even a limited plan into operation for several years.

On July 25, 1956, the G. I. Bill of Rights, set up for veterans of World War II on June 22, 1944, expired. Over the twelve-year period approximately 8 million veterans attended school and college at a cost to the government of $14 billion. Since many veterans pursued graduate work, the nation's supply of specialized talent was increased. Thus in social work the number of men taking graduate training expanded with the G. I. Bill. A total of 16,937 students—of whom 5442 were men—were graduated from accredited schools of social work in the United States during the ten-year period beginning 1945-1946. It was at the beginning of this ten-year period that World War II veterans had begun to register in schools and colleges under the G. I. Bill. The effect of termination of veterans benefits is indicated by the reduction in the number of men graduating in social work in 1956 and 1957. In 1952, a high of 798 men were graduated from all schools of social work; this number dropped to 579 in 1956, a reduction of 219 or 27 per cent. There was a decrease of only 10 per cent in the number of women graduated during this period.

If the nation is to keep pace with its need not only for social workers but for scientists, doctors, dentists, nurses, teachers, and so forth, a government-subsidized program of scholarships equivalent to the amount spent on the program of education for veterans in recent years may be necessary.[19]

Civil Rights and Civil Liberties

The decision of the United States Supreme Court on school desegregation in 1954 represented an important step toward the goal expressed in the Declaration of Independence. The minority problem represents the supreme test of whether or not a democracy can practice what it preaches. If democratic attitudes are deeply rooted and at work, the civil rights issues will be taken in stride. If they are not, legislation of and by itself will not bring an automatic solution. There is increasing evidence from the social scientists that legislation is one of the major methods of reducing not only discrimination but private prejudice as well. They base their opinion on the fact that many people who discriminate are not prejudiced but rather are unable to resist the group's demand for conformity. There is also agreement, however, that legislation of and by itself cannot be regarded as the total approach but only as an important step in the process. Roscoe Pound describes three limitations of law as an agency of social control.[20] Law, of necessity, deals with acts, and not with the "inside" of men. There are also limitations inherent in legal sanctions, that is, the limitations upon "coercion of the human will" by force. Law, furthermore, must rely upon some external agency to put the machinery in motion, since legal precepts do not enforce themselves.

Although the Supreme Court decision on desegregation in the public schools represents a milestone in the advance of civil rights, the seas ahead are still stormy. Some Southern states are resorting to subterfuges to avoid the intent of the Court's ruling. Another aspect of the problem is the fight for a civil rights bill. The House, on June 18, 1957, passed an all-encompassing bill by a vote of 282 to 126. The bill included the creation of a Civil Rights Commission, the appointment of a new Assistant Attorney General in the civil rights field, authorization for the Attorney General to utilize federal court injunctions to deal with any threat to civil rights and to obtain injunctions against violations of voting rights. The bill gave authority to federal judges to handle without a jury contempt charges in such violations. The Senate, on August 7, 1957, by a vote of 72 to 18, emasculated the bill. The authority given to the Attorney General to act in the case of any threat to civil rights was eliminated. The authority of federal judges to handle contempt charges without a jury was also amended. In the Senate version jury trials are required in cases of criminal but not civil contempt.

The direction of progress in civil rights has been chartered. To arrive at the cherished goal, however, much will have to be done on the political, economic, and social fronts. Sections of both parties jockey for political advantage in the fight for the soul of democracy. Their ability to play politics with a fundamental human issue in American life will depend on the extent to which the American people have the Bill of Rights at heart. Unless the legislation can be reinforced and supplemented with efforts by all institutions dealing with education for effective living, the results will be fragmented. The profession of social work can be important in helping to bring about necessary changes of attitude. If its intention is clear and its values strong, it can reinforce the momentum of the Supreme Court decision. If, however, it is hesitant or apathetic, then it will contribute little.

The problems of civil rights and civil liberties go hand in hand. A democratic climate is one in which both rights and liberties shine brightly. The nation has emerged from the gloomy climate of McCarthyism. The fears and insecurities present after World War II, fanned by international events, provided a favorable soil for growth of anti-civil-libertarian movements. These movements were essentially attempts, in the name of democracy, to challenge basic democratic values and beliefs. They combined an attack on civil liberties with an assault on those institutions basically responsible for developing democratic attitudes in our society. Congressional investigating committees, with the Senate Committee on Investigations headed by Senator McCarthy leading the way, adopted techniques foreign to our tradition and legal structure. Historians describing this era may perhaps refer to it as the "era of investigations" and of "guilt by association." Congressional investigations are not new or unnecessary phenomena, but previously they tended to respect basic democratic principles. In the atmosphere of McCarthyism, neither the dignity of the individual nor the hard-earned traditional rights were held sacred. The irony of the situation was that totalitarian methods were being employed supposedly to serve the American way of life. As Adlai Stevenson warned in the 1952 Presidential campaign: "Our farms and factories may give us our living, but the Bill of Rights gives us our life. Whoever lays rough hands upon it lays rough hands upon you and me, whoever profanes its spirit diminishes our inheritance and beclouds our title to greatness as a people."

The public attitude was affected by insidious suggestions. Americans have been traditionally adventurous in the intellectual as well as the physical realm. Our educational philosophy has encouraged the individual to reach out toward new experiences, even if there was danger involved, since our educators were fully aware that freedom to make one's own mistakes is essential to creative learning. The stimulation for these attitudes of independence and intellectual aggressiveness has come from parents, teachers, clergy, social workers—in brief, from all those engaged in education for effective living in a democracy. With the climate of distrust and intimidation, however, came a growing tendency toward restriction and conformity on the part of these "character builders." If this climate had continued for any length of time we would have been in danger of creating a generation of conformists and distrusters in whose hands democracy would face certain death, and totalitarianism would have a holiday. Even today, though we appear to have passed the danger point, we cannot afford to be complacent.

What of social work during this period? As might be expected, here, too, the repressive climate had its impact on policies and programs. Signs of repression were the attempts to malign the principles underlying government's responsibility in public welfare. In several of the large cities clients were accused of being "chiselers," and the publication of the names of those on relief was sometimes suggested as a method of dealing with the problem. An attempt was made to tag on to a federal bill a procedure making it mandatory for names to be published whenever federal funds were used in a relief program. *Common Human Needs* by Charlotte Towle, which was being distributed by a government agency, was attacked as subversive and dropped by the agency. Youth councils, which tended to reflect young enthusiasm for social change, faded into the background. Agencies involved in adult education were forced to become more conservative, both in the content of their programs and in the selection of speakers and teachers. Personnel under attack for union or political activities found themselves defenseless, with little support from boards of agencies or professional groups. Social action and social reform became subjects for pious speeches delivered occasionally at conferences but forgotten in practice. The period showed many similarities to that following World War I.

The first group in social work to show the full effect of the climate was the trade union movement. In 1948 two dissident groups broke away from the two large CIO unions in social work—the United Public Workers of America and the United Office and Professional Workers of America. The split reflected the fight in the trade union movement to oust the left-wing unions. Both new groups—the United Public Workers of America and the United Social Agency Employees—became constituents of the Industrial Union of Marine and Shipbuilding Workers, an affiliate of the CIO that was strongly opposed to the "extreme left-wing unions in the parent body." The split brought a gradual weakening in trade union ranks within social work and finally resulted in the demise of the two original unions. Today trade unionism plays a relatively small role in social work and some of the issues raised in the thirties are again being debated. They include the following:

1. A first problem is the appropriateness of trade unionism to professional workers.
2. A second issue, again not peculiar to social work unionism, is the scope of collective bargaining.
3. The problem that is perhaps the most fundamental of those reviewed here, and at the same time most relevant to the particular circumstances of unionism in social work, is the nature of reform activities as such. This problem may be phrased as whether it is the appropriate function of reform in general and social work in particular to aim at securing adaptation to the existing institutional order, or to seek fundamental changes in that order.[21]

The world was promised freedom from fear and want during World War II, but fear, anxiety, and insecurity increased manyfold since the termination of the war. "We live," says Robert Bondy, "in the uncertainty of the morrow—war or peace, full production or recession, a levelling off or a fall in the value of goods and services, fear of subversiveness or a confidence in our strengths and freedoms." [22] Several years of high employment and an increased standard of living are not enough to wipe away the specter of depression and war. These conditions are intensified by a huckster approach; public relations has become a substitute for hard thinking and facing the facts about basic issues. At times, it seems that the nation is like a ship which has ample power to travel fast and far but has thrown its compass overboard and so moves in circles issuing meaningless progress communiqués.

Our social and mental health problems are on the increase. The structureless and often contradictory attitudes of our day seem to be creating insecurities, anxieties, and tensions, which in turn contribute to an exceptionally high incidence of

divorce, broken homes, homicides, suicides, juvenile delinquency, alcoholism, psychosis, and so forth. In fact, the magnitude of the problem raises a vital question. Are we faced with
a situation analogous to that of unemployment during the depression, when it became clear a solution could be found by
looking not only at the unemployed person but also at the
problem of "structural" unemployment? In the same vein, is
the problem of emotional breakdown reaching a magnitude
where to find a solution one must look not only at the problem
of the "emotionally unemployed" but also at "emotional unemployment" or "structural emotional unemployment"? There is
a question as to whether the social institutions responsible for
the high standard of living can be regarded as separate and
apart from conditions responsible for social breakdown. Furthermore, may we not be dealing with problems so widespread
in the population, so serious in their consequences, so costly in
their solution that the individual, even with a high standard of
living, cannot deal with them unaided? When faced with such
problems in the economic sphere there has been no alternative
even on the part of the Eisenhower administration to see a major role for government in guiding the national welfare. Can
government assume less responsibility in a sphere of such great
significance both to man and to the democratic society of
which he is a part?

Social Work Trends and Developments

Professional Organizations

Three important organizational developments in the postwar period had their roots in the wartime atmosphere of unity.
The first in time was the reconstitution in 1946 of the National Social Work Council into the National Social Welfare
Assembly. The Assembly included both national voluntary and
government agencies, with local as well as national—and lay as

well as professional—representation. It attained the most advanced level reached to date in national social work cooperation, for it attempted to bring about not only better planning within the groups with shared interests but also among the key national interagency bodies, both public and private.

In 1952 the Council on Social Work Education was created. The first steps were taken in 1946, when a temporary study and coordinating body known as the National Council on Social Work Education was brought into being. The chief concern of this council was to help resolve the problem of two separate accrediting bodies in social work, namely the National Association of Schools of Social Administration and the American Association of Schools of Social Work. Through a grant from the Carnegie Foundation, the National Council was able to undertake the first comprehensive study in social work education since that done by James H. Tufts in 1922. The study was published in 1951 as the Hollis-Taylor report. One of the results of the study was the solution of the problem of dual accreditation, making it possible for both groups to give up their separate identities and to bring into being in 1952 the permanent and all-inclusive coordinating body called the Council on Social Work Education.

The council has a broad membership consisting of representatives not only from social work education but also from the professional group, the employing agencies, related educational fields, and the interested public. "The activities of the Council are carried on through a Council of Delegates, a Board of Directors, four standing commissions, numerous committees, and a professional staff." [23] The four commissions are: accreditation; program, services and publications; schools and departments of social work; and research. "Among the major program committees are those which give special attention to the following areas of activity: Admissions, the Advanced Curriculum, Careers in Social Work, Corrections, Evaluation of Students, Group Work, International Social Welfare Education, Program Planning for the Annual Meeting, Teaching Materials, and

Specialization in Social Work Education." [24] The council includes both graduate schools and undergraduate departments of social work education. By July 1956 there were fifty-nine graduate schools in the United States and Canada and ninety undergraduate departments affiliated with the council.

Another important organizational development was the creation of the National Association of Social Workers in October 1, 1955. Up to that time there were in existence seven separate membership associations. Five of these associations[25] were formalized professional bodies. The other two, the Association for the Study of Community Organization, organized in 1946, and the Social Work Research Group, organized in 1949, were still in the informal study stage. Since the war there had been an increasing effort to shift attention from the specializations that divided the social work field to the common core that united it. In line with this trend, a committee on interassociation structure was organized in 1949, through the initiative of several associations, to develop a plan for promoting closer cooperative relationships among the social work professional membership associations. The committee studied the objectives, programs, and procedures of the five associations, as well as areas of cooperation. Their deliberations caused them to realize that they had much in common and to explore the feasibility of a single professional association. An article in 1949 on the "Present Structure and Program of Membership Associations" made the following observations:

The five professional membership associations in social work have in common with each other and with counterpart associations in other fields the basic characteristics of any professional association of practitioners. These are: a stated purpose of program for improvement of competence in practice; criteria by which persons shall qualify for admittance into the association; group study and action to improve the quality and effectiveness of service to the public; and an organizational structure by which program can be sustained between meetings of the membership body. These, of course, constitute the basic Who, What and How of any professional association.[26]

In 1950 this committee, consisting of twenty representatives appointed by the boards of the five professional membership associations, was constituted into a Temporary Inter-Association Council of Social Work Membership Organizations. TIAC identified and studied the following three forms of organizational structure: (1) a permanently organized interassociation committee to further cooperation between the associations on special projects; (2) a federation of associations to insure more formally organized activities, but without loss of organizational autonomy; and (3) a single organization with the specialized interests served through a division or section structure. In 1952 representatives of the five professional associations and the two membership associations formulated a set of principles and policies on which specific plans for a new organization could be based. A plan built around the single organization structure was accepted in principle in the spring of 1953. Formal action on a statement of agreements and a set of bylaws was taken by all seven associations by February 15, 1955. The new association began operation on October 1, 1955.

The NASW states that its purpose is the promotion of the quality and effectiveness of social work practice and the improvement of the conditions of life in our society. Its structure and program were "designed to further a sound unification of objectives and activities," but allowing "for flexible diversification in line with the particular interests of members and the changing needs of a growing profession." Interests common to the field—such as social work practice, social work education, personnel standards and practices, social policy and action, recruitment, and interpretation—are served through commissions established by the board of directors. Specific interests—such as "practice in a specific setting, the development of a particular social work process, or the application of a related method in social work" [27]—are served through the establishment of sections and committees. At present, there are the following five sections: group work, medical social work, psychiatric social work, school social work, and social work research. There are also committees on community organization and international social welfare. The requirement for general membership is a degree from a graduate professional school of social work accredited by the Council on Social Work Education. Membership requirements for the sections are determined by the sections with the approval of the board of directors and are "defined in terms of training or experience in addition to the minimum standards provided for membership in the Association." [28] As of January 1, 1957, the NASW had a membership of approximately 22,500 functioning through approximately 143 chapters covering all of the states, Puerto Rico, and Hawaii.

Social Work Looks Inward

Social work once again has become introspective. It is proceeding, however, with an objectivity and a maturity that befit an older profession. Under scrutiny are its goals and objectives; its methodology and body of knowledge; its scope of services, including types of programs and clientele served; its professional resources; and its financial resources.

GOALS, SOCIAL POLICY, AND RESEARCH

Social work, although paying lip service to the dual approach, had found itself giving more and more emphasis to problems of adjustment and development and less and less attention to matters of broad social policy. The trend had become accentuated in the regressive postwar climate. There have been recent signs, however, of a renewed interest in social work's stake and role in social policy. Several questions are being raised. What is the element of social policy in the day-to-day operations of the social worker? What should all social workers know about the existing body of social policy? What knowledge and skills are necessary to evaluate existing social policy? What knowledge and skills are necessary to participate in changing existing social policy?

An examination of these questions points up the need for a better foundation in social philosophy than the social worker now gets in his educational training. It also exposes the weaknesses of training in such areas as social action, administration, and community organization. Social action had been regarded earlier as a primary professional obligation in social work. As early as 1922 Mary Richmond had referred to it as one of the four forms of social work. None of the schools of social work, however, has yet developed a special curriculum for social action; they see it rather as an integral part of the teaching in casework, group work, and community organization. The methods of social action, consisting as they do of research, planning, enlistment of public support, and interpretation to (and pressure on) those with authority to implement it, overlap a good deal with those of community organization. One of the major differences perhaps lies in the emphasis on the types of issues to be dealt with. There has been a growing tendency to leave social action to specialized agencies, to professional groups, and to social workers as individual citizens. Some social workers, however, feel that this represents a retreat from social work's full responsibility; for them "social action is as logical an outgrowth of the fundamental belief of the social work profession in the worth and well being of the individual as are more direct services to individuals." As John Hill states the case:

When in recognition of such circumstances [problems due to external conditions beyond the ability of the agency or the client to modify] the social worker turns to the forces of community or government, he is still striving for the same objectives as he was formerly seeking through individual action. . . . Social action is not restricted to problems which will not yield to individual treatment. . . . There are many problems which could be handled more effectively, efficiently and economically within a mass or preventive way than through the slower and more expensive one-by-one method.[29]

Although some schools have a course in social administration, few attempt a concentration in this area. The reason is that only a handful of students, primarily those who have entered school after years of experience in the field, are regarded as ready for administrative positions. Moreover, some social workers feel that when administration is reduced to an emphasis on method and process there is a good deal of overlap with the teaching in the three "core disciplines." Arthur Dunham sees the task of administration as including the following:

1. The determination and clarification of objectives, functions and policies.
2. The mobilization and maintenance of resources—personal, financial, material, even psychological—to the end that the agency may carry out its purposes and fulfill its functions effectively.
3. The development of program.
4. Organization and coordination.
5. Leadership, direction and supervision.
6. Planning, standardization and evaluation.
7. Recording, accounting and related activities.
8. Processing, or routine procedures.
9. Public relations.[30]

The preparation for some of these tasks is included in the training for casework, group work, and community organization. Other tasks, such as business methods and public relations, are specializations on their own which cannot be attained easily in a single course. Leadership depends on a degree of maturity and experience. As schools develop advanced studies beyond the master's level and require a period of experience after obtaining the master's degree for admission to advanced programs, more attention is being paid to preparation for positions of leadership in administration, community organization, and social policy.

The changing focus in research also has a bearing on both the goals and the method of social work. Until 1940 the dominant method of research had been the social survey, and the primary area of concern had been needs and services. There has been a decline in the quantity but an improvement in quality of this type of research since World War II. Greater attention is being paid to a proper definition of needs and the relationship between needs and need-satisfiers. Attempts are being made to relate services to needs. Methods of measuring the extent and prevalence of needs and tests of the adequacy and usefulness of services are also being developed and refined.[31]

With the ever-increasing expenditures of social welfare programs and services, the growing professionalization, the changing body of knowledge, a more mature attitude about facing research findings, greater ability in formulating problems for research, and a more adequate research methodology, has come a deeper sense of the need to account for the "why," the "what," and the "how" of social work activities. Social work has also shown greater freedom in joining with other related disciplines in tackling some of these problems.

The newly emerging areas of research interest in social work can be seen in the following list, compiled by the Committee on Research Function and Practice of the Social Work Research Group[32] in 1951:

1. Determination of need for services.
2. Evaluation of adequacy and effectiveness of services.
3. Investigation of the content of social work processes.
4. Investigation of the competence required for various operations.
5. Validation of social work theory and concepts.
6. Development of methodology and tools for research in social work.
7. Investigation of the development and sometimes decline of social work services, programs, and concepts.
8. Translation and testing of theory or knowledge drawn from other fields.[33]

The degree of progress varies in different areas of research. Some beginnings, however, are evident in all of them. In the area of administration, the studies of Hill and Ormsby[34] on cost analysis have laid the groundwork for fruitful research in determining priorities, the proper distribution of agency resources, and the formulation of social policy. The development of adequate cost accounting methods is essential both for sound administration and for accountability to the community.

Social work practice is recognized as a priority area for research but, for a variety of reasons, only "a modest beginning has been made. Social work is still a long way from having a scientifically tested and validated practice theory." [35] In Greenwood's view: "If we were to take what today passes for practice theory in social work and subject it to that major inventory taking that Gordon has called for, we would find that it has been built up in the main in a trial and error, crudely empirical and highly pragmatic manner. Social work practice theory was not developed via systematic research." [36] The problems in this area are complicated, for to deal with them one must be able to "develop adequate conceptual formulations," and to "properly identify, isolate and control the variables involved." [37]

Paralleling the desire for systematic analysis as to how social work proceeds is the interest in the consequences of social work practice. As Witmer indicates: "Evaluative studies seek answers to two main questions: How good is what we are trying to do? How well are we doing it? And these two questions merge into one: How does it compare with the way it ought to be?" [38] Evaluative research has taken on more importance since World War II.[39] The best-known work has been that by Dollard, and later by Hunt, Kogan, and others, conducted under the auspices of the Community Service Society of New York. The study of Hunt and Kogan, *Measuring Results in Social Case Work: A Manual on Judging Movement* (1950),[40] though wide in scope, marks only a beginning toward evaluative research. It measures movement in the clients as between two points of time, without trying to measure the effectiveness of casework service. A follow-up study has also been made.[41] Other studies in this field are: *Changing Attitudes Through Social Contact* (1951) by Festinger and Kelley;[42] *An Experiment in the Prevention of Delinquency* (1951) by Powers and Witmer;[43] and *Unravelling Juvenile Delinquency* (1950) by Sheldon and Eleanor Glueck.[44]

Evaluative research faces many obstacles that at times seem insuperable. Besides the problem of isolating and controlling many variables, there is the difficulty of developing adequate measuring devices and establishing the criteria to determine success or failure.

Research in social work education received an impetus through the Hollis-Taylor Study (1951). A new study of the social work curriculum is now in process under the aegis of the Council on Social Work Education. Directed by Dr. Werner Boehm, it is broad in its conception and will deal with social policy as well as with the social work method. The study is also taking into account the new sources of knowledge from the social sciences, the emerging trends of needs, and the patterns of service. The study faces several difficulties. It lacks as a starting point a definitive study of the nature and scope of social work practice. The plan is to utilize panels of experts in the various areas to establish judgments on present standards of practice. A fuller study of practice is, however, essential. The field must learn more about the various functions of the social worker so as to be able to determine whether all social work functions call for two years of training or whether some call for less and others for more. Is it possible, within a two-year program of social work education, to prepare a worker for all potential functions, or should there be continued schooling as one moves up the scale of responsibility? Even though social work wants to avoid training for a specific function and wants to train for continued growth, it needs answers to such questions about practice before it can study curriculum successfully.

It should be obvious that all of these new areas of research in social work overlap. It would be easier to get at the problems of results if we had a more systematic knowledge of practice, and vice versa. Research in curriculum and training would be simplified if there were more systematic knowledge of both results and practice. Because of these complications there is the danger of oversimplification and of dealing with borrowed concepts which are clearly defined in their original context but may have a different meaning for social work. Says William E. Gordon: "It is to the formulation, development, testing and organization of social work concepts, the building blocks of social work knowledge, that social work research is ultimately destined and should now be orienting itself if it is to be social work and not some other kind of research." [45]

As social work seeks to improve its scientific approach it finds that its historical emphasis on goals presents difficulties for the researcher. Social work must apply scientific knowledge to a specific individual, group, or community; and in so doing it is involved not only in "what is" but also in what "should be." The goals are derived from certain fundamental values. "Research," says Klein, "can discover, expose, explain and gauge the activating forces in social work. It cannot and, therefore, should not attempt to prove their validity. . . . Research does not make the choice: its function is exposition. . . . The choice of goals on the other hand, the determination of acceptable social values, the fixing of ethical and aesthetic aspirations, these are the function of a will, even of irresponsible will." [46] To emphasize scientific objectivity at the expense of goals and values can make of social work something completely apart from its traditional intent and purpose. Scientific objectivity without relation to goals and values can result in a "preoccupation with techniques and gadgets as an end in themselves," in a "directionless and conscienceless scientism." Social work, to live up to its intent of being both scientific and social minded, must meet the challenge of helping to integrate the two. Social work is most honest to its tradition when it views itself as science at work in the furthering of human values.

The problem of values and science is coming to the attention of the social scientists too as they attempt to utilize the life situation as their laboratory. They are beginning to recognize that "neither the body of knowledge, nor the activities of its seekers, is morally neutral." This point of view is clearly expressed by Kolb:

First, we must recognize and fully accept the dual character of the relationship between the sociologist and the people whom he studies. In the past we have recognized the relationship as a purely cognitive one existing between observer and observed. . . . It is now necessary that we see this relation as existing in a second dimension as one between the social scientist as a human being and the observed as a human being. As such it must be governed by the moral norms which regulate all such relationships. At the core of these values in our civilization is the belief that we are obligated to love one another. Because the word love has been sentimentalized in our culture, we have frequently substituted such terms as respect for human dignity or regard for the infinite importance of the person; but all these terms have ultimate roots in the Greek-Hebrew-Christian moral tradition, and perhaps it is time that we recover our older vocabulary. This ultimate value of love and the norms to which it gives rise are morally binding on the relationship between the social scientist and the object of his study, constituting that object essentially a subject. They take precedence over the purely cognitive standards and limit the degree to which the latter can shape our actual scientific procedure.[47]

Social work deals with people, their hopes, their aspirations, and their frustrations. Values affect the aspirations of men and through them social change. "No science can argue a man into having good will, and it is frightening when intelligence . . . which has characterized liberal societies has been based on the assumption that there existed in society a fund of good manners, good sense, and common decency which made it possible for men to understand one another and to negotiate their differences peacefully. In its larger aspect, the present resurgence of interest in philosophies of history is an attempt to find a fund of public values, or an element of shared purpose or common destiny, which might give men a basis for understanding and voluntary cooperation." [48] Although values do not lend themselves to scientific research, however, the consequences of following one set of values instead of another can be studied. The ordering of values into rules of conduct on democratic disciplines, as developed by Lindeman, should prove helpful in testing the consequences of the values under which social work operates.[49]

SCOPE OF SERVICES

The social breakdown following a war creates a demand not only for the intensification and expansion of existing services but also for the development of new ones. There has been, relatively speaking, a great expansion in mental health services and programs in both the private and public fields since the war. Increased attention has also been given to juvenile delinquency. This includes research and demonstration projects on how to work with gangs and the hard-to-reach groups. A good example of the expansion of efforts on problems growing out of the war is seen in the field of rehabilitation. Congress passed the Federal Vocational Rehabilitation Act in 1920. "A continually increased effort has been made to close the gap between the national need and the services which can be applied to it, but only during the past three or four years has there been a nationwide expansion in facilities, equipment, research, training and appropriations." [50] The field of probation, corrections, and parole is another in which research and demonstration are going on at an increased pace. Social workers have also entered the international field on a relatively large scale.

These new areas of activity have created new problems for social work. One is the growing shortage in trained personnel. For example, a study dealing with "Mobilization and Health Manpower," made for the Office of Defense Mobilization in 1956, reported that ". . . there are in the United States today an estimated 2,000,000 persons of employable age who need rehabilitation services. In addition to these 2,000,000 . . . there are hundreds of thousands of physically handicapped and chronically ill children of pre-school and school age. It has been universally recognized that the greatest single bottle-neck in the extension of services to these groups, is the lack of sufficient trained professional personnel." [51]

Another problem is the reluctance of agencies to seek new patterns of service. While the last few years have seen a trend toward greater integration and cooperation between agencies on the local and national levels, the agencies themselves have been slow to adjust their programs to changing needs. Thus there is a growing awareness that the answer to the problem of mental health and other unmet social needs will not be found merely in the increase of staffs and in the multiplication and extension of our present programs. Yet our social agencies, which took on their character in earlier generations, have lagged in taking care of the new functions. They often fail to recognize that "social agencies, like other institutions, need to change in sensitive association with the changing needs of society." The tendency is to expand and multiply the present prototypes. As Titmuss states:

The forces of the past in terms of how we live together in society create new situations; if the structure and functions of the social services cling too closely to the needs of the age when they originated, and if the interests which resist change become too powerful, these services will not meet the needs of the new situations. We shall not achieve a better balance between the needs of today and the resources of today by living out the destinies of tradition; by simply attending to the business of the State. Without knowledge of wind and current, without some sense of purpose, men and societies do not keep afloat for long, morally or economically, by baling out the water.[52]

A good example of this lag is the difficulty social work faces in meeting newly emerging programs in probation, corrections, and parole, and in rehabilitation. In both of these areas the traditional role and function of the social worker is being tested and challenged. In the former, the use of social work methods in a legally defined authoritative setting demands new attention, and points up the extent to which social work has ignored the importance of the setting as a part of treatment and has restricted itself for the most part to "deliberative" treatment. The agency has become to some extent a housing unit for individual practitioners, and the meaning of the agency qua agency, in the total process of treatment, has lost its significance. The recent work of sociologists on agency structure and its meaning for staff and clientele is providing a new dimension for understanding and dealing with behavior. It tends to give point to the view that behavior is a function not only of the individual and his unconscious drives but also of the individual in relation to his social institutions.

Rehabilitation in some respects is not so much a new field as a newly revived pattern for organizing existing services to meet a special need. Interestingly enough, social work helped create the vacuum that necessitated this new approach of coordinating services around the individual case. The community organization societies had originally performed this coordinating function until the field became more specialized, and they had to make a choice between coordination and direct service. When they chose the direct service and became the family agencies as we know them today, the coordinating function was taken over by the councils of social agencies. These councils, however, coordinated agencies only in relation to planning general resources to meet general needs. The task of coordinating services around an individual case was left to each agency through a system of referrals, and the individual frequently became lost in the referral procedure. In this field social work, while pushing toward new goals, is also relearning old techniques.

Another new problem, illustrated by the emerging program of rehabilitation, is that the role of the social worker is not so clearly defined as in the more orthodox settings such as the guidance clinic and the hospital. Part of this stems from the conflict with the psychologist, whose role in treatment is expanding, and part of it from the confusion of being thrown into new and still undefined situations. With an increasing number of clients being returned to the community, the social worker is being called upon to help evaluate readiness because of his knowledge of both the individual and the community. Is the family, for example, ready to absorb the individual? What will the return do to the family constellation? What kind of work must be done with the family during the period of readjustment? Are there essential community resources available and if not, how can such resources be developed? In brief, a stimulating new role and function seem to be evolving for the social worker—one that calls for an integration of knowledge and skills around both the individual and the social institutions. The new situation also contains the potential of an empirical, rather than a theoretical, approach to social policy. If resources are not available, the need must be interpreted in the light of best available knowledge whether it should be met through the resources of the local community, the state, or the federal government. On the basis of empirical data, a social action program can be built.

Social workers tend to resist their new role, however, and prefer to keep using the more orthodox conception of the social worker's function and responsibility on the team. In this connection, it might be well to keep in mind A. N. Whitehead's observation on the professions:

Each profession makes progress but it is progress in its own groove. Serious thought is confined to a narrow range of facts and experiences; the remainder of life is treated superficially. The fixed person for the fixed duties, who in older societies was such a godsend, in the future will be a public menace. The dangers arising from this aspect of professionalism are particularly great in democratic societies.[53]

PROFESSIONAL RESOURCES

A comprehensive study, made in 1950, estimated the social work force in the United States at 75,000. Of the 75,000 the largest single group, 30,000, was in public assistance. Of the other 45,000 all but a small percentage were engaged in direct services through casework and group work. The remainder were in community organization and teaching. Social work was still predominantly a woman's profession, approximately 70 per cent of the workers being women. There were more men than women, however, in the fields of probation and parole, group work, and community organization and in administrative positions. About 50 per cent of the workers had some graduate education, and a third did not have a college degree. Workers in mental hygiene programs had the most formal educational preparation, and workers in public programs on the state and local levels the least. Approximately 85 per cent of the social workers lived in urban areas whereas only 57 per cent of the general population lived in such areas.[54] The salaries for men were generally higher than those for women, but this difference was perhaps due more to the types of positions held than to a sex differential. The average salaries in social work compared favorably with those of nurses, librarians, dieticians, and teachers, which, however, were not high in the general competitive market. There were wide variations in social work salaries depending upon types of positions, fields, auspices of services, and geographical location.

The shortage of professionally trained personnel remains a problem:

A study published by the Council on Social Work Education shows that the social work profession is confronted with the worst personnel shortage in its history. . . . Between 125,000 and 150,000 social workers will be needed by 1965 to fill positions in public and voluntary agencies across the country. They will not be available. The study shows that in spite of the growth in the number of schools of social work the need for these workers has outdistanced the supply.[55]

The shortage can be attributed to several factors. With the expansion of the economy following the war and the increased emphasis on business, industry, and the physical sciences, the helping professions have been faced with difficulty in the competition for manpower. One of the key factors is the differential in salaries. In 1956 a comparison of social work salaries in the field of rehabilitation with salaries in fields which do not demand college training revealed the following:

Social workers	$4,600
Railroad conductors	$7,681
Railroad brakemen	$6,239
Tool and die makers	$5,574
Automobile manufacturing	$5,400 [56]

There is a telling comparison with salaries in other professions such as law, medicine, chemistry, chemical engineering, and accountancy, several of which do not require any more training than the two years of study beyond the B.A. degree required for social work. There is no question that if social work is to attract the necessary trained personnel, salary levels must be improved.

Any improvement in these matters rests ultimately on public opinion as to the relative worth of social work. While it is important that educational standards in the profession be raised (and better salary schedules can be used to achieve these ends), an improved educational level per se is not enough to elicit higher salaries and attract qualified students to the field. The public must be kept informed; indeed, it needs to be brought abreast of the progress which social workers have already made in establishing a profession.[57]

Another factor in the personnel shortage is the increasing cost of social work education, which is becoming one of the most expensive types of professional training. A recent study on "Scholarship Aid in Social Work Education" by Milton Wittman, reported the following:

1. Because of the high tuition costs, three out of four social work students now receive some form of scholarship assistance. Otherwise they would be unable to complete their graduate studies.
2. Fifty-six per cent of the students come from families with incomes below $5,000 a year.
3. More than a third of the students attending graduate schools of social work are married and have family obligations.
4. The students' share in the cost of their education ranges between $1,600 and $2,000 a year.
5. Social agencies, public and private, are spending more than $1,250,000 annually in the form of scholarship assistance. The grants range from under $500 to over $2,000.[58]

In view of the level of salaries and the high cost of social work education, increased scholarship assistance will be necessary from both public and private sources if the estimated shortage is to be met even partially.

The question of shortage is also tied up with the professional idea of the nature of the social work job in public assistance. Approximately 40 per cent of the total social work force is engaged in public assistance. From the time of the expansion of this program in 1934-1935 the question has been raised with more grinding insistence: How much time and money should be spent in determining eligibility for economic dependency, how much professional service would be offered to meet problems of emotional dependency? In brief, was the provision of relief within a given legal structure the primary function of the agency, or was relief only a tool in dealing with the total individual and his problems? The implications are broad. Thus, the question of whether or not all public welfare jobs necessitate two years of graduate training—aside from whether or not the program can ever afford this level of trained personnel—has not been clarified to this day. There are two schools of thought; one contends that the use of professionally trained staff throughout would, because of their understanding and handling of the basic problems, help to reduce the size of the case loads; the other points out that problems of economic dependency are not necessarily symptoms of emotional dependency, and that the job can best be accomplished through the concentration of professionally trained staff at such selective points as intake, supervision, special projects, and special case loads involving problems of emotional dependency. Thus a large part of the staff would only require a brief period of training, which would include less emphasis on treatment skills and greater focus on the special problems of a legal, economic, administrative, and psychological nature inherent in the setting. The same conflicting points of view are represented in discussions concerning the training program for the professional staff in the public welfare agency. Those who support the first view place primary emphasis on "core" methods, and contend that enough could be learned through field work placement, a basic course in public welfare, and a program of in-service training at the time of assuming the job to take care of the special problems of setting. The others, however, feel that the setting involves a special cluster of problems, demanding use of the basic principles and many of the skills taught in the "core disciplines" but within a context of social policy rather than psychological adjustment. Therefore they see the need for a sequence of courses in public welfare which would adapt the material of the "core disciplines" within this framework, and abstract problems of an administrative, supervisory, program, and policy nature for special consideration.

The answer to such important questions as these can only be found through an adequate study of practice. The field is aware of the need and is searching for an appropriate way to tackle the problem. The commission on practice of the National Association of Social Workers has projected a program over a five-year period which includes the following tasks:

1. To develop a working definition of social work practice to better enable the Commission to
   a. study and describe the nature and scope of social work practice;
   b. develop a base in setting standards;
   c. test any particular unit or segment of practice.
2. To study the trends, issues and problems relating to social work practice.
3. To study the use of personnel without graduate training to supplement and extend social work services.

Such a study may also shed light on another difficult problem, namely, the role of the volunteer. The volunteer has played an important part in the development of social work since its inception. It was through the volunteers' efforts that the organized health and welfare agencies were established in the latter half of the nineteenth century. As they brought first paid workers and then professionally trained staff into the agencies a conflict arose as to the role of the professional versus that of the volunteer. While volunteers were freely admitted to board and committee functions and fund-raising responsibilities, there was disagreement concerning the degree to which they should participate in the giving of services. Beginning in the thirties an organized effort was made to establish a pattern of collaboration among professionals and volunteers. Standards for volunteers were developed, types of services which they might render in the various functional fields outlined, and training programs established. During World War II numerous volunteer bureaus were created and the program for volunteers broadened. Although today there are literally millions of volunteers participating in the programs of social work throughout the nation, with the rapid trend toward professionalization in all areas of social work the role of the volunteer still lacks clarity.

FINANCIAL RESOURCES

The expansion of social welfare services under government auspices since 1934-1935 has raised the question of how much social welfare the nation can afford. Some critics have also suggested that the United States is drifting toward a welfare state. What has been the financial status of welfare over the past decade? The combined expenditures for civilian public programs such as social insurance and public assistance, public health and medical services, vocational rehabilitation, child welfare, veterans' pensions, and medical care, education, and public housing for the year 1954-1955 was approximately $32.5 billion. Compared with the expenditures for 1934-1935, which were approximately $7.9 billion, the total dollar cost of civilian programs has increased about four and one-half times. Adjustments must be made, however, for the change in price level and for the increase in population during this period. As Ida Merriam observes,[59] with an increase of 30 per cent in the total population and prices almost doubling during this period, "most of the programmes would have spent more money merely to maintain the same level of service per capita," and "a larger dollar outlay has been required for the same level of service." Miss Merriam suggests that a more accurate gauge is "social welfare expenditures as percentage of gross national product," since it reflects such factors as program development, population growth, price change, and improved levels of program adequacy. Utilizing this measure, she compares social welfare expenditures for selected fiscal years between 1934-1935 and 1954-1955 (see the table on page 302).

Thus when welfare expenditures are measured in relation to the gross national product there has been a decrease from 11.5 per cent in 1934-1935 to 8.7 per cent in 1954-1955. The

high figure in 1934-1935 can be explained, according to Miss
Merriam, "in part because national output had fallen sharply
and in part because of the emergency relief programmes, designed to mitigate and correct that situation." She attributes
the drop to 3.6 per cent in 1944-1945 to the "tremendous expansion in the output directed to war purposes." If one uses
1939-1940 as a base, there still has been a decrease from 9.6
per cent to 8.7 per cent.

SOCIAL WELFARE EXPENDITURES AS PERCENTAGE OF GROSS NATIONAL
PRODUCT, SELECTED FISCAL YEARS 1934–35—1954–55 [60]

Fiscal year	Gross national product (millions of dollars)	SOCIAL WELFARE EXPENDITURES AS PERCENTAGE OF GROSS NATIONAL PRODUCT						
		Total	Social insurance	Public aid	Health and medical services	Education	Other Welfare services	Veterans' programs
1934–35	68,700	11.5	0.6	5.9	0.9	3.2	0.2	0.7
1939–40	95,700	9.6	1.3	3.8	0.8	2.9	0.1	0.6
1944–45	218,300	3.6	0.6	0.5	0.5	1.6	0.1	0.4
1949–50	263,000	9.0	1.8	0.9	0.8	2.8	0.2	2.5
1952–53	357,900	7.4	1.8	0.8	0.8	2.6	0.2	1.2
1953–54	359,700	8.1	2.3	0.8	0.8	2.8	0.3	1.1
1954–55	373,100	8.7	2.7	0.8	0.9	2.9	0.2	1.2

In the private voluntary field figures are not so readily
available. The increase for the period 1929 to 1954 has been
approximately from $1.2 to $5.4 billion. These figures, however, include giving for religious purposes and, furthermore,
are not adjusted for change in price level. Miss Merriam estimates that approximately $2.8 billion in 1954 went to religious
organizations. Although there has been an increase in the
amount of funds raised by the private voluntary agencies, there
is no question that public moneys are providing an increasing
proportion of the total expenditures for social services. Professor Burns, in a paper presented at the National Conference
of Social Work in May 1954,[61] estimated that more than 90 per

cent of all welfare expenditures in the nation were for public programs.

A further analysis of public expenditures during this period, however, reveals that the largest growth has been in veterans' benefits, which have increased approximately tenfold. There has been a sharp decline in public aid and little change in civilian health and medical services. According to Professor Burns,[62] the major part of the growth in public social service expenditures can be accounted for by veterans' programs, social insurance, and public assistance. Only 1 per cent of the national income is being devoted to all other types of public welfare which, as Professor Burns points out, is a far cry from a welfare state. Professor Haber raises the moral issue:

Several elementary aspects of social welfare costs should be emphasized at the outset. A rather substantial proportion of what we spend for welfare—social security, public assistance, social services— are not items about which we have much choice. These expenditures cannot readily be evaded. We must provide for the aged who are in need, for the jobless whose incomes have ceased, for the ill and the disabled, for the veterans and their families. These obligations have had a high priority in our scheme of values throughout our history. Whether we can afford such expenditures is hardly a pertinent question.[63]

How much social welfare the nation can afford seems to be tied up as much with our attitude toward the place of welfare services in our society as with the economic question. Most economists agree that the constant growth of our national income will continue. If this rate continues, Ida Merriam estimates[64] that the gross national product will be about $425 billion by 1960, and if the present ratio of social welfare expenditures continues they will increase by $8 billion by 1960. The task, therefore, is an educational one, in which the private voluntary agencies have as much of a stake and responsibility as the public agencies. A change in attitude toward the responsibility of government in meeting our large areas of unmet needs will also bring a better understanding of social work in general. Furthermore, it will provide a greater opportunity for the private voluntary agencies to pioneer and set new sights and new standards.

BODY OF KNOWLEDGE

The developments in social science and research growing out of the war are having their impact on the body of knowledge underlying social work theory and practice. The demands of the war brought the social scientists close to the life situation, for they were called upon by the government to apply their research methods to everyday problems of human relations. As Dorwin Cartwright reports: "Practical problems of social engineering sprang up overnight which required solutions before lunch. Many of these problems were tackled by social psychologists; many by psychologists who had not thought of themselves as experts in the field; many were undertaken by social scientists from other academic disciplines." [65] Cartwright observes further that although social psychologists had dealt with social events and behavior prior to the war, the war provided new access to social groups and sufficient funds to study "real" social behavior.

Not only are the social sciences reflecting a dynamic new interest in the everyday plans of man, but they are also developing a greater feeling of interdependence.

Both in theory and practice, the social sciences are moving steadily in the direction of cooperation and integration. . . . The whole trend of twentieth century science is plainly toward integration, a fact indicated in the very names of the new disciplines: Psychosomatic Medicine, Biochemistry, Psychobiology and the like. The integrative movement in the social sciences derives further significance from this state of affairs. Our knowledge of the parts has now reached a stage when we can begin to seek a "holistic" understanding of larger wholes. Possessing now an anatomy of our various subjects, so to speak, we can begin to see the functioning physiology and relationships of these structures. Science, too, is discovering that there is only "one world." [66]

Social work, as one of the utilizers of social science knowledge in its work with individuals, groups, and communities, is feeling this impact. As social psychology, sociology, anthropology, economics, and political science thin out their boundaries and move more and more toward an interdisciplinary approach, social work is beginning to look more sharply at its own emphasis. It is beginning to re-examine the three dimensions essential to any theory and method for dealing with problems of human relations, namely, the individual or the psychological dimension; the social institutions through which the individual functions, or the sociological dimension; and the goals and values through which the individual orders his life, or the philosophical dimension. There is growing recognition that the challenge of the period is not merely to amass knowledge in all three areas but also to discover ways of integrating this knowledge for prevention as well as remedy.

Toward this goal, the Russell Sage Foundation is trying to create a group of "social engineers" to help bridge the gap between research in the social sciences and its use in the applied fields. Such an engineering pattern exists for the physical sciences but has been lacking in the case of the behavioral sciences. Through this program funds have been made available to schools of social work to employ social scientists on their faculties. The social scientists, with the help of their social work colleagues, are trying to introduce new elements into social work knowledge and also to learn more about social work for purposes of new research. Schools of social work have also stepped up their programs of training for research, especially in the advanced curriculum. Several schools have developed research centers. Students in the advanced programs are being required to take work in the basic social sciences and in research method in addition to their studies in practice. With their previous grounding in social work training and experience, and with the additional studies in social work, the social sciences, and research, they should be in a good position to help bridge the gap between social work and the social sciences and to contribute to basic research. Another important factor is that the teaching personnel for social work is being drawn more and more from the group who should be in a position to bring into their teachings the benefits of the closer integration with the social sciences and basic research.

Social work has moved far since the days of its humanitarian beginnings. The split that divided the early humanitarians, however, is still reflected in social work ranks. At times social work has veered toward emphasis on the environment, and at other times toward emphasis on the individual. The fluctuation of emphasis and the difficulty in integrating the two-pronged concern with which the humanitarians began can be attributed both to contemporary economic, political, and social demands and to the absence of essential knowledge. Of late social work has been accused of making professionalism an end in itself. To understand better the direction that social work has taken, it may be helpful to look more closely at historical developments within two contexts, namely, the dominant philosophical themes in the American scene, and the emergence of the trained specialist and the professional to service the increasingly complex society that has accompanied industrialization.

9

DOMINANT THEMES
IN THE
PHILOSOPHY OF
SOCIAL WORK

We have seen the growth and development of America's economic, political, social, and scientific heart, body, and mind in the various periods in American life. No period has stood alone; rather, each has been an episode in a continuous story of people and how they fared as the nation grew, developed, and changed. The story concerns not only the individual but also the collective efforts of people and their changing attitudes toward the needs and rights of others as well as themselves in the nation's struggle to fulfill its democratic aims.

The attitude toward people, toward human rights as contrasted with property rights, has been an area of concern and conflict in each period. Groups have differed both in the definition of the objective and in the means of achieving it. Thus there has been no consistent social philosophy, showing steady growth from period to period; rather elements of conflicting philosophies have been present in each period. At times, one point of view has represented the dominant theme, only to be replaced by another dominant theme at other times.

Social work, whose main concern is people, has been an integral part of the economic, political, social, and scientific atmosphere of these various stages in American history. It, too, has not had a consistent philosophy, and has tended to reflect the divergent themes present in the society as a whole. At times, it has been part of the rebellion against the prevailing theme, at times, a reflection of it, and at still other times it has appeared to ignore the philosophical climate and to escape into the technical and the practical. Social work has begun to realize the importance of the social climate, however, for it has discovered that the existing atmosphere tends to have a decisive impact on the objectives and methods of social work itself. It may be helpful, therefore, to review its past and present within the context of these dominant and conflicting themes in American life.

Early in the nation's history, before the impact of the industrial revolution, the dominant theme was political democracy. Economic and social affairs belonged outside the political realm. Political democracy reached deep into the works of Hobbes and Locke for its ideas. It was a liberal philosophy predicated on man's ability to govern himself and to agree collectively on and "observe common rules for the sake of certain definite advantages such as the preservation of life and the protection of property." [1] Basic to political democracy was its belief in parliamentary institutions and civil liberties; through such a structure the ever-present competition for social power was to be controlled and democratized rather than abolished. As Frankel observes:

Liberalism inherited from Thomas Hobbes the belief that the struggle for power is the persisting fact about political life, and it is a belief which has remained a fundamental assumption for the long line of liberal writers on politics, from John Locke to James Mill to Bertrand Russell to so recent an exponent of the philosophy of American liberalism as Professor J. K. Galbraith. Competition for power cannot be eliminated from human affairs; there is no perfect society which can guarantee that one man's interest will never collide with the interest of another man. The pursuit of a just society, therefore, is not the pursuit of an absolute which, when attained, will allow a liberal social movement to close up shop. The business of liberalism is a recurrent one—to correct imbalances of power and to organize social institutions in such a way that no one has too much power.[2]

This conception of political democracy, with its accompanying laissez-faire economic and social philosophy, had meaning in a rural economy where institutions like the family, the church, and the school were primary and played an important role in shaping the values of American life. The economy consisted of numerous small units with limited power. Large industries and controlling corporations lay in the future and unforeseen. Government too was decentralized in autonomous local units. In such an atmosphere not much government was required to keep the rules and to insure the liberties of the individual. Furthermore, it was sincerely believed that if the individual's liberties were not interfered with and if he could fend for himself, he would find ample resources to meet his basic economic needs of food, clothing, and shelter. In a land of endless opportunity only the lazy or morally weak would fail. Opportunities to succeed existed in the society if only the individual had the perseverance, industriousness, and shrewdness to find them.

The attitude toward pauperism reflected the prevailing philosophy, and the method for dealing with it stemmed not from the political liberalism of government but from the chief source of a philosophy of man's responsibility to man in social affairs, namely, the church. There was no scientifically defined method of dealing with people in trouble. The approach can best be described as moralistic and punitive. Since these people were regarded as morally weak, the answer to their problem could best be found in religious teachings. In accordance with Calvinistic philosophy, it was the moral self-controlling center of consciousness that needed strengthening. These individuals were reflecting the evil and sinfulness inherent in human nature, and the only way to remove evil and sinfulness was through pain and punishment.

In its narrowest sense the giving of alms was viewed as an obligation in the struggle for salvation. Emphasis was placed on the effect of giving on the soul of the giver rather than on what it did for the recipient. As religion received a broader interpretation, however, a distinction emerged between giving alms for personal salvation and helping people to change their ways. A distinction began to be drawn between deserving and undeserving misfits. The deserving, or more deserving, were those who had run into difficulty because of conditions beyond their control. This group included the widow, the orphan, the disabled, the aged, and so forth. The undeserving, on the other hand, were those who were victims of their own presumed moral weakness. This group included the criminal, the able-bodied unemployed, the alcoholic, the unmarried mother, and so forth. The methods of dealing with these two groups differed. In the case of the deserving, charity could be given without fear of destroying their moral character. In the case of the undeserving, however, the giving of charity without punishment and moral correction might encourage their moral defectiveness.

Nineteenth-century urbanization and industrialization brought many political, economic, and social problems. The nation had grown and changed so rapidly that its ability to function as a whole was constantly challenged. Civil war seemed to be the inevitable answer. After the war the growth toward unity was accelerated. As the nation developed, however, its eighteenth-century ideology no longer seemed adequate to guide it toward the objective of the priority of human rights over material rights; toward the realization of the self-evident truth that all men are created equal and endowed by their Creator with the unalienable right to life, liberty, and the pursuit of happiness. In a society that was becoming increasingly organic, the times called for a philosophy that recognized not only the importance of liberty and independence but also of social responsibility and interdependence. In Bertrand Russell's words:

. . . modern techniques make society more organic in the sense that its parts are more interdependent and an injury to one individual or group is more likely than it formerly was to cause injury to other individuals or groups. It is easier to kill a man than to kill a sponge because he is more highly organized and more centralized. In like manner it is easier to inflict vital damage upon a scientific community than a community of nomads or scattered peasants. This increase of interdependence makes it necessary to limit freedom in various ways which liberals in the past considered undesirable. There are two spheres in which such limitation is especially necessary: the one is in economics; and the other in the relations between states.[3]

With the emphasis on civil liberty, and without equal attention to civil and economic rights, one man's liberty was too frequently at the expense of another's freedom.

The nineteenth century was, in many respects, a turbulent one. As Frankel tells us:

. . . it had its revolutions, its riots in the streets, its outbreak of unreason, its dissolute ruling classes and its disoriented masses. It had its hard creeds and its insipid skepticism. Intellectually, technologically, sociologically, it was the period of speediest and profoundest change that the West had seen up to that time; everything from the relation of man to God to the relations between the sexes was altered. Old classes were disinherited, old skills displaced, old beliefs discredited; new classes emerged, a new public sensibility, a new education, a new kind of reading and writing, a new kind of town and a new kind of countryside.[4]

The American people struggled to keep democracy alive in this period of cataclysmic change. Three times during the century they were successful in electing a champion of the rights of the common man—Jefferson in 1800, Jackson in 1828, and Lincoln in 1860. Their attempt in 1896 to elect Bryan failed, but the groundwork was laid for success in the early decades of the twentieth century. The period witnessed marked changes in social philosophy.

Humanistic liberalism, with its emphasis on man's ability to control his fate by reason, opened new philosophical vistas. Man could not only control his own fate but also collectively could build a "brave new world." It was a point of view with man rather than God as the center of reference. Social arrangements could be understood in secular terms and man, through his rational powers, could be sufficiently objective to develop and utilize both physical and social science to shape his destiny. The potentialities of man were boundless when approached in terms not of what he was but of what he could become if dealt with justly and creatively and if given equal opportunity for life, liberty, and the pursuit of happiness. Man's collective efforts, his social institutions, could also be reformed and improved through the due process of "deliberately instituted legislative, judicial and administrative techniques, and by the piecemeal reconstruction of human institutions—and not by spiritual conversions, moral appeals for a change of heart or the sudden intervention of external powers." [5]

Humanistic liberalism did not accept economic determinism, as projected by Karl Marx, or the rugged individualism of Social Darwinism, as developed by Herbert Spencer and promulgated on the American scene by William Graham Sumner. It had abiding faith in the philosophy of consciousness advanced by Descartes. The pragmatism that emerged on the American scene was a practical philosophy for a practical nation and combined a concern for human values with an interest in science. Unlike the philosophy of Spencer, it did not deny idealism in the name of science and, unlike that of Hegel, it did not deny science in the name of idealism.

Religion also reflected the economic and sociological changes of the day, and shifted from the theologically centered approach to a more pragmatic one. The acceptance by humanistic liberalism of "the goodness of man" as a premise, in contrast to the view that evil and sinfulness are inherent in human nature, provided a positive atmosphere for social reform. "Good works" as well as prayer became important. Religious groups moved with zeal to reform the society as well as the individual.

In this atmosphere one phase of modern social work was incubated: namely, its interest in social reform and social policy. There was a growing recognition that many of man's problems could be traced to his environment rather than to moral inadequacy. Environmental reform became the order of the day. "Reform the environment in the service of the individual" was the battle cry. The method proposed was to use the knowledge of the social sciences, especially sociology, to tackle social problems and legislative channels to eliminate the ills. The first great leaders of the National Conference of Charities and Corrections, Bruno points out, acted on the tacit assumption that human ills (sickness, insanity, crime, poverty, and so forth) could be subjected to study and that methods of treatment and prevention could be formulated. They did not feel that social ills were the result of sin or fate, nor that they existed to provide one's fellow man with the opportunity to exercise charity. Their acceptance of the positive premise of the "goodness of man"—and his potentialities for change—provided an atmosphere for social reform.

It is not inevitable that a culture in which the belief in original sin is dominant will be harsher to children, more vindictive toward criminals, more unbending and unrealistic in its moral demands. . . . But when the doctrine of the goodness of man arose, it arose to combat an idea which had also been used in support of ruthlessness, intolerance and cruelty. When liberals talked about the goodness of man they were attempting to make education more responsive to the needs of children, to convert the treatment of lunacy from a scourging of devils into a medical art, to make penology something more than an exercise in sadism.[6]

This period in social work is sometimes described as focusing on cause, as contrasted with the focus on function that began to evolve in the latter part of the century through the efforts of the charity organization society movement. This distinction is oversimplified; for function—that is, a mode of action in which purpose is fulfilled—existed within the social reform approach, just as social objectives exist in the present-day context of social work. The social objectives today may be narrower or different; but Mary Richmond, in her search for a way of helping people, was just as cause-oriented as was Jane Addams.

The newly emerging techniques and methods, which were to reach fuller bloom in the early decades of the twentieth century, must also be viewed within the context of industrialization. "In general, advancing industrialization first moves people out of the primary industries' which extract or produce raw materials . . . into 'secondary industries' which convert raw materials into finished products. . . . At an advanced stage, industrialization then moves people out of both primary and secondary into tertiary industries . . . service professions and occupations of all kinds, from physicians and social workers to beauticians and television repair service man." [7] Social work was becoming one of the "tertiary industries," requiring specialized talents. This shift was marked by the introduction of the paid worker in the last two decades of the nineteenth century.

Between 1900 and World War I, the seeds sown by humanistic liberalism in the latter part of the nineteenth century began to bear fruit. First, in the administration of Theodore Roosevelt, and more fully in that of Woodrow Wilson, the concept of the use of government as a positive tool in furthering the welfare of people began to take shape. The more organized nature of society and its growing interdependence was being increasingly recognized. The principles and faith of democracy were being extended to our concepts of individualism and humanitarianism. We were moving from the earlier notion of aid as charity toward a new interpretation of needs, rights, and responsibility in a democratic society. Progressive forces, including political groups, labor, independents, and social workers, joined together in social action for bettering the health, living, and working conditions of the people. Government was becoming concerned about human rights as well as property rights.

Social work continued its interest in social reform; but at the same time it began to evolve a new method of approach to the individual that reflected the philosophy of pragmatism. It was an attempt to place the emerging scientific knowledge and approach within the framework of the new emphasis on human values. It rejected Utopian idealism, on the one hand, and rigid mores, laws, and traditions, on the other. It was moving toward a method of helping people that followed rational processes and permitted prediction and control.

The number of paid workers increased considerably during the first two decades of the century. Vocational training for social work began to develop, and it was a short step from the emergence of social work as a specialized talent to an interest in professional status and standards. Social work chose the medical profession as its model, for reasons described by Wilensky and Lebaux:

The nature of the claim to technical competence varies—with each profession emphasizing the distinctive features of its own background. Medicine, since its "reform" in the United States some fifty years ago, has emphasized its roots in a scientific body of knowledge along with high, rigorously defined and enforced standards of training designed to impart that body of knowledge. Contrast the ministry. It, too, stresses rigorous standards of training. But clearly it does not claim possession of a science-based body of knowledge (though its doctrines are well codified and systematized). It is medicine and not the ministry that has become the preferred model for social work, and a close relationship has developed between them.[8]

The fact that social work modeled its profession on medicine can perhaps be traced to its embracement of pragmatic philosophy, its early contacts with the medical profession through medical and psychiatric social work, and its interest in the theory and method of the newly emerging mental hygiene movement and psychiatry.

Social work was beginning to feel the impact of the new psychiatry. The Freudian approach, however, was not yet dominant. Mary Richmond, in her theories of social casework, leaned more heavily on the work and writings of Adolph Meyer, who had projected a philosophy of social psychiatry, than on the teachings of Freud. Meyer saw clearly the "interrelationships of the individual and the pathology of society," and in this sense, his approach came closer than Freud's to social work's interest in integrating its experience in social reform with its newly emerging approach to the individual. It was a philosophy that preserved the "social" in social work.

Following World War I the nation subsided into disillusionment, reaction, and despair. In search of a cure-all, it resisted taking the steps toward which the social philosophy of the previous decades had propelled it. Paralyzed by momentous decisions, and lacking the leadership to look ahead, it looked back, not to gain understanding, but rather to recapture a "normalcy" that was already history and, in the present, could only represent fantasy.

The United States had fought a war to make the world safe for democracy only to discover the real problems of the world and their meaning for it as a nation. It was faced with seeing itself as an integral part of the changing world and its problems and playing a leadership role in meeting these problems. The nation chose isolation instead, for it knew that to provide such leadership meant a change in its own social philosophy. It had joined in a fight between the family of nations and discovered that many of them contained "the sources of infection for Socialism and Communism." It did not want to acknowledge them as members of the family and ran from them as if from a plague, forgetting that the same forces that were creating this change were also affecting America, and that it was only a matter of time before it too would have to face the same problems. The nation refused to accept the growing interdependence of the world even though it had made some strides toward accepting the interdependence of its own various parts.

In this atmosphere of reaction, escape, and insecurity, social work turned inward. With social reform out of fashion or politically dangerous, social work turned to working more intensively with the individual and to sharpening its technical skill. It was not an easy task, for it was a period of structural immorality and not just a problem of the individual. There was a general collapse of values and the well-established patterns of action for social good seemed to be obliterated. The family as a social institution was breaking down and divorce and illegitimacy were on the increase. Speculation and gambling were seen as short-cuts to financial success and became a substitute for hard work and thrift. Moral laxness was the order of the day.

As social workers were forced to wrestle with problems of character and conduct on a large scale, they turned to psychiatry for magical answers. Meanwhile psychiatry had also turned the spotlight onto the "individual actor" and away from the "scenery, chorus, audience, and orchestra" on which his performance depended. It had shifted from a "social psychiatry" to the narrower conception of the medical and the clinical.

In embracing Freudian psychiatry, social work was taking on not only a method of treatment but also a new theory, which was to have a bearing on its social philosophy. Freud utilized the experimental approach to probe into the very core of empiricism, namely, man's rational processes. He followed the pattern and principles established in the physical sciences to get at "the forces behind observable phenomena." The principle, as summarized by Fromm,[9] was:

. . . that not sensory experience nor common sense nor tradition is a guarantee of the truth; that to grasp reality—outside of man and within him—we must know the nature and direction of forces which are not directly visible, but which can be inferred from the visible phenomena they produce. . . . Marx showed that man's social systems, and even his thought and culture, are determined by social forces which operate behind his back, as it were. Freud completed the process by showing that the conscious thoughts man has about himself and others are only a small part of what goes on within him. What is more important, he showed that most of the acknowledged thoughts are products of fears and desires which are not acknowledged.

In one respect, Freud contributed to the objective and scientific approach by pointing out to man that he should be skeptical and seek the truth about his own thoughts, feelings, and acts in the same way that he sought truth about the world around him. In another respect, he contributed to a growing uneasiness about the potentialities of man to control his destiny through intellect and reason. Part of the disquiet stemmed from the tendency to assume that since the individual was the entrepreneur in all social endeavors the total answer to human behavior could be found in psychoanalytic theory. Reliance on psychoanalytic theory alone represented too simple an attempt to get at cause and effect through the single dimension of the psychological mechanisms of the individual, regardless of external realities. Mindlin has stated the problem clearly:

It is my feeling that much of the misunderstanding surrounding psychoanalysis stems from the fact that it is expected to furnish a total answer to human behavior, which it does not presume to do. . . . The significance of the influence of external reality upon the rational activities of the individual lies in other disciplines than psychoanalysis. Parenthetically, it might be added that unfortu-

nately some psychoanalysts themselves do not always fully appreciate
the nature of the subject matter in their chosen field, so that at
times they wander into strange pastures and express opinions in
areas beyond the province of their specialized competence and
knowledge. Because psychoanalysis has emphasized the importance of unconscious forces, it does not follow that they are the only
factors or, in a given situation, the predominant factors involved.
This is particularly true with regard to the application of psychoanalysis to related fields.[10]

Freud had applied his theories to a study of society and
culture as well as to the individual.

He believed that primitive man lived out his instinctual desires
without too much frustration by society, but that because of this
there was a great deal of mutual hostility, and thus a great deal of
insecurity, in life. Progress in civilization was essentially an increasing repression of man's instinctual desires. These repressions resulted
in sublimation, that is, the transformation of the libido into cul-
turally valuable aims which have no direct connection with the
original instinctual aims. Culture, according to Freud, is thus an
effect of sublimation. But many people lack the capacity for sublimation which is required by the rigid rules and taboos of many societies; the conflict between their instinctual forces and the social
requirements for repression produces neuroses.[11]

This view of society, as Fromm points out, was pessimistic; for it
implied that society was a postulate to which man must adjust.
It lent itself to the erroneous interpretation that changing the
individual was the equivalent of eventually changing the society.
Some social work circles began to equate a theory of adjustment with a social philosophy: If man faced the truth about
himself, he would automatically change "for the better."
Change "for the better," however, is a moral question and, in a
democracy, implies movement toward democratic values. There
is no assurance that this will happen in the process of psychoanalysis where the individual is the entrepreneur seeking relief
from pain and not necessarily in pursuit of democratic values.
He may become more independent and feel more comfortable
about it without necessarily developing the sense of interdependence so essential in a democracy. Within the narrow con-

ception of adjustment the individual may be able to get along with people and hold onto a job, and still retain his prejudices and undemocratic behavior.

Social work had turned to psychiatry for help in developing a method of dealing with the individual who was facing problems of maladjustment. It took over, however, more than a method of treatment! It took over also a view of the nature of man and his social arrangements. It saw personal anxieties and maladjustments as rooted in the individual and his psychological past to the neglect of "structural" maladjustment—that is, maladjustment rooted in "quite objective social disorders." Concern for social institutions was almost neglected in the naïve belief that if one worked with enough individuals the social institutions would indirectly improve.

By the thirties, however, the external realities of a depression were so dominant that the role of internal factors had to be minimized. The nation was faced with "structural" unemployment and was back to the basic economic problems of feeding, clothing, and sheltering a third of its population. It was a period of great suffering and want that could no longer afford the fantasy of "normalcy" or the luxury of a laissez-faire and palliative philosophy of economics. It was a time of uncertainty not only in economic theory but also in scientific thought and political philosophy.

In science the view that almost everything in the world moved according to unchangeable and predictable physical laws came under attack. The emergence of functionalism in the biological sciences and of relativity in the physical sciences raised questions about the mechanistic concept of cause and effect. J.W.N. Sullivan, writing of "The Mystery of Matter" in the *Atlantic Monthly* in May 1936, stated: "We cannot say what must be, but only what the chances are that any one thing must happen rather than any other shall happen."

The new scientific thinking had a sharp impact on psychology. There was a move away from a psychology of elements to a study of the relationships within the whole. Kurt Lewin applied the new Gestalt theory to problems of behavior. He emphasized the importance of viewing all factors including the future—the individual's aspirations—as well as the present and the past, as a whole in dealing with a given situation. This approach raised doubts about the emphasis on the past in Freudian theory. Some social psychologists held that even if one could find in the past the cause of a present situation, the new pattern had now developed into an energy system of its own. Psychoanalytic schools began to vary in the amount of emphasis placed on the past, the present, or the future.

In the realm of human affairs man began to lose his confidence in the answers of science. He had witnessed an expansion of scientific knowledge and yet his sense of security was not improved. The assumption that with those scientific advances we could provide enough food, clothing, and shelter to raise the standard of living was not borne out by his present plight. Some turned away from science for the answer. For them, "the central dream, the demonstration that everything in the world moved by mechanical means, that all evils could be cured by appropriate technological steps, that there could exist engineers both of human souls and of human bodies, proved delusive." [12] Man's nature and his social arrangements had to be reassessed. More recognition had to be given to man's "selfish" and "base" side, which had been lost from view when humanistic liberalism conceived of man as a creature of reason. The new psychoanalysis could provide a factual and formal base for the conception of man's inherent fallibility that had formerly been expressed in theological terms. In regard to man's social arrangements, too, they felt that humanistic liberalism had gone too far; there was a need for a rediscovery of final causes and divine purpose. It was a neo-Aristotelian approach—"the explanation of phenomena in terms of the 'natural' tendency of every object to fulfill its own inner end or purpose—which was also to be the answer to the question of why it existed, and what function it was attempting to fulfill—motives for which no experimental or observational evidence can in principle be discovered. . . ." [13]

Other groups, however, did not lose faith in science but

saw the problem as related to our social and political philosophy. Science was not an end in itself but rather a means to an end. The goals toward which scientific knowledge were to be utilized depended on the social philosophy of the society. The pertinent question was: "Knowledge for what?"

The entire world, engulfed by the same forces that were creating economic deprivation, fear, and uncertainty in America, groped for a social philosophy that might provide a solution. Some turned to communism, with its emphasis on economic determinism, and others to fascism, with its regression to the "strong man" or "fuehrer" principle. America sought a solution that would permit it to retain its traditional political democracy. It moved from the "trust-busting" liberalism of Theodore Roosevelt and Woodrow Wilson to a philosophy of "national economic planning." National government took on a new role, formalizing a change of concept that had been growing since the latter part of the nineteenth century. Government had moved into a positive and active concern for the public welfare.

Social work reflected the ideological revolution of the thirties and was forced to reexamine its philosophy and goals, its method, its program, and its educational philosophy. The treatment of the individual had increasingly become the core of the professional approach. Moreover, most of this treatment had been conducted under private voluntary auspices. Now government in response to the depression had begun to move into public welfare on a large scale, and social reform was again becoming a dominant theme.

Was social work to view the new role of government, which sought to meet the needs of people through planning and social policy, as a concrete expression of a dominant theme in American life, or as merely a passing phase? Was this emphasis on "structural" causation, on human problems as the result of "quite objective social disorders," in conflict with the philosophy of society as the Freudians saw it? Would the emphasis on social policy and social planning pull the social worker too far afield from his new-won professional base? Could social work be practiced in settings dealing with mass needs, or did these require a different kind of approach? Since government was now concerned with social policy, did it not free social work to return to its emphasis on the adjustment and development of the individual? Could it continue to pursue its interest both in social reform and in the treatment of the maladjusted individual as related but separate entities?

The conflicting views in social work were as intense as those in the nation as a whole. The social worker began to discover that even though he had become a professional, his views could not be divorced from the attitudes and social philosophy of the agencies that provided his services. In the same way that self-determination of the client was limited by the presence or absence of alternatives, so too the self-determination of the professional was limited by the reality of the agency and its point of view.

There was no question that the steps taken by government had democratized the concept of charity. The right of people to aid in time of need and the responsibility of government to prevent suffering had become matters of law. A basic tenet of social work had been incorporated into public policy. There still remained the question, however, of whether people receiving economic aid did not also need help with their emotional problems. True, their problems might have been created "structurally," but did they not need psychological help before they could move ahead again? If so, how much help? Was not the problem really deep-rooted and more than the result of "quite objective social disorders"? Was it not based in the early family life of the individual, and did it not therefore have to be dealt with in a modified, analytic way? In raising these questions was social work trying to reconcile the problem with its new-found methodology, or was it really attempting to supplement the "structural" approach with the psychological?

Although social policy and social planning became a dominant theme for social work during this period, the major questions outlined above were not resolved. They continued to be debated by social workers even after the larger society found a temporary respite in the war. Examination of their full mean-ing and implications was postponed to a later date. In fact, they are only now coming to the fore. Essentially, these are the major questions:

Can social work, with its heavy emphasis on "psychic deter-minism," clarify its concern for, and role in, the develop-ment and execution of public social policies?

Can social work, with its emphasis on treatment, be differen-tiated from psychotherapy?

Can social work move with objectivity, flexibility, and maturity toward integrating into its body of knowledge the growing developments in related fields?

Can social work, with its emphasis on identification with par-ticular psychological points of view, develop professionals with the necessary attitudes and abilities to be critical and to contribute to change in the body of knowledge?

Can social work spell out more clearly not only the role and function of the professional and the volunteer but also of the agency as a social institution, with a function which goes beyond that of merely providing housing for a profes-sional and volunteer staff?

Can social work clarify its philosophy on the respective roles of public and private agencies in meeting the social wel-fare needs of people?

Can social work be utilized in all settings, authoritative as well as non-authoritative, or can it operate only in a limited number of settings conducive to its approach?

World War II and its aftermath resembled in many ways the previous war and postwar period. It was a war to make the world safe for democracy by defeating the threat of fascism. Of the three patterns that had emerged out of the forces of world-wide depression—fascism, communism, and national economic planning (national capitalism)—two joined hands to destroy the third. The union, however, proved to be temporary. After the war communism came to be regarded as part of the same brew as fascism, and a cold-war conflict between the two remaining forces is still in progress. Communism was feared not only from without but also internally and became a central issue in the American political scene.

The attitudes toward the threat of communism varied. On the one hand, a majority of the American people feared the expansion of Soviet Russia and were in favor of a program to check it as a possible external threat; many of these, however, were not opposed to the traditional free play of ideas that was an inherent part of American democracy. In matters of foreign policy, this group was aware of the fact that the containment of communism involved more than military strength and alliances. A program had to be developed, preferably through the United Nations, to help the underdeveloped countries that represent 51 per cent of the world's area and contain 46 per cent of the world's people. The way of life arrived at by these people could well determine the future course of the world. They were all entering a belated period of the industrial revolution and were groping for the form of society that would best meet their present-day needs. In a sense, they were the prospective customers before whom the samples of the conflicting ideologies were to be exhibited. The challenge was to be able to exhibit more than military strength. It was to reveal to them through actual demonstration, both at home and abroad, our deep concern for the fullness of the democratic way of life politically, economically, and socially.

On the other hand, some Americans were interested not only in meeting an external threat but also in destroying everything on the American scene that they regarded as a reflection of that ideology. For them this included not only the Communists but also all those who had been responsible for the social gains of the past twenty-five years. Because of this group we have witnessed a large-scale attack both on our principles of civil liberties and on those institutions basically responsible for developing democratic values and beliefs in our society.

Today we are going through an important transition in

American life. The unity prevalent during the war no longer exists. It was a temporary truce between conflicting interests to meet an external threat. Now that the external danger has been removed, the conflicting forces that emerged in the latter days of the New Deal are joining battle again. The cold-war atmosphere has prevented a complete recognition of the issues, for some form of unity can always be organized around a potential external danger—note the appeal from time to time for a bi-partisan foreign policy. On domestic issues, however, the battle for an extension of the principles of the New Deal has run into formidable opposition. In some circles, social reform has become a "nasty" word, linked to socialism and communism. There are those who refuse to face issues and seek to convince themselves that by standing still in the right spot—the center—they can avoid the pressures from the left and the right. Again they seek "normalcy" in nineteenth-century terms. but this time under the slogan "progress, peace, and prosperity."

Afraid to look ahead, they seek a conservative ideology to justify the middle-of-the-road position, but they cannot find one with sufficient meaning in a rapidly moving and changing world. As Mills observes: "Those who grope for ideologies with which to explain their conservative mood, would anchor this mood—as well as themselves—in some solid tradition. They feel that they have somehow been tricked by liberalism, progressivism, radicalism and they are a little frightened. What many of them want, it would seem, is a society of classic conservatism." [14]

Essentially, the conservative looks back and leans heavily on tradition for the answers to his problem. "The conservative defends the irrationality of tradition against the powers of human reason; he denies the legitimacy of man's attempt individually to control his own fate and collectively to build his own world." [15] Traditional conservatism does not limit religious beliefs to the personal concern of the individual but brings them into the consideration of political philosophy.

The conservative—Mr. Russell Kirk tells us—believes that (1) "divine intent rules society," man being incapable of grasping by his reason the great forces that prevail. Accordingly, change must be slow for "Providence is the proper instrument for change," and the test of a statesman is his "cognizance of the real tendency of Providential social forces." The conservative (2) has an affection for "the vanity and mystery of traditional life," perhaps most of all because he believes that "tradition and sound prejudice" check man's presumptuous will and archaic impulse. Moreover (3), "society longs for leadership," and the conservative holds that there are "natural distinctions" among men which form a natural order of classes and powers.[16]

We are told that the developments during the depression led us to the brink of communism and disaster. What had been interpreted as a creative and humane answer in a period of suffering and misery is now being reassessed as dangerous interference with the approach of "classic conservatism." In a period of moral uneasiness, pervading anxieties, loneliness, and confusion as to norms and values, we seek a leadership that will do our worrying for us, and that with divine help will lead us out of the wilderness. This is the period of the "great crusade" and of the good, kind, and all-knowing leader. It is the period of appeal—huckster fashion—to the nonrational, nonlogical, and emotional elements of man. It is the period when increased psychological knowledge is being utilized to manipulate rather than educate.

Philosophically, the attack on humanistic liberalism is reaching crescendo proportions. The experience over the past forty years, with its two World Wars, a major depression, and the emergence of fascism and communism, has created doubt and anxiety in the hearts and minds of men about their ability to be masters of their own fate and collectively to build a brave new world. The philosophy of consciousness and of the rational man is being gradually amended out of existence by the impact of biological, economic, and psychic determinism. Just as there was once an attempt to explain all behavior in rational terms, today the same mistake is made at the other extreme: an attempt to find the answers to human behavior only in nonrational and emotional terms.

This tendency reaches its apex in the existentialist movement. The existentialists describe the universal human predicament as characterized by anxiety, meaninglessness, loneliness, estrangement, emptiness, and guilt. Tillich points out that existentialism derives these characterizations ". . . from finitude, from the awareness of finitude which is anxiety; it derives them from estrangement from one's self and one's world. It points to the possibility and the danger of freedom and to the threat of non-being in all respects." [17] Tillich sees Freud, meanwhile, as having provided a scientific basis for some of the earlier theological and intuitive insights about the irrational element in man.

Freud in his discovery of the unconscious, rediscovered something that was known long since and had been used for many decades and even centuries to fight the victorious philosophy of consciousness. What Freud did was to give to all of this protest a scientific methodological foundation. In him we must see the old protest against the philosophy of consciousness. Especially in men like Heidegger and Sartre, and in the whole literature and art of the twentieth century, the existentialist point of view became aware of itself. It now is expressed intentionally and directly and not only as a suppressed element of protest.[18]

Tillich distinguishes between psychoanalysis and existentialism by suggesting that the philosophy of existentialism refers to a universal human predicament, "whereas depth psychology points to the ways in which people try to escape the situation by fleeing into neurosis and falling into psychosis." [19] His thesis is that psychoanalysis can deal with some of these illnesses in a limited way but cannot heal the underlying, fundamental feelings described by the existentialist.

Many psychoanalysts try to do it; they try with their methods to overcome the existential negativity, anxiety, estrangement, meaninglessness, guilt. They deny that they are universal, that they are

existential in this sense. They call all anxiety, all guilt, all emptiness, illness which can be overcome as any illness can be, and they
try to remove them. But this is impossible. The existential structures cannot be healed by the most refined techniques. They are objects of salvation.[20]

This approach utilizes the science and skill of psychology to
describe and analyze the human situation, but seeks the answer
outside the human situation and through other than scientific
methods.

The swing from man as rational to man as irrational has
brought with it an overemphasis on internal as contrasted with
external factors. A counterreaction to this development is an
emerging tendency to overemphasize the external factors. This
school views the moral uneasiness, pervading anxieties, loneliness, and confusion as "rooted in quite objective social disorders" which man can study and overcome. It believes that man
has been wallowing too much in his personal anxieties and
looking inward too much for the cause and the answer. Frankel
adopts this view. "It seems to me perfectly plain that most of
our personal anxieties and individual uncertainties are rooted
in quite objective social disorders; and if we do not know what
to believe, or what to believe in, the reason is not the turmoil
within but the fog outside. To see our way through this fog we
need social ideas, not personal therapy." [21] Mills, too, develops
the thesis of "structural immorality" and sees these problems
as emanating from a concentration of power in the economic,
political, and military groups.

Within American society, major national power now resides in the
economic, the political and the military domains. Other institutions
seem off to the side of modern history and, on occasion, duly sub-
ordinated to these. No family is as directly powerful in national
affairs as any major corporation; no church is as directly powerful
in the external biographies of young men in America today as the
military establishment; no college is as powerful in the shaping of
momentous events as the National Security Council. Religious, educational and family institutions are not autonomous centers of national power; on the contrary, these decentralized areas are increas-

ingly shaped by the big three in which developments of decisive and immediate consequence now occur.[22]

We seem to be having difficulty in breaking from the mechanistic conception of cause and effect, from the Cartesian view that the world moved according to unchangeable and predictable physical laws. Such a view leads us to seek oversimplified answers—either/or rather than both/and conceptions. It also encourages us to look for solutions in terms of the segment with which we operate and in which we specialize, rather than viewing it within the context of the whole of which it is a related part. As Mindlin suggests: "In some situations the external environmental factors dominate so completely as to minimize the role of internal factors and vice versa. Theoretically, however, neither the one nor the other can be completely excluded." [23]

Modern social work is caught up in this dilemma. With social reform as a mother and psychological individualization as a father, it has difficulty at times in establishing its legitimacy. There is a tendency to make one of the parents the skeleton in the family closet. Thus in recent years, social work has been accused of losing sight of its responsibility in helping to "shape the course of welfare events." [24] Hollis and Taylor warn of the effects of this trend:

The social work profession in the last quarter century has predominantly concerned itself with . . . the improvement of the quality of individualized services. Proportionately, less attention has been paid to . . . enriching and expanding social welfare programs. The profession has accepted too little of a unified responsibility for appraising and improving social welfare institutions. A continuation of the concern with improving the direct rendering of service to individuals and groups, to the neglect of a study of the causes of the individual and social maladjustment and the possibilities of broader programs of prevention, will seriously limit the expanding role of social work.[25]

Today, in an atmosphere of severe "emotional disability" and an attempt to turn the clock back to "classic conservatism," social work can no more seek escape into professional isolation than it could during the depression with its severe unemployment and attendant human hardships and misery. It has begun to show signs of rebellion in terms of its concern both for values and for the newly emerging holistic approach to man's problems. In the same way that it contributed to the view that man does not live by bread alone, so too must it help underscore the fact that man does not live by psychiatry alone. The tendency to divorce the individual from his social institutions and their constant impact on him must be checked. In so doing the importance of individual personality factors must not be ignored but rather seen within a total context.

Social work must continue to align itself with the new dynamic concepts emerging from sociology, social psychology, and cultural anthropology. In recent years, these behavioral sciences have been pointing up in dynamic terms the importance of understanding the social institution in dealing with asocial behavior. They have produced important thinking and research on problems of cultural value orientations, cultural values and social roles, age and sex determinants in the social structure, value conflicts, and so forth. Social work, with the help of social scientists, must continue to seek ways of enriching its own knowledge and skills from this source. In so doing, however, it must avoid the danger of mere substitution of sociology for psychology. What the times demand is a multidimensional and interrelated conception of need and function to meet this need. With such an approach many fields can find common ground for strengthening the mental health of the nation. Within social work it would also help to put into proper perspective the importance of broad welfare programming, social welfare policy, and social welfare administration.

Social work has had difficulty in limiting and defining its boundaries. Perhaps a weakness from the point of view of professional development, this difficulty may represent a strength in its goal of helping people in a changing society. Social work's pervasiveness places it in an excellent position to contribute to an holistic approach. Rather than be concerned because it is in everyone's backyard, it should remain mindful of its heritage, for this explains its reason for being there. The term "social" in social work is not an accident. It represents the context within which social work can cooperate fruitfully with other fields.

In the area of psychological individualization, social work finds itself in close relationship with medicine and psychology. If one draws three intersecting circles (Ballantine fashion) the three fields converge at the point where each is focused on therapy: medicine through psychiatry, psychology through clinical psychology, and social work through psychiatric social work. Interestingly enough, psychiatry and clinical psychology are just acquiring status in their respective circles. Psychiatric social work, however, has tended to overshadow in status the total circle of which it is a related part. Each discipline brings the contribution of its total circle into the common area. What should psychiatric social work bring? The traditional emphasis and experience around the social. If it brings only the emphasis on the psychological it is entering the common area with only borrowed finery. Thus, as a member of a psychiatric team, the social worker should be most helpful not merely in carrying out the orders of the psychiatrist but also in collaborating in a plan of action by bringing into the discussions the social dimension within which the medical and clinical diagnosis take on reality. As Dr. Bernard points out, in an article on the training program for medical psychotherapists, "Traditional biological emphases all along the line often threaten to overshadow or oppose the requisite socio-cultural background. . . ." [26]

On the other side of the fence, as social work operates within structures of an economic and political nature, it is in a position to help round out a one-sided approach that may fail to see the importance of understanding human behavior. Also important in the formulation of social policy is the contribution which social work can make by interpreting the impact of such policy on the individual and his need for independence.

If social work can remain focused on its goals and objectives, as well as on its techniques, it will find less difficulty with such problems as public versus private welfare, social policy versus psychological individualization, and professional versus volunteer. These issues are tied up with the kind of society we want, and are larger than questions of techniques and professional boundaries. For example, one of the important features of social work as a social activity is that the social agency, be it public or private, reflects the concern of people for their fellow men. The social agency, including its lay as well as its professional structure, is an important institution, an integral part of the democratic scene and a reflection of how a democratic society functions in meeting its human problems. If we are clear about the agency not only as a channel of service but also as a social institution in a democratic society, the question of the respective functions of public and private agencies becomes of secondary importance. It becomes easy to see them both "as branches of the same tree, nourished in the same soil of our religious, charitable and humanitarian traditions, fed by the same roots of belief in political democracy and in the basic equality and common brotherhood of man." [27]

If issues can be approached in an holistic and dynamic way, many of the problems which social work faces will fall into proper perspective. Then, as Dr. Davidson says, we will see that we are dealing not with cutting a given-sized pie into slices, but rather with a constantly changing and expanding situation in which "the horizons of human helpfulness are infinite and limitless. . . . If we can accept this concept of our democratic society and its application to our functions in the social service field, we will always find new fields for adventurous pioneering, new experiments to undertake, new social crusades to lead, new areas of human helpfulness in which the enterprise of our voluntary and public service agencies can make their contribution—ever changing—to the rich and full development of our community life." [28]

10

SOCIAL WORK
AS A
PROFESSION

WHERE IS social work as a profession today, when viewed within the general criteria of professionalism? The Hollis-Taylor study dealt with this problem. The authors pointed out that the "readiness of the profession to assume in full its professional responsibilities is estimated in two ways: By criteria which indicate the extent to which the workers constitute a profession; and by an analysis which shows the character of the professional activities undertaken." [1] In regard to the former, they were of the opinion that the social work profession is still in its "early adolescence," and that only the "hard core of social work in the United States can be said to have attained a satisfactory professional status." [2] It must be borne in mind that only approximately 30 per cent of the paid social workers are in the National Association of Social Workers. Furthermore, of the estimated total of 75,000 social workers in 1950 in the country, approximately only 16 per cent have had the full two-year graduate curriculum. Approximately another 11 per cent have had one to two years. Of the 73 per cent with less than a year of training, approximately 60 per cent have had no study at all in a graduate school of social work.

The character of the professional activities undertaken was the second major criterion regarded by Hollis and Taylor as indicative of readiness to assume professional responsibilities. In this connection, they pointed to two areas in which the least adequate job was being performed: (1) "in research and experimentation to test, refine and add to the body of professional knowledge and method"; and (2) "in developing and providing information about the profession to other professions, related disciplines and the public." [3] Since the Hollis-Taylor report social work has begun to make rapid strides in both of these areas.

Social work as a profession has traveled far since the challenging paper by Flexner in 1915. The causes and control of its growth are external as well as internal. Internally, the striving for professional status and standards has followed the pattern in related fields. In Lebaux's summary:

. . . at least three rewards of professional life provide impetus for this trend.

1. The professions have high status.
2. The professions have high income.
3. The drive toward professionalization, through stress on the moral and ethical aspects of work, through celebration of the service ideal and creation of a sense of internal community, may be seen as a way to give new meaning to the job.[4]

Externally, the increase of professionalism in social work must be viewed within the context of the trained specialists in our economy. Social work, as one of the specialized talents, has been part of the general growth of the trained specialist over the past fifty years. "During the past half century the number of school teachers in the United States has increased $1\frac{1}{4}$ times as rapidly as the total population. The number of professional health workers has increased $2\frac{1}{2}$ times as rapidly; the number of engineers 5 times and the number of scientists 10 times."[5] Accurate figures are not available for the number of social workers during this whole period, for they were not included in the census until 1930. The growth between 1930 and 1950, however, was approximately from 33,000 to 75,000, or twice as rapid as that of the total population.

Although the number of social workers shows a definite upward trend, it ranks far below that of all other helping professions except dentistry. There were approximately 2.2 times more clergymen, 14 times more school teachers, 2.5 times more doctors, and 6 times more nurses serving our society in 1954 than there were social workers. Furthermore, the increase includes a larger number of untrained workers than of graduates from schools of social work. In 1954-1955 there were only 1590 graduates from two-year accredited schools of social work. This number is not sufficient to correct the present balance between trained and untrained in a field of approximately 75,000, since the number leaving each year because of deaths, retirement, marriage, and shifts to other occupations is considerable.

Colleges are preparing for a marked increase in enrollment beginning in 1960 because of the rise in the birthrate during World War II. There is general agreement that the growth of specialization will continue in our society with its "expanding technology and dynamic social change," and that the helping professions will get their share of the increased number of college graduates. But there is no doubt that they will find the competition from the technological and business fields difficult to meet unless government takes a more direct interest in subsidizing the training programs. Moreover, even if such aid is forthcoming social work, because of peculiar problems of its own, may not get its share of the relative increase of students in the helping professions. Recent studies indicate that social work as a profession does not have full acceptance by the community; the social worker does not enjoy a level of remuneration commensurate with related professions, nor does he enjoy a prestige comparable to even low-payed related professions such as the ministry and teaching; and the social worker does not reveal the type of self-image which reflects personal satisfaction.[6]

Social work has made progress over the last several decades but has not been able fully to "convince the community that those who possess the professional skill deliver a superior service than those who do not; and that the community stands to benefit from and should prefer the superior performance."[7] As Dollard observes:

. . . of all forms of activity in which men and women engage, social work has at once the greatest claim to be a professional activity and the greatest difficulty in establishing its claim. The difficulty which has plagued social work in its development as a profession is that the social worker's dedication is to a degree shared by all good men and women. Most human beings have a deep need to be their brothers' keepers. Hence we all resist and resent the notion that the task of the social worker requires a pecular combination of temperament, intelligence, training and experience. The result is that social work has had to fight a constant rear-guard action against the pervasive notion that any man with love in his heart can do the job.[8]

As social work seeks greater professional acceptance in the community, it is caught up in conflicting currents. Inherent in the types of problems with which it deals and the objectives it pursues is a dedication to social reform greater than that of most other professions. This means that social work, more than other professions, is in the midst of the conflict in values in our society. Steeped in the democratic and humanitarian ethos, social work frequently meets resistance from those in the community who cling to their faith in the survival of the fittest in a competitive society.

Within social work itself there are conflicts, too, that affect agreement on what constitute the justifiable boundaries of the field. Opinions range all the way from seeing social work as a network of services, to social work as a unique method and process, to social work as social policy. Social work shares with related professions an interest in promoting broad human welfare. Viewed only in terms of this objective the line between social work and related fields would be fuzzy. It is not alone the objective so much as the method for accomplishing it, steeped in democratic principles, that begins to distinguish social work. Even here, however, the development and clarification of the social work method does not always make for an easy differentiation from such related fields as health, education, religion, recreation, and labor; for these are fields whose problems as well as purposes "sharply impinge upon the area of social work practice and interest," and whose practitioners "share with social workers the responsibility for service to a common group of clients." Furthermore, even among those agencies that are a recognized part of the social work family, the wide variations in auspices, settings, and over-all purpose affect the extent to which the method is utilized to the full or is modified and fragmented. The methods of social work can be, and are being, utilized in a variety of settings, but the fullness of their use is contingent upon the general social scene, the objectives of the agency, and the philosophy and skill of the staff.

Another necessary distinguishing characteristic, then, besides those of objective and method, is the social agency itself and the pattern of relationships between the various social agencies in the community. All social work agencies may be regarded as having in common the following:[9]

1. The provision of helping activities designed to give assistance to individuals, families and groups in respect to their social and economic problems. The method of providing the help, and the emphasis on the social or the economic, may vary.

2. These services whether under public or private, sectarian or nonsectarian, auspices are provided as social activities, that is, they are "carried on not for personal profit by private practitioners but under the auspices of governmental and-or non-governmental organizations established for the benefit of the community."

3. These agencies are linked together through various patterns of relationship such as exchange of information, referrals of clients, joint projects, federated fund raising and joint planning, thus making it easier for individuals, families, and groups to "tap the resources available in the community for their social and economic well-being," and to participate in changing these resources or creating new ones.

Several developments in recent years appear at first glance to challenge the second characteristic described above, namely social work as a social activity. I refer to the growth of the fee-service programs in casework agencies, and to the private practice of casework, that is outside of agencies and for personal profit.

Casework with its traditional role of service to the economically dependent found, as it moved more and more toward the treatment of emotional problems "in addition to and in relation to providing concrete services," that it also had a service that could be provided to the higher economic groups. "The traditional stigma of charity associated with the social agency, however, . . . prevented many individuals of other than the lower income groups from using casework services for non-material problems, even though the need was present. . . . Private agencies have therefore made an effort to reach other income groups by the establishment of fee service programs for individuals with emotional problems." [10] Fees for service were first instituted by two member agencies of the Family Service Association of America in 1941. By 1947 the number of agencies sponsoring this type of program had increased to twenty-two, and by 1951 there were more than fifty. Fee payments in social work are not new, however, having been used in medical and recreational settings for a long time. Furthermore, since fees are scaled on the ability to pay, and fee cases are dealt with as an integral part of the agency caseload, subject to the same procedures as nonfee cases; and since no personal profit accrues to the worker, this trend does not militate against the social activity in social work.

The same conclusion cannot be arrived at, however, in the matter of private practice. Although the skills being utilized may in many instances be similar to those in casework, they no longer represent social work practice in the full sense of the term. Perhaps the best answer to this problem is found in the study made by Peek and Plotkin of thirty former social workers in New York City engaged in private practice: ". . . for the most part, the practitioners (the thirty interviewed) regard themselves as psychotherapists or analysts. . . . The private practitioner's function in practice is found to be different than the function of the social agency. In her individual expression of her skills in a practice of her own, she has a different role in the community than the social agency with its broader social scope and responsibilities." [11] The trend toward private practice involves, among other factors, the search for higher financial gains and more status. The pertinent question is not whether a social worker has a right to move in this direction, but rather whether he is any longer engaged in social work. Professionals at times may become so absorbed in meeting their own financial and status needs that the purpose of the profession fades into the background. There is no doubt that an increase in the number of social workers in private practice does not constitute the answer to the national problem of mental health. Furthermore, it does not represent the primary contribution of the profession toward helping to find an answer. In brief, the movement into private practice must be seen within its proper perspective, and must not be rationalized as a higher level of development in social work.

With the spread and the change in the nature of the social work service, interest has grown in finding ways to safeguard the consumer against low standards of practice through some form of legal regulation. The internal differences concerning the definition of the field, as well as in imbalance between the number of untrained and trained workers, affect markedly the efforts to obtain legal sanction for the profession. The first formal consideration of legal regulation of social work practice began in the latter part of the 1930's, paralleling the period of great expansion in the public services. In 1945 the AASW established a committee to help bring about legal regulation. The delegate assembly of the AASW adopted a resolution in 1947 which placed the association on record as assuming responsibility for "the development of a long range program of study, education and action leading to the adoption of legislation in each state which would restrict the practice of social work to persons designated as qualified practitioners by an appropriate agency of the state." The NASW has taken over the responsibility of its predecessor association and is at present gathering information on the problem through its commission on personnel standards and practice.

Legal regulation of a profession can take several forms. One form of legal regulation is that which restricts a specialized title such as registered nurse or certified public accountant. One may still call himself an accountant, for example, and perform the function, but he may not publicize himself as a certified public accountant unless he has met the requirements stipulated in the law. . . . A second type of legal regulation is that which restricts a generic title. The new state law in New York certifying psychologists is an example of this type of legal control. It provides that to present oneself as a member of the profession and to render services under such a title, one must be certified and registered by the state. This type of legislation goes further than the first type mentioned in that it protects not just a specialized title but the title adopted by the profession, in this instance the title of psychologist. . . . The third type of legal control is that which restricts both the title and the performance of certain specified functions. This is the type of regulation which covers the practice of medicine. . . ." [12]

A national voluntary plan of registration has been proposed as a step toward preparing the public for legal regulation of social work practice. This is the procedure which was utilized in California in the early 1930's, when voluntary registration was introduced under the sponsorship of the State Conference of Social Work. This eventually led to a state registration law in 1945. Opponents of the national voluntary plan feel that it might retard rather than advance legal regulation. Even a national voluntary plan of registration presents many procedural and substantive problems. Some of the questions which must be faced are the following:

1. Should the plan be open to all persons employed in a social work capacity regardless of whether or not they are members of N.A.S.W.?
2. Shall there be a differential designation depending upon training?
3. Should there be one single designation? If so, shall there be blanketing in of persons now in social work jobs? If so, shall there be any training requirement in order to be blanketed in?
4. Should there be a set level of training for registration but a procedure through which those who did not meet the level of training could qualify by examination up until a specified cut-off date? [13]

The explorations of legal regulation to date indicate that the problems are complex. They bring to light many deep-rooted internal differences, which have lain dormant in recent years but will have to be faced and resolved before legal regulation can become a reality. Even for voluntary registration the field must be prepared to answer the question of who shall be considered a bona-fide social worker. If a decision is made to use the equivalent of one year of graduate training as the minimum requirement, there will be difficulty, on the one hand, with the large number of social workers who do not meet this requirement and, on the other hand, with the growing numbers who have two years of graduate training. The answer to the problem may have to await a study of practice suggested in Chapter 8. Through such a study there may emerge a clearer differentiation of function in professional and non-professional categories, similar to the developments in the field of nursing.

Social work today is at a crossroads much like that experienced by the early humanitarians. Again it must decide whether it can be satisfied to deal with the consequences rather than the causes of social breakdown. As the Beards [14] point out, the humanitarians, at the turn of the century, were taking advantage of the new knowledge emerging from economics, sociology, and political science about the existing doctrines of individualism, when they sought reform of the environment around the theory that "the individual, no matter how enterprising, derives the knowledge, the inventions he makes and uses and the security he enjoys from the common life of society and the government that holds it together." Today again the new knowledge emerging from the social sciences emphasizes the importance of social institutions in tackling the problems of social breakdown.

Social work thinking still leans heavily on what Mills [15] refers to as a classic view of democracy—of individualism, the market of free ideas, the power of free discussion, and the harmony of group interests. He regards this view as "a set of images out of a fairy tale." It is his view that although the United States "today is not altogether a mass society," it has "moved a considerable distance along the road to the mass society." The problem of the century, namely, how to live with bigness and yet avoid the depersonalization of life, has not been solved. The past several decades have revealed that neither the Marxian approach of attacking the social institutions regarded as responsible for the depersonalization of life, nor the Freudian emphasis on the importance of finding the spontaneous self, brings easy solutions. They represent but fragments of a necessary total approach.

Perhaps out of insecurity social work has clung to old ways, apparently with the hope that times would return to "normalcy" and make its methods current again. Furthermore, social workers have been trained so specifically within a single dimension that they tend to find it difficult to think in terms of new patterns, new wholes.

As the knowledge from the social sciences increases it must be translated into methods of dealing not only with the individual but also with social institutions. This involves, among other things, learning of how to deal with the power structure to bring about change. Social work, because of its experience in the humanitarian arena, and its ability to translate scientific knowledge into action, can perform a yeoman service during this period. On the other hand, it can become so absorbed in carving out a narrow professional niche for itself that it will no longer be a part of the historical stream.

If social work chooses the narrow road, what seems like a short-cut to status may prove to be a dead end. Social work is caught in a dilemma. It needs greater community recognition and acceptance to achieve its broad purposes. A step such as legal regulation might help to provide this enhanced status; but at the same time the definition necessary for legal regulation threatens to narrow the conception of social work to only a fragment of its full range. Part of the answer to this dilemma may lie in recognizing the fact that greater acceptance in the community involves the status not only of the social worker but also of social welfare as an institution in the democratic society. Unless the community is ready to see the value of social welfare services and pay for them through taxes and voluntary contributions, the role and status of the professional worker will not change significantly. In other words, the readiness of the community to accept social work is related not only to the social worker's performance but also to the community's attitude toward human values and democratic goals. Social work finds the community most receptive when the whole social climate is humanitarian and progressive rather than reactionary or conservative. Social work's difficulty in defining its function and boundaries may represent a strength in that it can maintain a desirable flexibility in a changing and expanding society.

The NASW can play an important role in providing leadership in this period of transition. The mere fact that seven associations with varying programs were able to give up their autonomy is evidence of flexibility and maturity. Furthermore, the purposes of the new association indicate that the profession is viewing social work in terms of broad objectives as well as of method and service. These purposes are:

. . . to promote the quality and effectiveness of social work practice in the United States of America through services to the individual, the group and the community; to further the broad objective of improving conditions of life in our democratic society through utilization of the professional knowledge and skills of social work, and to expand through research the knowledge necessary to define and attain these goals; to provide opportunity for the social work profession to work in unity toward maintaining and promoting high standards of practice and of preparation for practice and toward alleviating or preventing sources of deprivation, distress and strain susceptible of being influenced by social work methods and by social action.[16]

In its brief existence the NASW has begun to explore and act on the many problems described above. The commission on practice has evolved a long-range program for a basic and much needed study of practice. Paralleling this effort has been the work of the commission on social policy and action. This Commission has produced a document entitled, "Goals of Public Social Policy," where the responsibilities of social work are spelled out as follows:

Social work is the profession which concerns itself with the facilitation and strengthening of basic social relationships between individuals, groups and social institutions. It has, therefore, a social action responsibility which derives directly from its social function and professional knowledge. This responsibility lies in the following three areas: (a) the identification, analysis, and interpretation of specific unmet needs among individuals, and groups of individuals (b) advancing the standard of recognized social obligation between society and its individual members so that those needs will be met and a more satisfying environment for all achieved and (c) the application of specific knowledge, experience, and inventiveness to those problems which can be solved through social welfare methods.[17]

The document makes specific policy recommendations about social insurance, public welfare, juvenile delinquency, health, education, housing, public recreation and leisure-time services, community development, economic and labor conditions, military service, protection against common disaster, corrections, immigration, and civil rights and liberties. In order to facilitate its program of social policy and action, the NASW maintains an office in Washington, D.C., with a full-time staff person who devotes his energies to working with the various government agencies, making the association's views known to members of Congress, and keeping the chapter committees on social policy and action informed on pending legislation.

Further progress will depend on the cooperative efforts of the schools of social work through the Council on Social Work Education, the social work agencies, and the professional association. Schools of social work have a major responsibility in that they are shaping the minds of the future. These minds can be shaped in narrow and static ways or with emphasis on broad concepts and the sharpening of critical abilities. To move in this direction, the schools will need the cooperation of the social agencies. Agencies, too, must free themselves of the point of view that the answers to the problems of social breakdown have been found and that all that is needed is to train more workers to expand what is now being done. What is needed is an experimental mood that encourages staff to test new ideas and acquire new knowledge. The professional association, standing as it does between the schools and the agencies, can provide the necessary balance between the effort to find new patterns and the conservative demands of the day-to-day situation.

11

WHAT OF THE FUTURE?

To PROJECT into the future involves understanding not only where we are but also what has happened to us along the way. Social work has made tremendous strides in the past fifty years in response to industrialization and urbanization, two world wars, and a major depression. Now the second industrial revolution is unfolding in an atmosphere that reflects the strains of an uncertain international situation. Courageous and creative planning is necessary if the resulting social problems are to be prevented or minimized, if the health and welfare of our nation are to remain paramount. There is a sizable job ahead to deal with the myriad unmet needs that now exist and those that will grow out of the increasing pace of this new industrial revolution. In the next challenging decades social work can contribute much knowledge and wisdom if it remembers the whole of its heritage.

Our history has shown that no adequate progress can be made without expanding participation by government in the promotion of human welfare, as well as adventurous experimentation on the part of voluntary private agencies. The programs and social policies conceived in the depression can no longer be partisan issues. Fear of new developments is countered by the knowledge that we cannot turn back the clock. It is no coincidence that those who toy with the fantasy of a "return to normalcy" are also those who are gambling with the destruction of our basic human values. They know only too well that unless they can confuse and destroy our deeply rooted humanitarian and democratic values they cannot hope to win an all-out war against the social gains of the past several decades. Nor is it an accident that the personnel of those institutions that deal with education for democratic living, the transmitters of basic human values, have been singled out for attack. Their concern for the democratic pattern of meeting needs, based on the expansion of the philosophy of political democracy into the economic and social spheres, stands in the way of those who would destroy our democratic way of life. Social work cannot ignore this attack, or treat it as a nonprofessional problem; for social work methods and objectives are so intimately related to the system of humanitarian and democratic values that destruction of the latter means death to the former.

The place of social work in the fabric of the democratic society demands greater attention. This involves improving the status and prestige not only of the social worker but also of social work itself. To accomplish this goal, public responsibility as well as technical proficiency warrants a high priority in the concerns of both the professional organizations and the training programs. It should be possible to train the social worker of the future to be "skillful not only in the diagnosis and treatment of the individual and group problems which he meets in day-to-day practice" but also to be able "to speak with knowledge and understanding of the wider social issues involved" and with "authority on possible courses of action and development for society as a whole." [1]

Social work can best achieve its aims if it can help to shape the future course of social welfare events. To do so involves the development of leadership with the necessary knowledge, attitudes, and skills to administer large social welfare programs, evaluate existing policies, and help in the creation of new policies and programs. The training for such leadership has been foreign to social work curricula of the past several decades; however, recent trends in social work education provide a more consistent and productive basis for fulfilling this need.

Perhaps the most important influence on the future of social work will be the seriousness of its concern with prevention rather than with remedy alone. The magnitude of the mental health problem, and the limited dent we have made on it so far, are evidence that our present approach is not the whole answer. Prevention of "mental disability" necessitates not only a better knowledge of how to work with the individual but also a better understanding of and greater responsibility for the social conditions that affect mental health. The social worker of the future will have to be well versed in the interdependence of social institutions, social values and the psychology of the individual. There is growing evidence of a renewed interest in a social psychiatry more inclusive in its vision than the narrower emphasis on the medical and clinical that has dominated social work in past years.

The recent trend in the sciences toward interdisciplinary cooperation also is having its impact on social work. If social work training can be broadened to reflect the holistic approach of the social sciences, social workers can fulfill a significant function as the engineers who help translate the findings of "pure" science into action. Social work research is an important part of this process as it endeavors to interpret social science findings for use and to test out their validity in practice.

As social work continues in this spirit of objective self-scrutiny it will develop practitioners who are not committed to things as they are, but who have the objectivity and skill to contribute to an ever-changing and expanding body of knowledge. The growing acceptance of a multidimensional approach which provides consideration for man's rational as well as irrational side will contribute to the understanding of his problems as a product of both external and internal factors. This in turn will place in proper perspective the importance of a changing society as well as a changing individual. Such a broadened conception avoids an oversimplified interpretation of economic, political, and social phenomena. Above all it strengthens a basic belief of social work: that man can be master of his own fate and can, with his collective strength, build a brave new world.

The story of social work in America is a reflection of our faith in democracy not only as a form of government but as a way of life. It is the story of people and how they fare as the na-

354 • WHAT OF THE FUTURE?

tion grows, develops, and changes. Social work, therefore, is predicated on faith in the average man, in his ability to govern himself and to handle his rights and responsibilities maturely. It recognizes the potentialities of man regardless of race, creed, or national origin. It approaches him in terms, not of what he is but of what he can become if given equal opportunity and if dealt with justly. It further recognizes that man does not exist apart from his social relationships, and that in an increasingly inter-dependent society he has not only rights but also responsibilities to other men and their cooperative democratic undertakings. Social work makes its best contribution as it regards its professional knowledge and skill, not as ends in themselves, but rather as means to an end, a better life for all of mankind.

NOTES TO CHAPTERS

CHAPTER 1

Humanitarianism in Search of a Method

[1] E. W. Burgess, "Social Planning and the Mores," in *Publications of the American Sociological Society 29:3*, August 1935, p. 5.

[2] Gunnar Myrdal, *An American Dilemma* (Harper, New York, 1944, Vol. I, pp. 8-12).

[3] R. C. Snyder and H. H. Wilson, "The American Ideology," in *Roots of Political Behavior* (American Book, New York, 1949, pp. 558-59).

[4] Josephine Shaw Lowell in S. E. Morison and H. S. Commager, *The Growth of the American Republic* (Oxford Univ. Press, New York, 1937, p. 379).

[5] Address to 73rd Congress, June 8, 1934, in *Congressional Record 78:* 10, pp. 10, 770.

[6] Gordon Hamilton, *Theory and Practice of Social Case Work* (Columbia Univ. Press, New York, 1940, p. 4).

[7] Eduard C. Lindeman, "Functional Democracy in Human Relations," in *Toward Better Human Relations* (Wayne Univ. Press, Detroit, 1952, pp. 31-33).

[8] *Ibid.*, p. 33.

[9] *Ibid.*, p. 31.

[10] *Idem.*

[11] Charlotte Towle, "Social Case Work," in *Social Work Year Book* (Russell Sage, New York, 1947, p. 478).

[12] From the statement adopted by the Executive Board of the American Association of Group Workers—now the Group Work Section of the National Association of Social Workers—in 1949, as its official definition of group work.

[13] C. F. McNeil, "Community Organization for Social Welfare," in *Social Work Year Book* (American Association of Social Workers, New York, 1951, p. 123).

[14] Eduard C. Lindeman (*op. cit.*, p. 28).

CHAPTER 2

Defend Man's Natural Rights

[1] George Soule, *Economic Forces in American History* (Dryden, New York, 1952, pp. 153-54).

[2] S. E. Morison, *The Puritan Pronaos* (New York Univ. Press, New York, 1936, pp. 5-6).

[3] J. T. Adams, *March of Democracy* (Scribner's, New York, 1932, pp. 19-20).

[4] R. W. Kelso, *History of Public Poor Relief in Massachusetts, 1620-1920* (Houghton, Boston, 1922, pp. 121-22).

[5] Henry Steele Commager, *Living Ideas in America* (Harper, New York, 1951, p. 315).

[6] Adam Smith, *An Inquiry into the Nature and Causes of the Wealth of Nations* (Everyman's Library, Dutton, New York, 1910). See the introduction by Edwin R. A. Seligman.

[7] Kingsley Davis, "Mental Hygiene and the Class Structure," in *A Study of Interpersonal Relations,* edited by Patrick Mullahy (Hermitage, New York, 1949, pp. 370-71).

[8] George Soule (*op. cit.,* p. 13).

[9] *Ibid.,* p. 15.

[10] Henry Steele Commager (*op. cit.,* pp. 151-52).

[11] Charles A. and Mary R. Beard, *A Basic History of the United States* (Doubleday, New York, 1944, Chapter XIV).

[12] George Soule (*op. cit.,* p. 161).

[13] Mary Sophia Stevens Sims, *Natural History of a Social Institution* (Woman's Press, New York, 1936, p. 4).

[14] Catherine Drinker Bowen, *Yankee from Olympus* (Little, Boston, 1945, p. 86).

[15] *Ibid.,* p. 86.

[16] Charles A. and Mary R. Beard (*op. cit.,* p. 203).

[17] R. W. Kelso (*op. cit.,* p. 137).

[18] Ellen Winston, "Public Welfare," in *Social Work Year Book* (American Association of Social Workers, New York, 1951, p. 403).

[19] Josephine C. Brown, *Public Relief, 1929-39* (Holt, New York, 1940, p. 33).

[20] R. H. Felix, "Psychiatric Plans of the U.S.P.H.S.," *Mental Hygiene,* July 1946, p. 381.

[21] Natalie D. Spingarn, "St. Elizabeths, Pace-Setter for Mental Hospitals," *Harper's Magazine,* January 1956, p. 59.

[22] Josephine C. Brown (*op. cit.,* p. 33).

[23] See R. C. Morse, *History of the North American YMCA's* (Association Press, New York, 1913).

CHAPTER 3

Expanding Industrialism

[1] Philip M. Hauser and Conrad Taeuber, "The Changing Population of the United States," in *The Annals of the American Academy of Political and Social Science 237,* January 1945, p. 17.

[2] Henry Steele Commager (*op. cit.,* p. 292).

[3] William Graham Sumner, "The Challenge of Facts," in *The Challenge of Facts and Other Essays,* edited by Albert G. Keller (Yale Univ. Press, New Haven, 1914, p. 25).

[4] Gunnar Myrdal (*op cit.,* p. 9).

[5] S. E. Morison and H. S. Commager (*op. cit.,* pp. 355-56).

[6] New York Association for Improving the Condition of the Poor, *Twenty-ninth Annual Report,* 1872, pp. 63-64.

[7] J. T. Adams, *Frontiers of American Culture* (Scribner's, New York, 1944, pp. 113-14).

[8] Olive M. Stone, "What Can Social Case Work Contribute to the Social Sciences?" *American Sociological Review 15:* 1, February 1950, p. 67.

[9] E. G. Boring, *A History of Experimental Psychology* (Century, New York, 1929, p. 494).

[10] Frank J. Bruno, *Trends in Social Work* (Columbia Univ. Press, New York, 1948, pp. 72-73).

[11] David M. Schneider and Albert Deutsch, *The History of Public Welfare in New York State, 1867-1940* (Chicago Univ. Press, Chicago, 1941, p. 18).

[12] R. W. Kelso (*op. cit.,* pp. 191-92).

[13] *Ibid.,* p. 153.

[14] Frank D. Watson, *The Charity Organization Movement in the United States* (Macmillan, New York, 1922, pp. 76-93).

[15] Charles D. Kellogg, *Charity Organization in the United States* (Proceedings of the National Conference of Charities and Corrections, 1893, pp. 53-54).

[16] Frank D. Watson (*op. cit.,* p. 94).

[17] Joseph H. Crooker, *Problems in American Society* (Ellis, Boston, 1889, p. 71).

[18] Andre Karam, "A Glance at the Historical Development of Community Organization for Social Welfare in the United States" (unpublished student paper, New York School of Social Work, June 1956, p. 7).

¹⁹ Charles D. Kellogg (*op. cit.*, pp. 52 ff).

²⁰ John McDowell, "Settlements and Neighborhood Centers," in *Social Work Year Book* (American Association of Social Workers, New York, 1951, p. 450).

²¹ Jesse F. Steiner, *Community Organization: A Study of Its Theory and Practice* (revised edition, Century, New York, 1930, p. 155).

²² Sidney Dillick, *Community Organization for Neighborhood Development: Past and Present* (Woman's Press and Morrow, New York, 1953, pp. 37-38).

²³ Elizabeth Wilson, *Fifty Years of Association Work Among Young Women, 1866-1916* (Woman's Press, New York, 1916, p. 32).

²⁴ Charles Loring Brace, *The Dangerous Classes of New York* (Wynkoop, New York, 1872, pp. 1. f.).

²⁵ Marguerite T. Boylan, *Social Welfare in the Catholic Church* (Columbia Univ. Press, New York, 1941, p. 22).

²⁶ *Saint Vincent de Paul Quarterly 4:2*, May 1899, p. 146.

²⁷ John O'Grady, *Catholic Charities in the United States: History and Problems* (National Conference of Catholic Charities, Washington, 1930, p. 147).

²⁸ Martin M. Cohn, "Jewish Social Work," in *Social Work Year Book* (American Association of Social Workers, New York, 1951, p. 260).

²⁹ E. P. Cubberly, *Changing Conceptions of Education* (Houghton, Boston, 1909, p. 15).

³⁰ Frank D. Watson (*op. cit.*, p. 217).

CHAPTER 4

Expansion, War, and Aftermath

¹ Esther Eckstein, *The Relationship of the Social Work Field to the American Scene* (Master's Thesis, New York School of Social Work, April 1947, p. 6).

² P. M. Hauser and C. Taeuber (*op. cit.*, p. 14).

³ *Recent Social Trends in the United States* (McGraw-Hill, New York, 1933, Vol. I, p. 19).

⁴ George Soule (*op. cit.*, p. 436).

⁵ Woodrow Wilson, *The New Freedom* (Doubleday, New York, 1913, p. 20).

⁶ From Woodrow Wilson's First Inaugural Address, March 4, 1913, in *The Messages and Papers of Woodrow Wilson* (Doran, New York, 1917, Vol. I, pp. 2, 4).

⁷ George Soule (*op. cit.*, p. 440).

8 *Ibid.*, p. 362.

9 E. A. Ross, *Sin and Society* (Houghton, Boston, 1907, pp. 9-14, 40).

10 George Soule (*op. cit.*, p. 441).

11 Jane Addams, "Charity and Social Justice," Presidential Address in *Proceedings of the National Conference of Charities and Corrections,* 1910, p. 1.

12 Albert Deutsch, "American Labor and Social Work," in *Science and Society, 8:4,* Fall 1944, pp. 296-97.

13 "Politics and Social Work," *The Survey 29,* 1912, p. 9.

14 "Pragmatism in Politics," *The Survey 29,* 1912, p. 12.

15 George Soule (*op. cit.*, p. 471).

16 J. T. Adams, *The Epic of America* (Little, Boston, 1931, p. 391).

17 Charles A. and Mary R. Beard (*op. cit,* pp. 441-51).

CHAPTER 5

Social Work in Search of a Method

1 Albert Deutsch (*op. cit.*, pp. 295-96).

2 Anna Leibowitz, *Homer Folks: A Study of His Professional Growth in Terms of His Contributions to the Field of Social Work and the Milieu in Which He Developed* (Master's Thesis, New York School of Social Work, 1950, p. 29).

3 The mental hygiene movement was formally launched by Clifford Beers in 1908 with his book, *A Mind That Found Itself.* In 1909 the Connecticut Mental Hygiene Society was established; then followed the national organization and the spread of the movement into many states.

4 F. J. Bruno (*op. cit.*, p. 193).

5 Frank D. Watson (*op. cit.*, p. 436).

6 L. A. Halbert, "Board of Public Welfare; a System of Government Social Work," in *Proceedings of the National Conference of Social Work,* 1918, pp. 220-21.

7 Irma Stein, unpublished paper, New York School of Social Work, p. 12.

8 Howard W. Odum, "Public Welfare," in *Recent Social Trends in the United States* (Vol. 2, p. 1239).

9 John A. Fitch, "Labor Standards," in *Social Work Year Book* (Russell Sage, New York, 1947, p. 287).

10 James H. Tufts, *Education and Training for Social Work* (Russell Sage, New York, 1923, p. 111).

11 Timothy Nicholson, "A Glance at the Past, A Look at the Present, A Vision of the Immediate Future," in *Proceedings of the National Conference of Charities and Corrections,* 1902, p. 10.

[12] Abraham Flexner, "Is Social Work a Profession?" in *Proceedings of the National Conference of Charities and Corrections*, 1915, pp. 576-90.

[13] F. J. Bruno (*op. cit.*, p. 141).

[14] E. G. Boring (*op. cit.*, p. 509).

[15] R. T. LePierre and P. R. Farnsworth, *Social Psychology* (McGraw-Hill, New York, 1936, p. 18).

[16] *Ibid.*, p. 23.

[17] E. Pumpian-Mindlin, "The Position of Psychoanalysis in Relation to the Biological and Social Sciences," in *Psychoanalysis as Science* (Stanford Univ. Press, Stanford, 1952, p. 133).

[18] Valer Barbu, "The Commonsense Psychiatry of Adolf Meyer" (book review), *American Journal of Psychoanalysis*, 1950, p. 71.

[19] Fay B. Karpf, *American Social Psychology and Its European Background* (McGraw-Hill, New York, 1931, Appendix).

[20] Elizabeth Wisner, "War and the Social Services," in *Proceedings of the National Conference of Social Work* (Columbia Univ. Press, New York, 1944, p. 2).

[21] F. J. Bruno (*op. cit.*, p. 284).

[22] Irma Stein (*op. cit.*, p. 15).

[23] Elizabeth L. Grover, "History and Philosophy of Social Welfare, 1918-1932," (unpublished paper, New York School of Social Work, April 1956).

[24] F. J. Bruno (*op. cit.*, pp. 201-02).

[25] Elizabeth Wisner (*op. cit.*, p. 4).

[26] Mary E. Richmond, *What Is Social Case Work?* (Russell Sage, New York, 1922, p. 98).

[27] *Ibid.*, p. 259.

[28] Milford Conference Report, *Social Case Work; Generic and Specific* (American Association of Social Workers, New York, 1929, p. 3).

[29] *Ibid.*, p. 16.

[30] Mary E. Richmond, *The Long View* (Russell Sage, New York, 1930, p. 374).

[31] Virginia P. Robinson, *A Changing Psychology in Social Case Work* (Univ. of North Carolina Press, Chapel Hill, 1930, pp. 42-52).

[32] E. W. Burgess, "Interdependence of Sociology and Social Work," *Journal of Social Forces 1:4*, May 1923, p. 368.

[33] Irving A. Hallowell, "Anthropology and the Social Worker's Perspective," *The Family 5:4*, June 1924, p. 91.

[34] Virginia P. Robinson (*op. cit.*, p. 35).

[35] *Ibid.*, p. 61.

[36] United States Bureau of the Census, *Fifteenth Census of the United States*, June 1932 release.

[37] Bertha C. Reynolds, "Rethinking Social Case Work," in *Social Work Today*, April 1938, p. 8.

[38] Quoted by Ewan Clague in "Research in Social Work," in *Social Work Year Book* (Russell Sage, New York, 1935, p. 421).

[39] Harry L. Lurie, "Social Research," in *Social Work Year Book* (Russell Sage, New York, 1929, pp. 415-20).

[40] Harry L. Lurie, "Research in Social Work," in *Social Work Year Book* (Russell Sage, 1933, pp. 437-41).

[41] Saiyid Zafar Hasan, "Development of Research in Social Work" (unpublished paper, New York School of Social Work, 1956).

[42] *Ibid.*

[43] Pauline V. Young, *Scientific Social Surveys and Research* (2d ed., Prentice-Hall, New York, 1949, p. 27).

[44] Shelby M. Harrison, "Social Surveys," in *Social Work Year Book* (Russell Sage, New York, 1929, pp. 432-33).

[45] Harry L. Lurie, "Social Research," (*loc. cit.*, p. 418).

[46] M. J. Karpf, *The Scientific Basis of Social Work* (Columbia Univ. Press, New York, 1931, p. 17).

[47] James H. Tufts (*op. cit.*, pp. 1-32).

[48] *Ibid.*, pp. 30-31.

[49] *Ibid.*, p. 91.

[50] *Ibid.*, pp. 97-98.

[51] Albert Deutsch (*op. cit.*, pp. 300-01).

[52] *Ibid.*, p. 302.

[53] Howard W. Odum (*op. cit.*, p. 1239).

[54] Herbert Hoover, "Lincoln's Birthday," Feb. 12, 1931, in *The State Papers and Other Public Writings of Herbert Hoover* (collected and edited by W. S. Myers, Doubleday, New York, 1934, Vol. I, pp. 502-03).

[55] Howard W. Odum (*op. cit.*, pp. 1266-67).

[56] *Ibid.*, p. 1268.

CHAPTER 6

The Great Depression

[1] *Unemployment Relief: Hearings before a Sub-Committee of the Committee on Manufactures, U. S. Senate, December 28-30, 1931, Jan. 4-9, 1932* (Government Printing Office, Washington, D. C., 1932, p. 75).

[2] George Soule (*op. cit.*, p. 345).

[3] Shepard B. Clough, "The New Economic Insecurity," in *Economic Security for Americans* (American Assembly, Columbia Univ., 1953, pp. 62-65).

[4] *Ibid.*, p. 64.

[5] Frederick Lewis Allen, "A Look Back and a Look Ahead," in *Economic*

Security for Americans, p. 12.

[6] Jerre S. Williams, *The Supreme Court Speaks* (Univ. of Texas Press, Austin, 1956, p. 293).

[7] *Ibid.,* pp. 305-308.

[8] Arthur M. Schlesinger, Jr., *The Age of Roosevelt: The Crisis of the Old Order, 1919-1933* (Houghton, Boston, 1957, p. 25).

[9] Robert L. Heilbroner, *The Worldly Philosophers* (Simon and Schuster, New York, 1953, pp. 315-316).

[10] E. W. Burgess, "Social Planning and the Mores" (*loc. cit.,* p. 10).

[11] Thomas Parran, "Relation of Maternal and Child Health to the General Health Program," *American Journal of Public Health 28:3,* March 1938, p. 256.

[12] *Youth and the Future* (General Report of the American Youth Commission, American Council on Education, Washington, D. C., 1942, p. ix).

[13] *Ibid.,* p. 33.

[14] *Ibid.,* p. 30.

[15] Shepard B. Clough (*op. cit.,* p. 70).

[16] Arthur Larson, "The American Social Insurance System," in *Economic Security for Americans,* p. 21.

[17] Frank J. Bruno, "The First Twenty-five Years of the AASW," *The Compass 27,* June 1946, p. 12.

[18] Bertha Reynolds (*op. cit.*).

[19] Virginia P. Robinson (*op. cit.,* see pp. 115-166).

[20] Grace Marcus, "Changes in the Theory of Relief-Giving," *Social Work Today 8:3,* June-July 1941, pp. 6-9.

[21] Jesse Taft (ed.), *A Functional Approach to Family Case Work* (Univ. of Pennsylvania Press, Philadelphia, 1944, p. 6).

[22] *Idem.*

[23] Ernest V. Hollis and Alice L. Taylor, *Social Work Education in the United States* (Columbia Univ. Press, New York, 1951, p. 32).

[24] Henry W. Thurston, *The Dependent Child* (Columbia Univ. Press, New York, 1930, p. 40).

[25] Charles E. Hendry, "A Review of Group Work's Affirmations," in *Proceedings of the National Conference of Social Work* (Columbia Univ. Press, New York, 1940, p. 543).

[26] *Ibid.,* p. 550.

[27] Grace L. Coyle, "Case Work and Group Work," *The Survey,* April 1937, pp. 102-104.

[28] Ray Johns, "An Examination of Group Work's Practices," in *Proceedings of the National Conference of Social Work* (Columbia Univ. Press, New York, 1940, p. 560).

[29] *Ibid.,* p. 557.

[30] Frank J. Bruno, *Trends in Social Work,* p. 194.

[31] Jesse F. Steiner (*op. cit.,* p. 99).

[32] Robert P. Lane, "The Field of Community Organization," in *Proceedings of the National Conference of Social Work* (Columbia Univ. Press, New York, 1939, pp. 496-97).

[33] *ASCO Newsletter*, February 1947, pp. 11-12.

[34] Ernest V. Hollis and Alice L. Taylor *(op. cit., p. 24)*.

[35] Grace L. Coyle *(op. cit., pp. 103-04)*.

[36] Grace L. Coyle, "Limitations of Social Work in Relation to Social Reorganization," *Papers*, American Sociological Society, August 1935, p. 177.

[37] "Rank and File Speak," in *Proceedings of the Pittsburgh Convention*, published by the National Coordinating Committee (pamphlet), n.d.

[38] Mary Van Kleeck, *Creative America* (Covici-Friede, New York, 1936, p. 281).

[39] George Soule *(op. cit., p. 365)*.

[40] Thomas Parran, "The Health of the Nation," *American Journal of Public Health 28*:12, December 1938, p. 1376.

[41] Odin W. Anderson, "Compulsory Medical Care Insurance, 1910-1950," in *The Annals of the American Academy of Political and Social Science 273*, January 1951, p. 112.

[42] Robert L. Heilbroner *(op. cit., pp. 291-92)*.

[43] Arthur Larson *(op. cit., p. 37)*.

CHAPTER 7

New Frontiers, New Methods, New Unity

[1] Shelby M. Harrison, "Attacking on Social Work's Three Fronts," in *Proceedings of the National Conference of Social Work* (Columbia Univ. Press, New York, 1942, pp. 3-21).

[2] Luther E. Woodward, "Social Case Work in Relation to Selective Service and the Rejectee," in *Proceedings of the National Conference of Social Work* (Columbia Univ. Press, New York, 1943, pp. 85-96).

[3] Robert E. Bondy, "Special Welfare Services to Families of Men in Service," in *Proceedings of the National Conference of Social Work* (Columbia Univ. Press, New York, 1943, p. 83).

[4] Ray Johns, Margaret Creech, Hedley S. Dimock, and Louis Kraft, "The Experience of the United Service Organizations and Social Work Practice," in *Proceedings of the National Conference of Social Work* (Columbia Univ. Press, New York, 1944, p. 193).

[5] Douglas P. Falconer, Clifford D. Moore, and Bertha C. Reynolds, "World-Wide Service for American Merchant Seamen," in *Proceedings of the National Conference of Social Work* (Columbia Univ. Press, New York, 1944, pp. 181-82).

[6] Lyman S. Ford, "The Effect of World War II on Community Organiza-

tion for Health and Welfare," in *Proceedings of the National Conference of Social Work* (Columbia Univ. Press, New York, 1944, pp. 392-401).

7 Quoted in *Community*, March 1944 (publication of United Community Funds and Councils of America, Inc.) from an address delivered by Thomas L. Carroll at a conference of the National War Fund in New York.

8 Howard A. Amerman, "State War Fund Experiences in Rural Areas," in *Proceedings of the National Conference of Social Work* (Columbia Univ. Press, New York, 1944, pp. 416-17).

9 From a speech at the Seventh Constitutional CIO Convention, reported in National CIO War Relief Committee, Community Services Newsletter, December 1944, p. 3.

10 Donald S. Howard, "Foreign Relief and Rehabilitation," in *Social Work Year Book* (Russell Sage, New York, 1947, pp. 190-202).

11 *Ibid.*, p. 201.

12 Eveline M. Burns, "The Security Report of the National Resources Planning Board," in *Proceedings of the National Conference of Social Work* (Columbia Univ. Press, New York, 1943, pp. 376-78).

13 William C. Menninger, "Psychiatric Social Work in the Army and Its Implications for Civilian Social Work," in *Proceedings of the National Conference of Social Work* (Columbia Univ. Press, New York, 1945, p. 89).

14 *Ibid.*, p. 87.

15 *Ibid.*, p. 86.

16 Kurt Lewin, *Resolving Social Conflicts* (Harper, New York, 1948, p. 73).

17 Ellen C. Potter, "The Year of Decision for Social Work," in *Proceedings of the National Conference of Social Work* (Columbia Univ. Press, New York, 1945, p. 13).

18 *Ibid.*, p. 11.

19 *Ibid.*, p. 12.

20 *Ibid.*

21 Marion Hathway, "Social Action and Professional Education," in *Proceedings of the National Conference of Social Work* (Columbia Univ. Press, New York, 1944, p. 373).

CHAPTER 8

After World War II

1 George Soule (*op. cit.*, p. 520).

2 *The American Federationist*, March 1951, p. 5.

3 Arthur J. Altmeyer, "Social Insurance," in *Social Work Year Book* (American Association of Social Workers, New York, 1951, p. 480).

4 Samuel Lubell, *The Future of American Politics* (Harper, New York, 1952, p. 19).

5 *The New York Times,* Thursday, September 2, 1954, pp. 1, 9.

6 *Ibid.,* Saturday, August 21, 1954, p. 8.

7 A. H. Raskin, "How Eisenhower Plans to Deal with Depression," in *Commentary,* May 1954, p. 430.

8 James Reston, "Eisenhower's Four Years," *The New York Times,* Sunday, July 22, 1956, p. 42 L.

9 *Idem.*

10 For comparison of social welfare expenditures between 1952-53 and 1954-55 see the section in the latter part of the chapter on financial resources.

11 Frederick Lewis Allen (*op. cit.,* p. 18).

12 H. L. Wilensky and C. N. Lebaux, *Industrialization and Social Welfare* (Russell Sage, New York, November 1955, p. 80).

13 Ida C. Merriam, *Social Security Bulletin 16:2,* February 1953, p. 12.

14 J. H. S. Bossard, "Eight Reasons Why Marriages Go Wrong," *The New York Times Magazine,* Sunday, June 24, 1956, p. 5.

15 Howard A. Rusk, "The State of the Union's Health," *The New York Times Magazine,* Sunday, July 22, 1956, p. 22.

16 H. L. Wilensky and C. N. Lebaux (*op. cit.,* pp. 53-54).

17 *Ibid.,* p. 91.

18 Cabell Phillips, " 'H.E.W.'—How Much Welfare?" *The New York Times Magazine,* Sunday, August 28, 1955, pp. 32, 34.

19 Ida C. Merriam (*op. cit.* p. 12).

20 See Roscoe Pound, *Social Control through Law* (Yale Univ. Press, New Haven, 1942).

21 Wilbert E. Moore, "Unions in Social Work," in *Social Work Year Book* (Russell Sage, New York, 1949, pp. 520-21).

22 Robert E. Bondy, *Annual Report of the National Social Welfare Assembly,* 1953, p. 1.

23 Katherine A. Kendall, "Education for Social Work," in *Social Work Year Book* (National Association of Social Workers, New York, 1957, p. 219).

24 *Idem.*

25 *Association*	*Date of Organization*	*Membership (Jan. 1951)*
American Association of Medical Social Workers	1918	2,254
National Association of School Social Workers	1919	635
American Association of Social Workers	1921	12,492
American Association of Psychiatric Social Workers	1926	1,646
American Association of Group Workers	1936	1,902

[26] C. R. Thompson and L. E. Woodward, "Present Structure and Program of the Membership Associations," *Social Work Journal 30,* July 1949, p. 110.

[27] Plans for a Single New Organization of Social Workers (Temporary Inter-Association Council of Social Work Membership Organizations, 1952, p. 1).

[28] Proposed By-Laws and Memorandum of Understandings (National Association of Social Workers, November 1954, p. 19).

[29] John G. Hill, "Social Action," in *Social Work Year Book* (American Association of Social Workers, New York, 1951, p. 456).

[30] Arthur Dunham, "Administration of Social Agencies," in *Social Work Year Book* (Russell Sage Foundation, New York, 1947, pp. 15-16).

[31] S. Z. Hasan (*op. cit.,* pp. 12-13). Cited as examples of this development are: Virginia K. White, "Measuring Leisure Time Needs," Group Work Council, Welfare Federation of Cleveland, Ohio; Henry S. Maas and Martin Wollins, "Concepts and Methods in Social Work Research," in Cora Kasius, ed., *New Directions in Social Work* (Harper, New York, 1954).

[32] Now the Research Section of the National Association of Social Workers.

[33] *The Function and Practice of Research in Social Work* (Social Work Research Group, May 1955, p. 4).

[34] John G. Hill and Ralph Ormsby, *Cost Analysis Method for Casework Agencies,* Family Service of Philadelphia, 1953.

[35] S. Z. Hasan (*op. cit.*).

[36] Ernest Greenwood, "Social Science and Social Work: A Theory of Their Relationship," in *Social Service Review,* March 1955, pp. 27-28.

[37] For full discussion see Alfred J. Kahn, "Some Problems Facing Social Work Scholarship," in *Social Work 2:2,* April 1957, pp. 54-62.

[38] Helen L. Witmer, "What Is Evaluation?" in *Casework Papers from the National Conference of Social Work* (The Family Service Association of America, New York, 1954, p. 142).

[39] S. Z. Hasan (*op. cit.*).

[40] J. McV. Hunt and L. S. Kogan, *Measuring Results in Social Case Work: A Manual on Judging Movement* (Family Service Association of America, New York, 1950).

[41] L. S. Kogan, J. McV. Hunt, and P. F. Bartelme, *Follow-up Study of the Results of Social Casework* (Family Service Association of America, New York, 1953).

[42] L. Festinger and H. H. Kelley, *Changing Attitudes through Social Contact* (Institute for Social Research, Univ. of Michigan, Ann Arbor, 1951).

[43] Edwin Powers and Helen L. Witmer, *An Experiment in the Prevention of Delinquency* (Columbia Univ. Press, New York, 1951).

44 Sheldon and Eleanor Glueck, *Unraveling Juvenile Delinquency* (Commonwealth Fund, New York, 1950).
45 William E. Gordon, "The Professional Base of Social Work Research—Some Essential Elements," *Social Work Journal,* January 1952, p. 21.
46 Philip Klein, "The Contribution of Research to the Progress of Social Work," *The Contribution of Research to Social Work,* A.A.S.W. Pamphlet, 1949, p. 6.
47 William L. Kolb, "The Impingement of Moral Values on Sociology," *Social Problems,* October 1954, pp. 68-69.
48 Charles B. Frankel, *The Case for Modern Man* (Harper, New York, 1955, p. 19).
49 Eduard C. Lindeman (*op. cit.*).
50 Sidney G. Tickton, *Rebuilding Human Lives: The Rehabilitation of the Handicapped* (Seventh Company, New York, May 1957, Part 1, p. 9).
51 *Ibid.,* p. 10.
52 Richard M. Titmuss, "Social Administration in a Changing Society," *Social Work 9: 2,* April 1952 (Damson House, London), p. 668.
54 From "A Report on the Study of Salaries and Working Conditions in Social Work—Spring 1950," prepared by the United States Department of Labor, Bureau of Labor Statistics.
55 Benjamin Fine, *The New York Times,* Sunday, July 14, 1957, p. 46.
56 Sidney G. Tickton (*op. cit.* p. 21).
57 Ernest V. Hollis and Alice L. Taylor (*op. cit.,* pp. 103, 105).
58 Benjamin Fine (*op. cit.*).

CHAPTER 9

Dominant Themes in the Philosophy of Social Work

1 Charles B. Frankel (*op. cit.,* p. 31).
2 *Ibid.,* p. 30.
3 Bertrand Russell, "Science and Human Life," in James R. Newman, ed., *What Is Science?* (Simon and Schuster, New York, 1955, pp. 9-10).
4 Charles B. Frankel (*op. cit.,* p. 21).
5 *Ibid.,* p. 47.
6 *Ibid.,* p. 111.
7 H. L. Wilensky and C. N. Lebaux (*op. cit.,* p. 66).
8 *Ibid.,* p. 177.
9 Erich Fromm, "Psychoanalysis," in *What Is Science?,* p. 363.
10 E. Pumpian-Mindlin (*op. cit.,* pp. 133-34).

11 Erich Fromm (*op. cit.*, p. 371).
12 Isaiah Berlin, *The Age of Enlightenment* (New American Library, New York, 1956, p. 29).
13 *Ibid.*, p. 17.
14 C. Wright Mills, *The Power Elite* (Oxford Univ. Press, New York, 1956, p. 326).
15 *Ibid.*, p. 327.
16 *Ibid.*, pp. 326-27.
17 Paul Tillich, "Psychoanalysis, Existentialism and Theology—Interdependence," *The Christian Register* (now *Universalist Register*), March 1956, p. 34.
18 *Ibid.*, p. 17.
19 *Ibid.*, p. 34.
20 *Ibid.*, p. 35.
21 Charles B. Frankel (*op. cit.*, pp. 2-3).
22 C. Wright Mills (*op. cit.*, p. 6).
23 E. Pumpian-Mindlin (*op. cit.*).
24 H. L. Wilensky and C. N. Lebaux (*op. cit.*, p. 198).
25 E. V. Hollis and A. L. Taylor (*op. cit.*, p. 142).
26 Viola W. Bernard, "Qualifications for Psychotherapists," *American Journal of Orthopsychiatry* 26:1, January 1956, p. 45.
27 George F. Davidson, "Responsibility to Meet Social Service Needs," in *National Policies for Education, Health and Welfare Services* (Doubleday, New York, 1955, p. 154).
28 *Ibid.*, p. 171.

CHAPTER 10

Social Work as a Profession

1 E. V. Hollis and A. L. Taylor, Abridgment of *Social Education in the United States*, 1952, p. 10.
2 *Ibid.*, p. 11.
3 *Idem.*
4 H. L. Wilensky and C. N. Lebaux (*op. cit.*, p. 175).
5 Dael Wolfle, *America's Resources of Specialized Talent* (Harper, New York, 1954, p. 2).
6 Clyde R. White, "Prestige of Social Work and the Social Worker," *Social Work Journal* 36:1, January 1955, pp. 21-23; Norman Polansky, William Bowens, Lucille Gordon, and Conrad Nathan, "Social Workers in Society: Result of a Sampling Study," *Social Work*

Journal 34, April 1953, pp. 74-80; William Oldys, "Wages, Budgets, Recruitments, Expectations," *Social Work Journal 36*:1, January 1955, p. 24.

7 Ernest Greenwood, *Toward a Sociology of Social Work* (Welfare Council of Metropolitan Los Angeles, November 1953, p. 11).

8 Charles Dollard, *Bulletin of the New York School of Social Work*, September 1952, p. 4.

9 Based on the normative characteristics of social work as developed in the study by the United Nations on *Training for Social Work: An International Survey*, 1950.

10 Josephine Peek and Charlotte Plotkin, "Social Caseworkers in Private Practice," *Smith College Studies in Social Work 21*:3, pp. 165-66.

11 *Ibid.*, pp. 196-97.

12 Ernest H. Smith, unpublished paper, presented at a meeting sponsored by the New York City Chapter of N.A.S.W. at the New York State Welfare Conference, December 10, 1956.

13 Memorandum to Chapter Chairmen from Bertram Beck, Associate Executive Secretary, N.A.S.W., February 18, 1956.

14 Charles A. and Mary R. Beard, *Basic History of the United States* (*op. cit.*, pp. 393-95).

15 C. Wright Mills (*op. cit.*, Chap. 13).

16 *Proposed By-Laws and Memorandum of Understanding* (*loc. cit.*, p. 3).

17 *Goals of Public Social Policy* (National Association of Social Workers, 1957, Part 1, p. 4).

CHAPTER 11

What of the Future?

1 E. R. Hoban, unpublished report on "Observation of Social Work in the United States." For an excellent discussion of this problem as it applies to social group work see Clara A. Kaiser, "Social Group Work Practise and Social Responsibility," in *Social Welfare Forum, National Conference of Social Work* (Columbia Univ. Press, New York, 1952, pp. 161-67).

SELECTED BIBLIOGRAPHY

I. General History of the United States

Charles A. Beard and Mary R. Beard, *A Basic History of the United States* (New York, Doubleday, 1944).

S. E. Morison and H. S. Commager, *The Growth of the American Republic* (New York, Oxford Univ. Press, 1930 and revisions).

Arthur M. Schlesinger and Dixon R. Fox (eds.), *History of American Life* (13 vols., New York, Macmillan).

II. Historical Analysis
(Intellectual, Economic, Social, Political)

Frederick L. Allen, *The Big Change* (New York, Harper, 1952).

Thomas C. Cochrane, *The Age of Enterprise* (New York, Macmillan, 1951).

Henry Steele Commager, *The American Mind* (New Haven, Conn., Yale Univ. Press, 1950).

—— *Living Ideas in America* (New York, Harper, 1951).

Merle Curti, *The Growth of American Thought* (New York, Harper, 1951).

Harold U. Faulkner, *The Quest for Social Justice, 1898-1914* (New York, Macmillan, 1931).

Eric Goldman, *Rendezvous with Destiny* (New York, Knopf, 1952).

Richard Hofstadter, *The American Political Tradition* (New York, Knopf, 1948).

—— *The Age of Reform* (New York, Knopf, 1955).

—— *Social Darwinism in American Thought* (New York, Beacon, 1955).

Harold J. Laski, *The American Democracy* (New York, Viking, 1948).

Vernon L. Parrington, *Main Currents in American Thought* (New York, Harcourt, 1927).

Arthur M. Schlesinger, Jr., *The Age of Jackson* (Boston, Little, 1945).

—— *The Crisis of the Old Order* (Boston, Houghton, 1957).

George Soule, *Economic Forces in American History* (New York, Dryden, 1952).

III. Historical Perspectives in Related Fields

Harry Elmer Barnes, *Historical Sociology, Its Origin and Development* (New York, Philosophical Library, 1948).

Howard Becker and H. E. Barnes, *Social Thought from Lore to Science* (2d ed.; New York, Dover, 1956).

Edwin G. Boring, *A History of Experimental Psychology* (2d ed.; New York, Appleton-Century-Crofts, 1950).

R. F. Butts and Lawrence A. Cremin, *A History of Education in American Culture* (New York, Holt, 1953).

Charles Gide and Charles Rist, *A History of Economic Doctrines from the Time of the Physiocrats to the Present Day* (2d ed.; Boston, Heath, 1948).

Alfred C. Haddon, *History of Anthropology* (London, Watts, 1949).

William C. Menninger, *Psychiatry, Its Evolution and Present Status* (Ithaca, N.Y., Cornell Univ. Press, 1948).

Gardiner Murphy, *Historical Introduction to Modern Psychology* (2d ed.; New York, Harcourt, 1949).

Howard W. Odum, *American Sociology: The Story of Sociology in the United States through 1950* (New York, Longmans, 1951).

George H. Sabine, *A History of Political Theory* (rev. ed.; New York, Holt, 1951).

Richard Harrison Shryock, *The Development of Modern Medicine* (Philadelphia, Univ. of Pennsylvania Press, 1947).

Gregory Zilboorg, *A History of Medical Psychology* (New York, Norton, 1941).

IV. Historical Perspectives in Social Work

Jane Addams, *Forty Years at Hull House* (New York, Macmillan, 1935).

Lillian Brandt, *Growth and Development of the A.I.C.P. and C.O.S.* (New York, Community Service Society, 1942).

Frank J. Bruno, *Trends in Social Work* (New York, Columbia Univ. Press, 1948).

Eveline M. Burns, *The American Social Security System* (Boston, Houghton, 1949).

Karl De Schweinitz, *England's Road to Social Security* (Philadelphia, Univ. of Pennsylvania Press, 1947).

Edward J. Devine, *When Social Work Was Young* (New York, Macmillan, 1939).

E. V. Hollis and A. L. Taylor, *Social Work Education* (New York, Columbia Univ. Press, 1951), Chap. 1.

Mary Hurlbutt, "Rise of Social Work," *Annals,* Vol. CLXXVI (1934), pp. 1-13.

Philip Klein, "Social Work," *Encyclopedia of the Social Sciences,* Vol. XIV, pp. 165-183.

Harry L. Lurie, "The Development of Social Welfare Programs in the United States," *Social Work Year Book* (New York, National Association of Social Workers, 1957), pp. 19-45.

Stuart Queen, *Social Work in the Light of History* (Philadelphia, Lippincott, 1922).

Virginia Robinson, *A Changing Psychology in Social Case Work* (Chapel Hill, N.C., Univ. of North Carolina Press, 1930), Part I.

Amos G. Warner, *American Charities* (New York, Crowell, 1908), Chap. 1.

A. Warner, S. Queen, and E. Harper, *American Charities and Social Work* (New York, Crowell, 1930), Chap. 1.

Frank D. Watson, *The Charity Organization Movement in the United States* (New York, Macmillan, 1922), Chap. 2.

V. *Philosophical Perspectives*

K. D. Benne and G. E. Swanson (issue eds.), "Values and the Social Scientist," *Journal of Social Issues,* Vol. VI, No. 4 (1950).

Herbert Bisno, *The Philosophy of Social Work* (Washington, D. C., Public Affairs Press, 1952).

Antoinette Cannon, "Recent Changes in the Philosophy of Social Workers," *Proceedings of the National Conference of Social Work* (Chicago, Univ. of Chicago Press, 1933).

Morris R. Cohen, *Law and the Social Order* (New York, Harcourt, 1933), especially Chaps. 1, 2.

Nathan E. Cohen, "Desegregation—A Challenge to the Place of Moral Values in Social Work Education," in *Education for Social Work* (New York, Council on Social Work Education, 1955).

Henry S. Commager, *The American Mind* (New Haven, Conn., Yale Univ. Press, 1950).

Rev. T. J. Cooke, *Thomistic Philosophy in the Principles of Social Group Work* (Washington, D. C., Catholic Univ. Press, 1951).

J. F. De Jongh, "Self-Help in Modern Society," *Social Work Journal,* Vol. XXXV, No. 4 (October 1954).

Charles Frankel, *The Case for Modern Man* (New York, Harper, 1956).

David E. Hailman, "A Code of Ethics for the Social Worker," *Social Work Journal,* Vol. XXX, No. 2 (April 1949).

Gisela Konopka, "Social Work's Search for a Philosophy, with Special Reference to Eduard C. Lindeman" (doctoral dissertation, New York School of Social Work, Columbia University, 1957).*

Hilary Leyendecker, *Problems and Policy in Public Assistance* (New York, Harper, 1955), Chaps. 6, 7.

Alfred Lief, *The Social and Economic Views of Mr. Justice Brandeis* (New York, Vanguard, 1930).

Mary J. McCormick, *Diagnostic Case Work in the Thomistic Pattern* (New York, Columbia Univ. Press, 1954).

Gunnar Myrdal, *An American Dilemma* (New York, Harper, 1944), Vol. I, pp. 3-25.

Reinhold Niebuhr, *The Contribution of Religion to Social Work* (New York, Columbia Univ. Press, 1932).

Roscoe Pound, *Social Control through Law* (New Haven, Conn., Yale Univ. Press, 1942).

Delafield Smith, *The Right to Life* (Chapel Hill, N.C., Univ. of North Carolina Press, 1955), especially Chaps. 1-7, 12.

Charlotte Towle, *Common Human Needs* (New York, American Association of Social Workers, 1952), pp. 1-95.

B. E. Youngdahl, "Social Work at the Crossroads," *Social Work Journal*, Vol. XXXIV, No. 3 (July 1953).

* Contains excellent bibliography of all the writings of Eduard C. Lindeman.

VI. *The Field of Social Work*

Arthur Fink, *The Field of Social Work* (New York, Holt, 1949).

Walter A. Friedlander, *Introduction to Social Welfare* (New York, Prentice-Hall, 1955).

E. V. Hollis and Alice L. Taylor, *Social Work Education* (New York, Columbia Univ. Press, 1951), Chap. 2.

Social Work Year Book (New York, National Association of Social Workers, 1957).

Herbert Stroup, *Social Work* (New York, American Book, 1948).

Helen Witmer, *Social Work* (New York, Farrar and Rinehart, 1942).

VII. Social *Work in Periods of American History*

1. COLONIAL PERIOD

Edith Abbott, *Some American Pioneers in Social Welfare* (Chicago, Univ. of Chicago Press, 1937), pp. 1-59.

Grace Abbott, *The Child and the State* (Chicago, Univ. of Chicago Press, 1938), Vol. I, pp. 195-213.

Carl Bridenbaugh, *Cities in Revolt; Urban Life in America, 1743-1776* (New York, Knopf, 1955), Chap. 3, pp. 319-331.

———— *Cities in the Wilderness* (New York, Knopf, 1955).

Karl De Schweinitz, *England's Road to Social Security*, pp. 28-29, 39-99.

Albert Deutsch, *The Mentally Ill in America* (New York, Doubleday Doran, 1937), Chaps. 2, 3.

Robert W. Kelso, *History of Public Poor Relief in Massachusetts* (Boston, Houghton, 1922).

Aileen E. Kennedy, *The Ohio Poor Law and Its Administration* (Chicago, Univ. of Chicago Press, 1934), Chap. 3.

David M. Schneider, *History of Public Welfare in New York State (1609-1886)* (Chicago, Univ. of Chicago Press, 1938), Chaps. 2-4.

Henry W. Thurston, *The Dependent Child* (New York, Columbia Univ. Press, 1930), Chap. 2.

2. EARLY NATIONAL LIFE (1790-1860)

Edith Abbott, *Some American Pioneers in Social Welfare*, pp. 59-150.

Sophonisba Breckinridge, *Public Welfare Administration in the United States* (Chicago, Univ. of Chicago Press, 1927), pp. 30-54, 170-174, 149-151, 196-234.

Thomas Chalmers, *The Parochial System without a Poor Rate* (New York, Collins, 1841), pp. i, iv, v, vii, xi, xiii.

De Schweinitz, *England's Road to Social Security*, pp. 66-139.

Deutsch, *The Mentally Ill in America*, Chaps. 7-9.

Leah Feder, *Unemployment Relief in Periods of Depression* (New York, Russell Sage, 1936), Chap. 2.

Kennedy, *The Ohio Poor Law and Its Administration*, Chaps. 4, 5.

Schneider, *History of Public Welfare in New York State (1609-1866)*, pp. 211-215, 265-287.

Thurston, *The Dependent Child*, pp. 27-113.

Mary B. Treudley, "The 'Benevolent Fair': Charitable Organization among American Women Before 1835," *Social Service Review*, Vol. XIV, No. 3 (September 1940), pp. 509-522.

Watson, *The Charity Organization Movement in the United States*, pp. 66-68, 76-93.

3. EXPANDING INDUSTRIALISM (1865-1890)

Edith Abbott, *Some American Pioneers in Social Welfare*, pp. 151-189.

American Social Science Association, *Journal of Social Science*, No. XII (December 1880), pp. 84-124 (symposium on associated charities).

Boris Bogen, *Jewish Philanthropy* (New York, Macmillan, 1917).

Charles Booth, *Labour and Life of the People* (East London, England, Williams and Norgate, 1889), Vol. I.

Breckinridge, *Public Welfare Administration in the United States*, pp. 142-148, 237-258, 368-380.

Bruno, *Trends in Social Work*, pp. 3-129.

R. De Forest and L. Veiller, *The Tenement House Problem* (New York, Macmillan, 1903).

Deutsch, *The Mentally Ill in America*, Chaps. 13-14.

Sherwood Eddy, *A Century with Youth: The History of the Y.M.C.A. from 1844 to 1944* (New York, Association Press, 1944).

Feder, *Unemployment Relief in Periods of Depression*, Chap. 3.

Octavia Hill, *Our Common Land* (New York, Macmillan, 1877), pp. 18-88.

Josephine S. Lowell, *Public Relief and Private Charity* (New York, Putnam, 1884).

Allan Nevins, *The Emergence of Modern America, 1865-1878* (New York, Macmillan, 1935), especially Chap. 12.

John O'Grady, *Catholic Charities in the United States* (Washington, D. C., National Conference of Catholic Charities, 1930), Chaps. 5, 6, 9.

Proceedings of the National Conference of Charities and Corrections (Boston, George H. Ellis Press, 1893), pp. 33-262 (summaries of the history of sections on twentieth anniversary).

Benjamin Rabinowitz, *The Young Men's Hebrew Association, 1854-1913* (New York, National Jewish Welfare Board, 1948).

Mary S. Sims, *The Natural History of a Social Institution, the Y.W.C.A.* (New York, Woman's Press, 1935).

Thurston, *The Dependent Child*, pp. 113-201.

4. AGE OF REFORM (1890-1918)

Grace Abbott, *The Child and the State*, Vol. II, pp. 229-246.

Addams, *Twenty Years at Hull House*, pp. 81-127.

Clifford Beers, *The Mind That Found Itself* (New York, Doubleday, 1935).

Robert Bremner, *From the Depths: The Discovery of Poverty in the United States* (New York, New York Univ. Press, 1956).

Bruno, *Trends in Social Work*, pp. 133-230, 257-269.

Ida M. Cannon, *On the Social Frontier of Medicine* (Cambridge, Mass., Harvard Univ. Press, 1952), Chaps. 4, 5, 8, 11, 15, 17.

Deutsch, *The Mentally Ill in America*, Chap. 15.

Feder, *Unemployment Relief in Periods of Depression*, Chaps. 4-10.

Abraham Flexner, "Is Social Work a Profession?" *Proceedings of the National Conference of Social Work* (Chicago, Univ. of Chicago Press, 1915), pp. 576-590.

Paul Kellogg, "The Spread of the Survey Idea," *Social Surveys*, Russell Sage Foundation Publications, No. 1, 1912.

Joseph Lee, *Constructive and Preventive Philanthropy* (New York, Macmillan, 1902).

Porter R. Lee, "The Professional Basis of Social Work," *Proceedings of the National Conference of Social Work* (Chicago, Univ. of Chicago Press, 1915), pp. 596-606.

Owen D. Lovejoy, "Report of the Committee on Standards of Living and Labor," *Proceedings of the National Conference of Social Work* (Chicago, Univ. of Chicago Press, 1912), pp. 376-394.

Elizabeth Meier, *A History of the New York School of Social Work* (New York, Columbia Univ. Press, 1954), Chaps. 1-3.

"Politics and Social Work," *The Survey*, Vol. XXIX, No. 1 (October 5, 1912), pp. 8-12.

Jacob Reis, *How the Other Half Lives* (New York, Scribner, 1890).

Margaret Rich, "Mary E. Richmond: Social Worker, 1861-1928," *Social Casework*, Vol. XXXIII, No. 9 (November 1952), pp. 363-374.

Mary Richmond, *Social Diagnosis* (New York, Russell Sage, 1917), pp. 38-50, 342-363, 367-370.

——— *The Good Neighbor* (Philadelphia, Lippincott, 1908).

Arthur M. Schlesinger, *The Rise of the City, 1878-1898* (New York, Macmillan, 1933), Chaps. 11, 12.

Amos G. Warner, *American Charities*, Parts II and III.

White House Conference on the Care of Dependent Children, *Report* (Washington, D. C., Government Printing Office, 1909), especially pp. 8-18.

Robert Woods and Albert Kennedy, *The Settlement Horizon* (New York, Russell Sage, 1922), Chap. 4.

5. WORLD WAR AND AFTERMATH (1917-1928)

Ethel S. Dunmer, "Life in Relation to Time," in Lawson Lowrey (ed.), *Orthopsychiatry, 1923-1948: Retrospect and Prospect* (New York, American Orthopsychiatric Association, 1948), pp. 3-14.

Mary Parker Follett, *Creative Experience* (New York, Longmans, 1924), especially Chaps. 4, 5, 9.

——— *The New State* (New York, Longmans, 1918), especially Chaps. 2, 3, 7, 13.

W. H. Healy and A. F. Bronner, "The Child Guidance Clinic: Birth and Growth of an Idea," in Lawson Lowrey, *op. cit.*, pp. 14-50.

William Hodson, "Is Social Work Professional?" *Proceedings of the National Conference of Social Work* (Chicago, Univ. of Chicago Press, 1925), pp. 629-636.

Porter R. Lee, *Social Work as Cause and Function* (New York, Columbia Univ. Press, 1937), pp. 1-24.

Eduard C. Lindeman, *The Community* (New York, Association Press, 1921).

L. G. Lowrey, "The Birth of Orthopsychiatry," in Lawson Lowrey, *op. cit.*, pp. 190-208.

Meier, *A History of the New York School of Social Work*, Chaps. 4, 5.

Milford (Pa.) Conference Report, *Social Casework, Generic and Specific: An Outline* (New York, American Association of Social Workers, 1929).

William J. Norton, *The Cooperative Movement in Social Work* (New York, Macmillan, 1927), pp. 35-49, 131-153.

G. S. Stevenson, "Child Guidance and the National Committee for Mental Hygiene," in Lawson Lowrey, *op. cit.*, pp. 50-82.

James H. Tufts, *Education and Training for Social Work* (New York, Russell Sage, 1923), Chaps. 1, 2.

6. THE GREAT DEPRESSION (1928-1940)

A. The Social Scene

Grace Abbott, *From Relief to Social Security* (Chicago, Univ. of Chicago Press, 1941), especially pp. 3-48, 121-160, 199-225.

Josephine C. Brown, *Public Relief, 1929-1939* (New York, Holt, 1940), especially Chaps. 4, 5, 10, 11, 12, 17.

Grace Browning, *Rural Public Welfare* (Chicago, Univ. of Chicago Press, 1941), pp. 3-16, 101-131, 518-526.

Eveline M. Burns, *Towards Social Security* (New York, McGraw, 1936).

Friedlander, *Introduction to Social Welfare*, pp. 135-155.

Herbert C. Hoover and Gifford Pinchot, "The Case Against and For Federal Relief," *The Survey*, Vol. LXVII, No. 7 (January 1, 1932), pp. 346-349 ff.

Donald S. Howard, *The W.P.A. and Federal Relief Policy* (New York, Russell Sage, 1943), Chaps. 4, 5.

Paul Kellogg, "A Century of Achievement in Democracy," in *Proceedings of the National Conference of Social Work* (New York, Columbia Univ. Press, 1939), pp. 3-29.

Porter R. Lee, *Social Work as Cause and Function*, pp. 177-200.

Leyendecker, *Problems and Policy in Public Assistance*, Chap. 3.

National Resources Planning Board, *Security, Work, and Relief Policies* (Washington, D. C., 1942).

Report of the American Youth Commission, *Youth and the Future* (Washington, D. C., 1942).

B. Professional Developments

Bruno, *Trends in Social Work*, pp. 239-364.

—— "The First Twenty-five Years of the AASW," *The Compass*, Vol. XXVII, No. 5 (June 1946), pp. 9-12.

Antoinette Cannon, "Where the Changes in Social Case Work Have Brought Us," in Fern Lowry (ed.), *Readings in Social Case Work* (New York, Columbia Univ. Press, 1939), pp. 109-121.

Grace Coyle, "Social Work at the Turn of the Decade," *Proceedings of the National Conference of Social Work* (New York, Columbia Univ. Press, 1940), pp. 3-26.

—— "Social Workers and Social Action," *op. cit.*, pp. 565-568.

Jacob Fisher, *The Rank and File Movement in Social Work, 1931-1936* (New York, New York School of Social Work, 1936).

John Gambs, "Relief Workers' Unions," *The Survey*, Vol. LXXII, No. 1 (January 1936), pp. 11-13.

Marion Hathway, "Twenty-five Years of Professional Education for Social Work—and a Look Ahead," *The Compass*, Vol. XXVII, No. 5 (June 1946), pp. 13-18.

Clara A. Kaiser, "Coordination of Group Work and Case Work Services," in Joshua Lieberman (ed.), *New Trends in Group Work* (New York, Association Press, 1938), pp. 190-199.

—— "Record Keeping in Group Work," *op. cit.*, pp. 221-229.

Robert P. Lane, "The Field of Community Organization," *Proceedings of the National Conference of Social Work* (New York, Columbia Univ. Press, 1939), pp. 495-511; *ibid.*, (1940), pp. 456-473.

Fern Lowry, "Current Concepts in Social Case Work Practice," *Social Service Review*, Vol. XII, No. 3 (September 1938), pp. 365-373; *ibid.*, No. 4 (December 1938), pp. 571-597.

Grace Marcus, "Status of Social Case Work Today," in Fern Lowry (ed.), *Readings in Social Case Work* (New York, Columbia Univ. Press, 1939), pp. 122-135.

Meier, *A History of the New York School of Social Work*, Chap. 6.

Wilbur I. Newstetter, "What Is Social Group Work?" *Proceedings of the National Conference of Social Work* (Chicago, Univ. of Chicago Press, 1935), pp. 291-299.

Virginia Robinson, *A Changing Psychology in Social Case Work*, Chaps. 12, 13, Conclusion.

7. WORLD WAR II (1939-1945)

Eveline M. Burns, "The Security Report of the National Resources Planning Board," *Proceedings of the National Conference of Social Work* (New York, Columbia Univ. Press, 1943), pp. 370-381.

Almena Dawley, "Professional Association in a World Crisis," in Henry S. Maas (ed.), *Adventures in Mental Health* (New York, Columbia Univ. Press, 1951).

Douglas P. Falconer, Clifford D. Moore, and Bertha C. Reynolds, "World-wide Services for American Merchant Seamen," *Proceedings of the National Conference of Social Work* (New York, Columbia Univ. Press, 1944), pp. 181-192.

Lyman S. Ford, "The Effects of World War II on Community Organization for Health and Welfare," *Proceedings of the National Conference of Social Work* (New York, Columbia Univ. Press, 1944), pp. 392-401.

Gordon Hamilton, "The Underlying Philosophy of Social Case Work," *Family*, Vol. XXII, No. 5 (July 1941), pp. 139-147.

Shelby Harrison, "Attacking on Social Work's Three Fronts," *Proceedings of the National Conference of Social Work* (New York, Columbia Univ. Press, 1942), pp. 3-21.

Marion Hathway, "Social Action and Professional Education," *Proceedings of the National Conference of Social Work* (New York, Columbia Univ. Press, 1944), pp. 363-373.

Donald S. Howard, "Foreign Relief and Rehabilitation," *Social Work Year Book* (New York, National Association of Social Workers, 1947), pp. 190-202.

Ray Johns, Margaret Creech, Hedley S. Dimock, and Louis Kraft, "The Experiences of the United Service Organizations and Social Work Practice," *Proceedings of the National Conference of Social Work* (New York, Columbia Univ. Press, 1944), pp. 193-207.

Wayne McMillen, *Community Organization for Social Welfare* (Chicago, Univ. of Chicago Press, 1945), especially Chaps. 1, 16, 17.

Ellen C. Potter, "The Year of Decision for Social Work," *Proceedings of the National Conference of Social Work* (New York, Columbia Univ. Press, 1945), pp. 1-16.

Kenneth Pray, "Social Work in a Revolutionary Age," *Proceedings of the National Conference of Social Work* (New York, Columbia Univ. Press, 1946), pp. 399-410.

"Return of the Serviceman to His Family and Community," *Proceedings of the National Conference of Social Work* (New York, Columbia Univ. Press, 1945), pp. 92-116.

Bertha C. Reynolds, *Learning and Teaching in the Practice of Social Work* (New York, Farrar and Rinehart, 1942), pp. 3-30.

M. J. Rockmore and F. Greving, "Adapting Civilian Practice to Military Settings," in Maas, *op. cit.*, pp. 3-23.

——— "Practice Today," in Maas, *op. cit.*, pp. 261-280.

Roy Sorenson, "Planning for Group Work Needs," *Proceedings of the National Conference of Social Work* (New York, Columbia Univ. Press, 1944), pp. 136-147.

Jesse Taft (ed.), *A Functional Approach to Family Case Work* (Philadelphia, Univ. of Pennsylvania Press, 1944), Introduction.

Elizabeth Wisner, "War and the Social Services," in Taft, *op. cit.*, pp. 1-15.

8. 1946——

Gordon Allport, "The Limits of Social Service," in J. E. Russell (ed.), *National Policies for Education, Health and Social Services* (New York, Doubleday, 1955), pp. 194-213.

Lucille Austin, "Trends in Differential Treatment in Case Work," *Proceedings of the National Conference of Social Work* (New York, Columbia Univ. Press, 1949), pp. 271-283.

—— "An Evaluation of Supervision," *Social Casework*, Vol. XXXVII, No. 8 (October 1956), pp. 375-382.

S. Bowers, "The Nature and Definition of Social Casework," in Cora Kasius (ed.), *Principles and Techniques of Social Casework* (New York, Family Service Association of America, 1950), pp. 97-126.

Nathan E. Cohen, "The Future of Graduate Training for Social Work," *The Educational Record*, April 1951, pp. 142-151.

—— "The Over-all Look," in Russell, *op. cit.*, pp. 214-241.

Grace Coyle, "Proposed Areas for Concentration and Study," *The Group*, Vol. XVII, No. 5 (June 1955), pp. 7-10.

Karl De Schweinitz, "The Development of Governmental Responsibility for Human Welfare," in *Social Work as Human Relations* (New York, Columbia Univ. Press, 1949), pp. 19-35.

Ernest Greenwood, *Toward a Sociology of Social Work* (Los Angeles, Welfare Council of Metropolitan Los Angeles, 1953).

Gordon Hamilton, "Helping People, the Growth of a Profession," in *Social Work as Human Relations* (New York, Columbia Univ. Press, 1949), pp. 3-18.

Alfred J. Kahn, "Some Problems Facing Social Work Scholarship," *Social Work*, Vol. II, No. 2 (April 1957), pp. 54-62.

Katherine Kendall, *Training for Social Work: An International Survey* (New York, United Nations, 1950).

Outlook for Women in Social Work, U.S. Women's Bureau Bulletin, 1952, pp. 235-238.

David M. Schneider, "Perspectives on Social Work," *Social Work Journal*, Vol. XXXII, No. 2 (January 1951), pp. 26-30.

"Social Security in Review," *Social Security Bulletin*, Vol. XVI, Nos. 1-12 (1953); *ibid.*, Vol. XVII, Nos. 1-12 (1954).

Social Workers in 1950 (New York, American Association of Social Workers, 1952).

H. D. Stein, "Social Work Science in Social Work Practice and Education," *Social Casework,* Vol. XXXVI, No. 4 (April 1955), pp. 147-154.

Anthony R. Stone, "The Private Practice of Social Casework," *Social Work Journal,* Vol. XXXV, No. 2 (April 1954), pp. 61-64.

Damon Turner, "The Licensing Effort—Seven Years Later," *Social Work Journal,* Vol. XXXV, No. 2 (April 1954), pp. 68-72 ff.

"A Twenty-Year Perspective on Services to Children: Developments in Child Health and Welfare Since the Passage of the Social Security Act," *Children,* Vol. II, No. 4 (July-August 1955), pp. 123-160.

"What's Past Is Prologue," final issue of *Social Work Journal,* Vol. XXXVI, No. 3 (July 1955), pp. 79-130.

INDEX